Organized Crime

Policing Illegal Business Entrepreneurialism

Organized Crime

Policing Illegal Business
Entrepreneurialism

Geoff Dean,
Ivar Fahsing,
and
Petter Gottschalk

UNIVERSITY PRESS

Great Clarendon Street, Oxford OX2 6DP
Oxford University Press is a department of the University of Oxford.
It furthers the University's objective of excellence in research, scholarship,
and education by publishing worldwide in
Oxford New York
Auckland Cape Town Dar es Salaam Hong Kong Karachi
Kuala Lumpur Madrid Melbourne Mexico City Nairobi
New Delhi Shanghai Taipei Toronto
With offices in
Argentina Austria Brazil Chile Czech Republic France Greece
Guatemala Hungary Italy Japan South Korea Poland Portugal
Singapore Switzerland Thailand Turkey Ukraine Vietnam

Oxford is a registered trade mark of Oxford University Press
in the UK and in certain other countries

Published in the United States
by Oxford University Press Inc., New York

© Geoff Dean, Ivar Fahsing, and Petter Gottschalk, 2010

The moral rights of the author have been asserted

Crown copyright material is reproduced under Class Licence Number
C01P0000148 with the permission of OPSI and the
Queen's Printer for Scotland

Database right Oxford University Press (maker)

Reprinted 2011

All rights reserved. No part of this publication may be reproduced,
stored in a retrieval system, or transmitted, in any form or by any means,
without the prior permission in writing of Oxford University Press,
or as expressly permitted by law, or under terms agreed with the appropriate
reprographics rights organization. Enquiries concerning reproduction
outside the scope of the above should be sent to the Rights Department,
Oxford University Press, at the address above

You must not circulate this book in any other binding or cover
And you must impose this same condition on any acquirer

ISBN 978-0-19-957843-6

Printed and bound by CPI Group (UK) Ltd, Croydon, CR0 4YY

Foreword

The huge expansion of organized crime that has accompanied globalization has presented policy makers, police practitioners, and academics with many challenges. Two of the most significant are: understanding how organized crime operates and developing effective interventions to address it. The first of these is a problem because, in addition to the usual difficulty of uncovering information about criminal behaviour, it is not always easy to see how local manifestations of organized crime relate to the wider picture. The second is a problem because a successful intervention against a particular type of crime or operations against individuals or groups often simply provides others with a new business opportunity. The result is that despite the apparent success of the initiative or operation, economies, communities, and individuals continue to be victimized.

The authors of this book are uniquely well placed to help the reader deal with these challenges. They bring together a wealth of knowledge and practical experience in policing, knowledge management, and business to provide a coherent way of understanding how organized crime operates and how best to develop effective responses to it. The use of case examples, crime scenarios, and extended case studies helps the reader to relate the conceptual 'enterprise model' of organized crime into the real business world of criminal entrepreneurialism that will support both policy development and operational activity. This book provides a valuable addition to the literature on organized crime for police practitioners, policy makers, and academics.

Dr Peter Stelfox
Head of Investigative Practice
National Policing Improvement Agency

Acknowledgements

To write anything worthwhile requires much time, lots of patience, and a supportive environment. To get the time requires pinching it from somewhere or someone. For that, I owe a debt I can't repay in kind to my family, especially my life partner, Robyn and children, Megan, Amber, Simon, and Jeremy.

Moreover, a book like this can't happen without the support of many dedicated police and scholars. The ones I know personally, work with, and consult around the globe have provided invaluable assistance. Top of this list are my two co-authors. They have supplied buckets of material to make sense of, valuable insights, and wonderful companionship on the tough road of the writing craft.

Finally, this book started as a spark of an idea which has now seen the light of day. I and my co-authors owe a deep sense of gratitude to the commissioning editor, Peter Daniell at Oxford University Press. He had and held the faith in us to produce, what we hope, many others will come to regard as a very important and worthwhile contribution to the betterment of society.

Geoff Dean

To partake in writing books like this can sometimes be a very isolated and lonely experience. However, my co-authors have made it a thrilling affair ranging all over the mood scale. With Petter onboard you are guaranteed some serious work and lots of entertainment and surprises. Thank you. And thanks to Geoff for making this book come through with his fantastic effort, insight, and patience on all phases of the project. You should be really proud of yourself. Furthermore, I wish to send my warm regards to my colleagues at the Organized Crime Section in the Amsterdam Police, especially to Chu Man and Rene Bulstra. I especially want to thank Andy Griffiths in the Sussex Police, David Murthwaite, Merseyside Police, Jan Glent at the Norwegian National Authority for Prosecution of Organized and Other Serious Crime, as well as all my colleagues at the Norwegian Police University College. Then last, but not least, I want to thank Vivian, Steffen, Tuva, Kristian, and the rest of my family for making it all worthwhile.

Ivar Fahsing

It has been a strange, but interesting and exciting experience to apply what we teach in business administration and management to illegal enterprises and organized crime. So many management scholars have contributed to this book in terms of their theories and models of entrepreneurs, markets, leadership, and strategy. Without encouragement from and discussions with experienced police officers and criminology faculties in many parts of the world, this book would

Acknowledgements

never have achieved the quality we are proud of. They know who they are—I thank them all.

To Grethe and our two wonderful adult daughters Anne and Mette, who provide fantastic support, I extend my heartfelt thanks. I am especially grateful to my life companion Grethe, who is excited about this new book. We have a weekend deal where I can get up in the middle of the night to write so long as I have morning tea ready for her when she wakes up. I am truly thankful for such a partnership of mutual joy and benefit.

Petter Gottschalk

Contents

Special Features   xiii
Abbreviations   xv
List of Figures and Tables   xvii
List of Case Examples and Case Studies   xix
Introduction   xxi

Part One   The Business of Crime

1 Entrepreneurialism of Organized Crime   3
Introduction   3
Focal Framework: Business Enterprise Paradigm   5
Entrepreneurial Framework: Individual Capabilities   6
Opportunity Perspective   7
Resources Mobilization   8
Decision-Making under Uncertainty   10
People Cooperation   11
Profit Maximization   12
Case Study: Criminal Entrepreneurship   14
Summary   17

2 Criminal Enterprises, Markets, and Industries   19
Introduction   19
Operating Framework: Model of Business Development   19
Case Study: The Business of Organized Crime in Lithuania   23
Market Mechanisms   24
Criminal Markets   33
Criminal Enterprises as Global Industries   37
Case Study: Crime in the Commerce Industry   38
Summary   40

Part Two   Crime Business Phases

3 Establishing the Crime Business   43
Introduction   43
Criminal Business Modelling: Establishment Phase   43
Entrepreneurial Capability: Opportunity Perspective   45

Entrepreneurial Vision 46
Business Planning 48
Crime Money Management 52
Entrepreneurial Capability: Resources Mobilization 55
Financial Capital 56
Operational Logistics 57
'Fuzzy' Mapping of *Establishing* Crime Business 63
Summary 67

4 Expanding the Crime Business 68

Introduction 68
Criminal Business Modelling: Expansion Phase 68
Entrepreneurial Capability: Decision-Making under Uncertainty 70
Business Intelligence 70
Violence 73
Corruption 76
Counter-intelligence 81
'Fuzzy' Mapping of *Expanding* Crime Business 83
Summary 86

5 Consolidating the Crime Business 87

Introduction 87
Criminal Business Modelling: Consolidation Phase 87
Entrepreneurial Capability: People Cooperation 89
Criminal Business Connections 90
Legitimate Business Connections 93
Influential People Connections 96
'Fuzzy' Mapping of *Consolidating* Crime Business 100
Summary 102

6 Positioning the Crime Business 103

Introduction 103
Criminal Business Modelling: Positioning Phase 103
Entrepreneurial Capability: Profit Maximization 105
'Local' Market Share 107
'Global' Market Share 109
Competitive Advantages 111
'Fuzzy' Mapping of *Positioning* Crime Business 117
Summary 119

Part Three Policing Crime Businesses

7 Knowledge-Managed Policing: Principles and Practices 123

Introduction 123
Application of 'Knowledge' in Policing 123
Knowledge Categories in Policing 126

Knowledge Levels of Police	126
Knowledge Depth to Police	127
Police Knowledge Framework: Knowledge Cubes	130
Case Study: Knowledge Failure of Suspected Terrorist	133
Summary	142

8 Policing Criminal Businesses   143

Introduction	143
Policing in Context	143
Criminal Structures	144
Business Models: Cultural Variations	146
Case Study: The Business of Human Trafficking	146
Market Spheres: Dynamic Interconnectivity	150
Case Study: Business, Crime, and Politics in Montenegro	152
Operational Knowledge Framework: Crime Business Analysis Matrix	153
Case Study: Outlaw Motorcycle Gangs—Bandidos in Norway	156
Summary	166

9 Future Policing of 'Organized Crime'   168

Introduction	168
Morphing of 'Organized Crime'	169
Combating Organized Crime: UK Approach	171
Knowledge War: Policing Criminal Entrepreneurialism	173
Strategic Knowledge Framework: 'Policing Sector' Positioning	174
Intervention Strategies against Illegal Business Activities	177
Knowledge Sharing: Local and Global Policing Partnerships	178
International Cooperation in Policing	182
Future Directions	185

References	**189**
Index	**203**

Special Features

This book is designed for police practitioners, executives, policy makers, and students in the criminal justice/criminological domain and related government and non-government agencies. It is also applicable to specific industry sectors of business, economics, and finance. There are a number of special features to aid your understanding, reflection, and study of the content contained within this work.

- **Figures**—there are some 34 diagrams that illustrate various ideas, processes, and relationships. They convey complex information and act as conceptual graphics for teaching and training purposes.
- **Case Examples**—these contain some 52 case examples and brief vignettes of the operation of various business factors associated with the entrepreneurial capabilities of crime groups.
- **Case Studies**—there are seven case studies that present a more extended and in-depth study of particular illegal business activities in various crime markets.

Abbreviations

ABCI	Australian Bureau of Criminal Intelligence
ACC	Australian Crime Commission
ACS	Australian Customs Service
AFP	Australian Federal Police
AMRS	Alternative Money Remittance Schemes
ASIO	Australian Security Intelligence Organization
BCB	Big Circle Boys
BE	Business Enterprise
CBAM	Crime Business Analysis Matrix
CDPP	Commonwealth Director of Public Prosecutions
CMM	Crime Money Management
DIKW	Data-Information-Knowledge-Wisdom
FATF	Financial Action Task Force
FBI	Federal Bureau of Investigation
FCBP	Fuzzy Crime Business Profile
IBC	International Banking Corporation
IBS	Informal Banking Systems
KC	Knowledge Cube
KM	Knowledge Management
KMP	Knowledge-Managed Policing
ML/TF	Money Laundering/Terrorism Financing
MPS	Metropolitan Police Service
MPS-CTC	Counter Terrorism Command of the Metropolitan Police Service
NAGIA	National Alliance of Gang Investigators Association
NCA	National Crime Authority (Australia)
OCTA	Organized Crime Threat Assessment
OMCG	Outlaw Motorcycle Gang
OSCA	Office of Strategic Crime Assessments
PACO	Program against Corruption and Organized Crime in South Eastern Europe
SOCA	Serious Organised Crime Agency
SOP	Standard Operating Procedure
SWOT	Strengths-Weaknesses-Opportunities-Threats
TraCCC	Transnational Crime and Corruption Centre
WODC	*Wetenschappelijk Onderzoek- en Documentatiecentrum* (Research and Documentation Centre for the Dutch Ministry of Justice)

List of Figures and Tables

List of Figures

1.1	Entrepreneurial capabilities framework	7
2.1	Model of business development applied to organized crime	20
2.2	Key factors in a competing market environment	26
2.3	Market price determined by intersecting supply and demand curves	29
2.4	Market price fluctuations due to law enforcement	29
2.5	Market price when 'demand elasticity' is low	30
2.6	Global spheres of influence in criminal markets	34
2.7	Dynamic interconnectivity in criminal market global spheres	35
3.1	Crime business model: Phase 1—'establishment' business factors	44
3.2	Entrepreneurial capability by business factors at 'establishing' phase	45
3.3	Fuzzy scenarios of entrepreneurial capability at 'establishment' phase	64
4.1	Crime business model: Phase 2—'expansion' business factors	69
4.2	Entrepreneurial capability by business factors at 'expansion' phase	69
4.3	Conceptualization of police crime and organized crime	78
4.4	Fuzzy scenarios of entrepreneurial capability at 'expansion' phase	84
5.1	Crime business model: Phase 3—'consolidation' business factors	88
5.2	Entrepreneurial capability by business factors at 'consolidation' phase	88
5.3	Fuzzy scenarios of entrepreneurial capability at 'consolidation' phase	101
6.1	Crime business model: Phase 4—'positioning' business factors	104
6.2	Entrepreneurial capability by business factors at 'positioning' phase	104
6.3	Fuzzy scenarios of entrepreneurial capability at 'positioning' phase	117
7.1	Two sides of knowledge-managed policing	125
7.2	Matrix of knowledge categories and levels within policing	128
7.3	A 'Knowledge Cube' of policing	129
7.4	Plotting knowledge points on 'Knowledge Cube'	132
7.5	Knowledge Cube of failed terrorism investigation	140
8.1	Interrelationship of crime business phases to criminal market spheres	151
8.2	Criminal Business Analysis Matrix for policing organized crime groups	155
8.3	Application of CBAM tool to Bandidos crime business in Norway	160
9.1	UK approach to combating organized crime	172
9.2	Strategic knowledge framework for sector policing of organized crime	175
9.3	Intervention strategies against organized criminal entrepreneurialism	179

9.4 Integrating emergent and engineering models of
     knowledge sharing   181
9.5 Balanced alignment of enabling factors in international
     cooperation   184

List of Tables

7.1 Sequence of events in Haneef case   134

List of Case Examples and Case Studies

List of Case Examples

1.1	Entrapping Young Women as Unsuspecting Drug Mules	3
3.1	Verhagen Group (Dutch)	46
3.2	Computer Chips (Vietnamese)	47
3.3	Hijacking Technology (Australia)	48
3.4	Thinking Man's 'Red Daisy' Fraud (Russian)	49
3.5	Value-Added Illegal Immigration (Chinese)	49
3.6	Fake 'Versace Jackets' (Italian Camorra in Canada)	50
3.7	Systemic Corruption in Pharmaceutical Industry (Ukraine)	54
3.8	Variations on Smurfing: 'Cuckoo' Fraud (Europe and Australia)	55
3.9	Financing Backing for Cigarette Trafficking (Europe)	57
3.10	Pooling Resources in Drug Trade (United Kingdom)	57
3.11	Cyber Crime: Electronic Gambling Machines (Canada)	58
3.12	Human Smuggling and Trafficking (Belgium)	59
3.13	Trafficking in Illegal Weapons (Europe)	59
3.14	'Criminal Heaven' for Organized Crime (Canada)	60
3.15	Employment Pool: Criminal Lifestyle (Global)	61
4.1	'Patching Over' Business Strategy (OMCGs)	71
4.2	Brokering 'Street War' (Canada)	72
4.3	'Baby's Bonnet': Indirect Brutal Violence (Chinese)	73
4.4	'Operation Kronos': Human Smuggling Twist (United Kingdom)	74
4.5	'Reputational Violence': Branding Strategy (Sicilian Mafia)	75
4.6	Violence 'Asian-style' (Vietnamese)	75
4.7	Perfecting a Criminal State: Systemic Corruption (Post-Soviet Russia)	77
4.8	Vladimir 'The Poodle' Podatiev (Russia)	79
4.9	Corruption as a 'Corrosive Agent' (Global)	80
4.10	'Criminal Intelligence Service' by Hash-Smuggler (Netherlands)	82
4.11	Hells Angels' Surveillance Programme on Police (Canada)	82
5.1	Avoiding Turf War: Hells Angels and Italian Mafia (Canada)	90
5.2	Syndicated Criminal Networks: Big Circle Boys (Chinese)	92
5.3	Banking Scam: 'Mafiya' [*vory v zakone*] (Russian)	93
5.4	Triad Infiltration of 'Tongs' (Chinese)	94
5.5	Publicly Traded Company 'Shares Scam' (Australia)	95
5.6	Lawyers as Go-betweens for Organized Criminals (Italy)	96
5.7	Lawyers as Enablers of Human Trafficking (Italy)	97
5.8	'Mafiaocracy' (Post-Soviet Russia)	97
5.9	'Triads as Water': Triads in Czech Republic (Chinese)	98

5.10 Money-Laundering via Derivatives Market (Australia) 98
5.11 Risky Business of CMM (Netherlands) 99
6.1 'One way' Russian-Style Joint Ventures (Russia) 107
6.2 'New Kids' on Block: the Case of MS-13 (Salvadorans) 108
6.3 'The Corporation': Albanian Organized Crime (United States) 109
6.4 Spreading the Organized Crime Virus (Global) 109
6.5 'Black Hole' of Nigerian Crime Groups (Africa) 110
6.6 Strategy 1: Operate a 'Decentralized Command Structure' 111
6.7 Strategy 2: Create Specialists' Roles 112
6.8 Strategy 3: Utilize 'Little and Often' Principle 112
6.9 Strategy 4: Recycle 'Crime Networks' and Utilize 'Porous Borders' 113
6.10 Strategy 5: Exploit 'Failed States' and Civil Wars 114
6.11 Strategy 6: Capitalize on Police Crackdowns 115
6.12 Strategy 7: Make Strategic Alliances 115
6.13 Strategy 8: Ensure Impenetrability 116
6.14 Strategy 9: Keep a 'Low-Profile' 116

List of Case Studies

Case Study: Criminal Entrepreneurship 14
Case Study: The Business of Organized Crime in Lithuania 23
Case Study: Crime in the Commerce Industry 38
Case Study: Knowledge Failure of Suspected Terrorist 133
Case Study: The Business of Human Trafficking 146
Case Study: Business, Crime, and Politics in Montenegro 152
Case Study: Outlaw Motorcycle Gangs—Bandidos in Norway 156

Introduction

Organized criminals are good at adapting things to fit their illegal activities. Take for example the oft quoted saying in business that *it is not what you know but who you know that counts*. The spin entrepreneurially-oriented criminals put on this goes something like—*it is not what you know but 'what you know about' who you know that really counts*. Our book is about this 'high-end' of organized crime and its manifest forms of illegal business entrepreneurialism.

This is a hard subject to write about, not because it is difficult, but because we do not want to unduly assist organized crime groups to get better at their illegal business activities. Consequently, considerable thought has gone into what to put in and what to leave out. Hence for reasons of security, the 'left out' bits are better discussed in the context of police educational and training programmes. However, even what we have 'left in' will no doubt 'unfortunately' provide some crime groups with useful knowledge for them. But the greater danger, in our view, is in not making the innovative knowledge in this book available to policing, security, law enforcement, and related government departments, politicians, and the various sectors of banking, economics, and finance. Agencies and practitioners in the criminal justice field need to be smarter, more educated, and better trained than criminal entrepreneurs. There is no alternative. Our book seeks to bridge this knowledge gap between 'high-end' organized crime and 'knowledge-managed' policing.

We have endeavoured to pack this book with numerous, highly relevant, and practical case examples, crime scenarios, and extended case studies to illustrate the business of profit-driven, market-oriented, entrepreneurially-led crime. We trust our work in producing this book will well serve the interests of society in general and practitioners, in particular, in the criminal justice field.

Geoff Dean, Ivar Fahsing, and Petter Gottschalk
(Brisbane, Australia, Lillesand, Norway,
and Oslo, Norway)

PART ONE

The Business of Crime

This first section deals with the twin themes of this work—illegal businesses and entrepreneurial criminality. The section consists of two interrelated chapters (1 and 2). These chapters lay the groundwork for understanding organized crime as a profit-oriented, market-driven business, and more importantly, focus on 'high-end' illegal enterprises. High-end illegal businesses are characteristically run by criminals with entrepreneurial talent.

Chapter 1 outlines and discusses specific capabilities which form the entrepreneurial framework used throughout this book. This is the focal reference point for analysing and planning policing and law enforcement intervention strategies to combat entrepreneurially-driven organized criminals.

Chapter 2 links this entrepreneurial capabilities framework to a business development model of organized criminality. It explores how a crime business is subject to market mechanisms and therefore must operate in a global competitive criminal market context. A competitive market context presents both obstacles and opportunities for policing intervention. Case studies are presented throughout these first two chapters to illustrate the workings of profit-driven, market-oriented, and entrepreneurially-led, criminal business enterprises.

1

Entrepreneurialism of Organized Crime

Introduction

This chapter lays the foundation for understanding organized crime as, first and foremost, a criminal business. Organized crime is about making money, lots of it. This book focuses on 'high-end' organized criminality; that is, criminals with entrepreneurial talent who want to make huge profits from their illegal business activities. To understand the business dynamics of high-end, entrepreneurially-driven organized crime in its ruthless pursuit of profits and relentless desire to outwit law enforcement, consider the following case.

> **Case Example 1.1 Entrapping Young Women as Unsuspecting Drug Mules**
>
> In May 2008 three young Norwegian women and a two-year old toddler were caught at the airport in Cochabamba in Bolivia with more than 22 kilos of cocaine in their luggage. The three women have since been remanded in custody on drug smuggling charges.
> They deny they were deliberately trying to smuggle cocaine, which would have had a street value in Norway of around NOK 20 million (US $4 million). They told a Norwegian broadcasting company (NRK) that they had been on holiday in Bolivia for three weeks, that they did a lot of shopping, and needed to buy extra luggage to cart all their purchases home.
>
> *continued*

> The three women, aged 17 to 22, claim they had no idea their luggage was stuffed with cocaine. The cocaine, they claim, must have been stashed in the new bags that they bought, without their knowledge. One report in Bolivian newspaper *La Razon* said one suitcase had a double bottom. Bolivian police not only found the drugs but also claim the suitcases were coated with a sort of coffee paste, often used by smugglers in an attempt to confuse dogs specially trained to sniff out narcotics (Aftenposten, 2008).
>
> Norwegian defence attorney Dietrichson claims the young women were victims of professional narcotics dealers: 'Whether they knew it or not, someone is behind all this and used the girls'.
>
> A further investigation led by the police in Norway has shown that the three girls were not the only ones trapped into this shady business. In October 2008 another two girls with exactly the same story were arrested with 6 kilos of cocaine at Stockholm airport Arlanda in Sweden. A 24-year old man, with family ties to Bolivia and studying theology in Oslo, has been arrested and identified as the man behind this recruitment of the young female drug-traffickers. So far, the police have identified almost 30 Norwegian girls who have been tempted to go for what seemed to be an all expenses holiday in South-America (VG, 2009).
>
> The *modus operandi* of the entrapment scam works along the lines of the following: individual criminal group members 'befriend' young adult women at parties and, over the course of several party scenes, get to know them as casual acquaintances on a social level. Then, at some point, the individual crime member asks the 'trusting' young female if she could help him out. He had paid for a two-week holiday to South America but now has to forgo the planned trip owing to some unforeseen circumstance that has just arisen—work commitments, sick relative, and such like. The nature of the 'pay back' to the 'friend' (crime group member) for providing the 'free' holiday to the young women varies in some details depending on circumstances. For instance, in some cases the young women may be asked to catch up with an acquaintance of the 'friend' while holidaying in South America. The rationale being that this acquaintance has some very good bottles of wine/spirits he was going to give to him as a 'special gift' so can they bring the wine back to Norway as a small favour in return for the 'paid-for' holiday. The import tax on liquor to Norway is extremely high so it is not unusual for Norwegians to 'hide' a few bottles in their luggage upon returning from an overseas country. Such a request would not be seen as particularly suspicious by naïve young adult Norwegian women. The 'gift' of liquor bottles will contain some type of drug mixture like cocaine. Another rationale used is to connect up the young women with one of his 'close friends' in the South American country they will be holidaying in to show them a good time and where to get the 'best shopping bargains'. Naturally, specially prepared drug-courier luggage is provided during the shopping spree. The naïve and unsuspecting young adult females, if they agree to go on the 'paid-for' holiday, have inadvertently become unsuspecting 'clean skin' drug mules, with no criminal history to alert custom officials or police upon their return to Norway after the 'free' holiday.

Manipulating human needs for profit

The great tragedy is that ensnared victims like these young women can be anyone's daughters. They could be a politician's daughter, a police officer's daughter, or a grocer's daughter. Organized criminals don't care whom they use or abuse to make profits. The notion that organized criminality is of little concern to society, apart from the economic harm it can do, because it is essentially about 'victimless', crimes is a nonsense. The social harm that entrepreneurial criminality does to the fabric of families, to communities, and to society-at-large is incalculable. All criminality has victims, the difference with so-termed 'organized crimes' is that their victims, because of the nature of crime market business arrangements for illegal goods and services, are more hidden from view. 'Customers' of organized crime often want anonymity because of the illegality of the goods or services they desire. Such customers can become 'victims' owing to the poor quality of the goods or services provided by crime groups. For instance, health problems through using contaminated drugs, unprotected sex, and so on. But the invisibility of victims is also due to clever scams, entrapment strategies as in the case above, or feeding on victims' human needs to get out of a poverty trap or to find a better, more secure life for their children. This is often the case with people smuggling and sex trafficking operations organized by criminal groups. There are no limits on the extent to which organized crime groups will go to in manipulating human needs and emotions to make money. Large-scale frauds like Nigerian scams rip off millions a year from victims that are too trusting, gullible, or naïve to know better. The online grooming of children by paedophile networks does untold harm to such victims, their families, and the global community.

The point is that the seriousness of organized crime in terms of economic and social harm goes largely unnoticed by the general public, most politicians, and some police executives because of its invisibility and the aim of our book is to expose this. This will be done by demonstrating how criminal businesses start, grow, develop, and embed themselves in a cloak of legitimacy within the global community. In doing so entrepreneurial criminals maximize their profits and, at the same time, inflict massive body blows on the social fabric of communites and the global economy. Thus, in this first chapter we will define the characteristics and contours of what being a high-end 'criminal entrepreneur' looks like through a blend of research findings from business, management, and organizational studies, as well as organized crime and general criminological literature.

Focal Framework: Business Enterprise Paradigm

The central dynamic we are exploring throughout this work is the notion of 'organized crime as entrepreneurialism' and its relationship to a set of concepts that make up what is termed a 'Business Enterprise' (BE) paradigm. This paradigm is the focal framework drawn upon in our work for understanding organized crime and its variant forms of illegal activity.

We do not claim any originality for this business enterprise focus as other researchers most notably Smith (1974, 1994), (Block, 1983) and, more recently, Symeonidou-Kastanidou (2007) have explicitly drawn attention to the notion of organized crime as foundationally being about a business enterprise involving illegal entrepreneurialism. As Smith (1974: 10) points out organized crime operates on 'the same fundamental assumptions that govern entrepreneurship in the legitimate marketplace: a necessity to maintain and extend one's share of the market'. Symeonidou-Kastanidou (2007) argues that there is a need for a new definition of organized crime, where entrepreneurial structure is included as an important element. This view is in line with the Australian Crime Commission's finding that 'Organized crime is becoming more entrepreneurial, flexible, and increasingly resistant to law enforcement intervention'. (Milroy, 2007).

What we do claim as an original contribution to the literature in this area is that for the first time this 'entrepreneurial model' is developed in a far more organizationally-relevant manner than previous efforts and conceptually linked to current knowledge management thinking in the policing and law enforcement field. Therefore, our work will explore and apply in more detail a number of key concepts like entrepreneurialism and market forces that constitute a 'business enterprise' paradigm as it relates to organized crime.

Entrepreneurial Framework: Individual Capabilities

A simple definition of entrepreneurialism is that it involves 'risk-taking individuals who undertake industrial and commercial activities (businesses) with a view to making a profit' (Moles and Terry, 1997). With regard to organized crime, such 'entrepreneurial' risk-taking focuses on illegal activities as the core business strategy for profit-making by those involved in the enterprise. Hence, a person seeking to be an entrepreneur, legitimately or criminally, will need to possess or develop in themselves particular attributes or mental capacities in order to embark on an entrepreneurial career. This section outlines the core or essential set of capabilities for an entrepreneur. Figure 1.1 below lists five essential capabilities that drive entrepreneurial behaviour.

As can be seen on Figure 1.1 the core capabilities are numbered from 1 to 5. The reason is to indicate the logical interlocking sequence for how each capability builds upon the other. That is, an entrepreneur has to possess or develop the ability *first* to 'see' an *opportunity* to make money. *Secondly*, once an entrepreneur has identified an opportunity then they have to mobilize some *resources* in order to seize or exploit that opportunity. *Thirdly*, getting resources requires some *decision-making under conditions of often extreme uncertainty and high risk* about how best to allocate such resources to maximize a profit. *Fourthly*, such a high-risk exploration and exploitation of a perceived opportunity to make substantial money will of necessity involve at some point the need for the *cooperation of other people*. *Fifthly*, the end result of entrepreneurial behaviour is to make a substantial *profit*—that is the goal which orients and focuses all other capabilities.

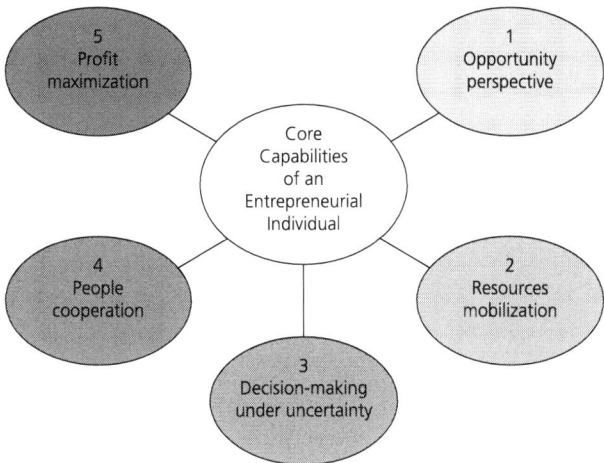

Figure 1.1 Entrepreneurial capabilities framework

Such a logical structure aids analytical discussion but should not to taken to imply there is, necessarily, a temporal sequence to these capabilities. In some situations the career of an entrepreneur will neatly follow such a temporal order, while in other circumstances it may not. Reality rarely fits comfortably into our conceptual categories. However, the usefulness of conceptualizing is that it allows us to get a hold of reality to a degree whereby we are in a better position to control and exploit parts of it. Hence, further elaboration of each of these five core capabilities follows.

Opportunity Perspective

In relation to the first entrepreneurial capability, 'opportunity perspective', it is important to appreciate that this capability is more than just having a positive outlook as an entrepreneur. The capability to 'see' an opportunity involves 'perception' and that is not about 'seeing with the eyes' but about 'perceiving with the brain'. Hence, where one individual will 'see' problems and difficulties another individual will 'see' solutions and opportunities to exploit. Such individual differences in *entrepreneurial perception* are often related in the literature to having a positive mental outlook or 'can-do' mentality (Jacobides and Winter, 2007). However, we would argue that while having a belief in the power of positive thinking is clearly an asset for an entrepreneur is should not be taken as a given necessity for success.

For this reason, we define this first core capability as one of having an 'opportunity perspective'. For entrepreneurship involves much more than just personality dynamics, as it is primarily about the study of sources of opportunities; the processes of discovery, evaluation, and exploitation of opportunities; and the set of individuals who discover, evaluate, and exploit them (Langlois, 2007).

'Seeing' opportunities is about perspective and resides in the realm of 'perception'. The capability of having an entrepreneurial 'opportunity perspective' first of all revolves around the individual's ability to identify an opportunity. For it is the identification of an opportunity which triggers the decision to engage in entrepreneurial action (Audretsch and Keilbach, 2007). Such 'opportunity identification' is a function of cognition and perception, not personality.

Therefore, in relation to criminal entrepreneurs, their task is to discover and exploit opportunities, which can be simply defined as a situation in which there is profit to be made by engaging in illegal business activity. In this sense the identification or discovery of an opportunity is about valuable goods and services for which there is a market. Accordingly, the identification of valuable goods and services also involves the identification of the valuable markets that they serve (Hsieh, Nickerson, and Zenger, 2007).

Some criminal entrepreneurs are assisted in 'seeing' business opportunities as they have grown up in a 'familial entrepreneurial culture' (Thomas and Mancino, 2007). Exposure to such a family culture in their early formative years greatly assists their entry into a criminal business enterprise. Similarly, starting life with doing petty crimes can often lead to a criminal career where exposure to more experienced criminals and a 'criminal sub-culture' full of contacts can be a determining factor in developing a more entrepreneurial vision (Witt, 2007) and search for new criminal business opportunities to exploit. In this regard Grennan and Britz (2006: 15) argue that '. . . gangs may simply be a less evolved criminal group, because the vast majority of organized crime members trace their criminal history to youth gangs'. Some entrepreneurs may engage in criminal businesses out of 'necessity' or simply 'opportunistically'—by being in the right place at the right time while other entrepreneurs are more 'innovative' (Markovski and Hall, 2007) and generally smarter, or at least more sophisticated, talented, and creative in the way they will run their criminal businesses.

In sum, a criminal's entrepreneurial vision can be rooted in a familial criminal culture, a gang sub-culture, out of necessity, opportunism, or simply innovative talent. However such entrepreneurialism comes about the research literature makes it very clear that entrepreneurially-oriented individuals have strong convictions and a belief in the superiority of their ideas, as well as the self-confidence to act on them (Jacobides and Winter, 2007). In other words, entrepreneurs are people of strong will and are determined to prove that the 'opportunities' they have 'perceived' are going to make big money for them.

Resources Mobilization

It is essential for an entrepreneur to get a business opportunity off the ground and/or take it to the next stage of business development. This is where the next entrepreneurial capability of 'mobilizing resources' comes into play. Rarely, does an entrepreneur have enough of their own resources available to be completely independent of the need for securing further resources from others. Particularly for new business ventures it takes money to make money. In other words, a criminal entrepreneur will need capital to set up a crime business.

Capital, in the financial sense, is start-up money. For example, if the business enterprise is to begin smuggling drugs then capital will be needed to buy drugs, store, and transport them to customers. In the legal sector of the economy, corporate finance fulfils the role of providing the funds for a corporation's activities. It generally involves balancing risk and profitability, while attempting to maximize an entity's wealth and the value for its stakeholders. Long-term funds are provided by ownership equity and long-term credit. Short-term funding, in terms of working capital, is mostly provided by banks that are extending a line of credit. The balance between these types of funding forms the company's capital structure. To start up a criminal business enterprise, some of these options are not available to a criminal entrepreneur. Typically, the entrepreneur will need to search for funding from crime money. Crime money will be available if the potential profit is high and the potential risk is low (Duyne, 2007).

While such resource mobilization often comes down to securing financial backing to exploit the 'perceived' business opportunity, this is not always the case. Mobilizing resources could be as simple as getting premises or transport or equipment or other logistics support to start a business venture. In most cases, mobilizing resources will also run parallel with the fourth capability (Figure 1.1), namely that of getting cooperation from others. Unless the would-be entrepreneur can get the resources from influential people to back their business proposal in one way or another, it can only ever remain a 'good idea' that has not yet been realized. This point of getting the cooperation of other people for a 'perceived' business opportunity will be discussed in more detail under that capability.

However, the point being made is that alongside getting capital, another way in which a criminal business can mobilize resources that are not available to a legitimate entrepreneur is through *corruption strategies*. As Markovska (2007) notes, an important part of financing criminal activities for start-up enterprises is corruption. To get into a market, corruption is often used by criminal entrepreneurs and, indeed, required in some situations. Corruption is a strategy that 'buys' people like government officials and is more useful than capital in some circumstances because it provides influence and leverage that money may not be able to buy. For example, the famous 'honey traps' used by Russian spies to ensnare politicians through blackmail over their sexual exploits with prostitutes can provide substantial power to criminal entrepreneurs in a way that straight capital cannot.

Finally, with regard to mobilizing resources it is clear in the entrepreneurial literature that the emergence of business enterprises is strongly associated with *entrepreneurial innovation* (Casson and Godley, 2007). By definition, entrepreneurialism involves some level of innovation and creative thinking to venture out into unknown or partly known new territory where the likelihood of failure is high. Hence, a criminal with a talent for entrepreneurial innovation could mobilize resources to start up a crime business in a number of ways. For example, a criminal entrepreneur may be innovative in finding new ways to smuggle drugs through scanning devices like concealing them in lead containers. Or they could be innovative in the production of designer drugs by securing the services of a talented chemist to make a new variant and so open up a new product and avenue for the illicit drug market.

Decision-Making under Uncertainty

This third entrepreneurial capability, 'decision-making under uncertainty', often occurs at the same time as 'resources mobilization', in that decisions have to be made about whom to approach for financial backing or equipment and so forth. Once an entrepreneur has secured some support, financial or material, for their business proposal it is no longer just an 'idea'—now they have money and/or equipment to make it happen.

However, the type of decision-making this capability is focused on has more to do with the conditions under which entrepreneurs have to make decisions. An entrepreneur again, by definition, operates in an *uncertain and highly risky environment*. This environment is even more volatile, aggressive, and dangerous in the criminal underworld where both competitors and the police are trying to take a would-be entrepreneur down. Hence, getting a criminal business going and growing will always involve making decisions under conditions of uncertainty and risk that can vary to extreme uncertainty and high risk on a daily basis.

In this regard, Lyman and Potter (2007) make the point that compared to legal businesses, criminal enterprises will often need to have a 'tighter control structure' since they operate in a hostile and uncertain environment as noted previously. The need for secrecy and security to conduct their illegal operations is a constant constraint on a crime business. Hence, structural control is a high priority for a criminal entrepreneur. Thus, there can be a strong drive by criminal entrepreneurs to develop a more 'concrete structure' (Symeonidou-Kastanidou, 2007) through possessing their own assets for their business in order to have more security over the production and/or distribution of their illegal operations.

Another characteristic closely associated with doing business in an uncertain environment (Foss *et al.*, 2007) is that of *entrepreneurial judgment*. For instance, a drug dealer who buys before they know the price at which it can be resold must make a judgment about what the future price will be. Judgment, therefore, refers primarily to business decision-making when the range of possible future outcomes is generally unknown. Judgment is required when no obviously correct model or decision rule is available or when relevant data is unreliable or incomplete (Foss *et al.*, 2007). In relation to entrepreneurial judgment, it is ultimately judgment about the control of resources. An entrepreneur must exercise judgment in terms of resource acquisition and allocation to prosper from criminal business opportunities.

An entrepreneur that wants to stay in business in an uncertain, high-risk environment will need to have or develop the capacity to utilize and build on *knowledge*. Research clearly indicates that entrepreneurial decision-makers tend to notice new information that relates to and can be combined with knowledge they already have (Zander, 2007). Knowledge of the strategic type is a necessary capacity for a would-be criminal entrepreneur to develop as their business may not survive in the longer term if they fail to notice or take heed of new law enforcement techniques, strategies, or technologies that can do their business harm. Criminal entrepreneurs who have this capacity will also invest in anti-policing countermeasures and anti-surveillance technological devices to ensure the continuation of their illegal business activities.

People Cooperation

It is a necessary core capacity for criminal entrepreneurs to make and maintain *cooperative connections* with influential people. This is what this fourth entrepreneurial capability of 'people cooperation' is all about. Securing such cooperation requires both active, direct influence and/or more passive, indirect means of exerting influence by criminal entrepreneurs on people.

Criminal entrepreneurs need directly to seek out various kinds of influential people in the legitimate environment, like bank managers, financiers, backers, lawyers, accountants, partners, shareholders, technical experts, industry leaders, government officials, and so forth. Such people will have to be consulted, harnessed, or otherwise dealt with by the criminal entrepreneur. The input or support of these people is needed to assist the business opportunity to be realized.

More indirect ways of gaining people's cooperation are necessary, through activities like misinformation, scams, entrapment and bribery of others in positions of influence or power that have the potential to affect the outcome of the business venture. These are influential people in government departments and/or police executives who can stand in the way of the entrepreneurial opportunity. Such people at least are capable of inflicting damage on the criminal business venture and will need to be dealt with by organized criminals either through co-opting them, corrupting them, or in some other manner neutralizing their power or influence.

An entrepreneur also needs to be able to 'connect' with people, in the sense of having good communication and relationship-building skills, to get their cooperation. Unless an entrepreneur is able to persuade others to put money or other resources behind their business venture then they will not be able to get very far with exploiting the opportunity. It is unlikely that a 'good idea' sells itself or else it would have been done before and, hence, there is little need for an entrepreneur.

To what extent a criminal entrepreneur needs 'good communication/relationship-building skills' is less of a consideration. Depending on the type of 'business opportunity' being undertaken, a big gun in someone's face or the threat of violence has the potential to turn even the most reluctant participant into a supporter, if only for a limited time. Moreover, bribes and corruption of government officials, police, customs officers, and others is a SOP (standard operating procedure of organized criminality) that will ensure a business venture can be established with the minimum level of communication skills by a criminal entrepreneur. It is a well documented fact that *bribery and corruption, combined with violence* and threats of violence, is an effective strategy for many criminal organizations to employ as a type of 'business insurance' (Kugler, Verdier, and Zenou, 2005).

Getting people's cooperation and making the right connections with suppliers, producers, influential persons, and so on is essential to operate a successful business. Such connectedness is perhaps even more important for running a criminal business as suppliers and producers are not as readily available in a criminal context as they are in the legal business environment. A criminal entrepreneur is not able to just go and look up the telephone book for another supplier of illegal drugs when his previous supplier is arrested. Hence, the *'social microcosm'* of the criminal underworld is of critical importance for an aspiring criminal entrepreneur. Lampe (2007) elaborates this notion of a criminal social microcosm in the following manner:

> The concept of the 'social microcosm of illegal entrepreneurs' encompasses three aspects that have variously been addressed in the criminological and organised crime literature: co-offending, the social embeddedness of criminal networks, and the interaction between illegal and legal spheres of society. Co-offending includes the joint execution of criminal activity. Social embeddedness includes relatives, friends and others in the personal network that participate in social transactions that do not have a criminal connotation as such, but do nevertheless have some bearing on the criminal activity. Interaction between illegal and legal institutional environments is typically visible in terms of corruption and infiltration (Lampe, 2007: 132)

Thus, the 'social microcosm' of a criminal entrepreneur includes all those individuals they encounter in the course of their criminal activities, who are in a position to influence the success or failure of their particular criminal enterprise.

Profit Maximization

The fifth and final entrepreneurial capability, that of 'profit maximization', may seem self-evident but in relation to running a criminal business there are points of difference about this capability that require some discussion. Organized criminals, like legitimate business entrepreneurs, seek to make substantial money from their business venture in order to compensate themselves financially for the high risks taken in exploiting the business opportunity in the first place.

An entrepreneur running a legitimate business has time to devote to establishing institutional support and building up the business whereas, for a criminal running an illegal business, 'time' can often be an enemy. For instance, a criminal entrepreneur can be impulsively driven by simple greed or an inability to wait or postpone the satisfaction of making lots of money. Often there is the need to make quick profits to pay back a crime loan or, more strategically, to not attract police attention or operate for too long in a hostile environment. In other words, there is a *time pressure* to making a profit with a criminal business enterprise that is not as pressing or urgent for a legitimate business entrepreneur. This is not to imply that a legitimate business entrepreneur does not have urgent timelines to make money. Often they do, especially when monthly repayments on borrowed money are required. But they do not have the added pressure of operating their business in a highly volatile, dangerously competitive, and hostile environment where they can be arrested, closed down, or even killed at any point in time. The need to make big money quickly is a constant danger faced by criminal entrepreneurs.

Given such time pressure on criminal entrepreneurs it is likely that they will aggressively pursue, both in the sense of physical aggression and having an aggressive mentality, money-making opportunities more quickly than a legal entrepreneur. In this regard the aggressive pursuit of profit will involve both 'strong' and 'weak' entrepreneurial 'innovators'[1]. Knowing the likely characteristics of who you are dealing with allows police to 'know thy enemy' and hence places policing in a superior strategic position to plan and execute targeted operations against organized crime groups and networks.

Finally, making money occurs in a market context. Business markets are not perfect mechanisms as the economics of supply and demand are constantly changing. Hence, *market imperfections* exist which can be exploited by the smart criminal entrepreneur. Therefore, opportunities to create new economic value exist because of demand for goods and services in illegal markets. A criminal entrepreneur who realizes this reality of market imperfections due to changes in technology, demand, or other factors is in a position to exploit these competitive imperfections in illegal markets. For example, Ismael Zambada-Garcia is a Mexican drug lord. He is capo (captain) and head of the Sinaloa cartel in Mexico. He is 'El Mayo', Mexico's number one drug dealer. He climbed to the top by eliminating rivals and victory over Columbian cocaine producers. Zambada-Garcia got help indirectly from the police, because police in Mazatlan shot and killed his most powerful rival Ramon Arellano Felix in 2002. The Tijuana cartel run by Felix was weakened, while the Sinaloa cartel of Zambada-Garcia was strengthened (Small and Taylor, 2006). Competitive imperfections (killing of a rival by police) were created for Zambada-Garcia, which he then purposely exploited to his advantage.

---

[1] Entrepreneurs with a *strong* sense of innovation tend to champion radical changes in resource allocation, for example in making new product markets and pioneering new processes, whereas entrepreneurs with a *weak* sense of innovation tend to seek small changes in resource allocation by exploring profit making opportunities between already established activities (Markovski and Hall, 2007).

Such market imperfections can create volatility in the larger social environment and global context. Volatility reflects the fact that the economic, competitive, and law enforcement environment is continually subjected to shocks (Casson and Godley, 2007). Shocks are extremely varied: they include disruptions because of police actions, fads and fashions in consumer tastes, and rivalry among competitors. Under conditions of *global volatility* such 'shocks' again present opportunities for the smart criminal entrepreneur to exploit at either the local level or global level.

Interrelated entrepreneurial capabilities

In sum, this discussion of the nexus between a criminal entrepreneur's core capabilities, that of *opportunity perspective, resources mobilization, and decision-making under uncertainty, people cooperation, and profit maximization*, as well as the range of characteristics linked to these various capabilities provides a useful starting point for our work and will be developed further in subsequent chapters. For now, a relatively simple case study is presented below to show the interrelated nature of these five entrepreneurial capabilities.

Case Study: Criminal Entrepreneurship

The following case study is of a once very 'successful' criminal entrepreneur, Curtis 'Cocky' Warren (Barnes, Elias, and Walsh, 2001), before he was finally brought to some form of belated justice on drug smuggling charges (*Guardian*, 2009 [e]). The case is analysed in the light of the preceding discussion of the five entrepreneurial capabilities identified from the literature as core components for a criminal entrepreneur.

Synopsis of case

Warren was one of Britain's biggest ever drug traffickers; at his peak he made it on to The Sunday Times Rich 500 List (*Guardian*, 2009 [c]), the highest-placed mixed-race plutocrat in the country. The odd thing about all this wealth is that he had, as they say, no visible means of income. Curtis Warren is said to be a highly intelligent force and to have a photographic memory for telephone numbers, bank accounts details, and so forth. Unlike most other criminals, Warren doesn't drink, smoke, or use drugs. He started selling heroin as a teenager and, in a few years, he became the main drug supplier in all of Britain, moving tonnes of cocaine, heroin, and Ecstasy, working in close cooperation with the Colombian Cali Cartel and Moroccan and Turkish criminal organizations.

First capability: opportunity perspective

Curtis Warren was born on 31 May 1963 in Liverpool, England. His father was a mixed-race sailor with the Norwegian Merchant Navy and his mother was the daughter of a shipyard boiler attendant in Liverpool. Warren grew up in the Granby district of Toxteth—a tough neighbourhood with a bad reputation. When he reached his teens

Warren became a bouncer at a Liverpool night club. In this position he saw how the local drug trade was organized. He soon realized (*entrepreneurial vision—perception*) that a bouncer was in a unique position. A bouncer has the power to let the dealers (and the drugs) in or out.

After some time Warren was promoted to main bouncer and had the task of bossing around the other bouncers. This position allowed him to exploit the dealers fully and to establish a good hold on the drug trade. He got his 'in' and began selling and controlling drugs. Owing to Warren's individual entrepreneurial capacity to identify, explore, and exploit the drug business opportunity through his position as a bouncer, he established his own business venture.

Second capability: resources mobilization

By the late 1980s Curtis Warren had risen to become the leading drug dealer in the Liverpool area. He made good money and could have decided to stabilize his business in Liverpool. Instead he decided to expand through resource mobilization. Warren teamed up with another drugs trafficker with style, Brian Charrington, who worked the north-east of England, to Cocky's north-west. Like Warren, Charrington was already wealthy.

By forming an alliance these two criminal entrepreneurs had between them the financial capital derived from crime money and other asset resources to make it into the big time criminal league. Charrington had a yacht and the two men went to France on British visitor passports. Once in France, they were able to fly to Venezuela and Colombia to organize their joint drug importation syndicate. In Colombia the two men fixed a deal to import huge amounts of cocaine. The first shipment of hundreds of kilos of cocaine arrived safely for the British market in spite of a thorough HM Customs' inspection.

The next shipment was already on its way, when the British Customs received a tip from their Dutch colleagues and they launched a new inspection. This time the cocaine was found and Warren, Charrington and several others were arrested by HM Customs. It seemed Warren's criminal career was over and that he was going away to prison for a very long time. Warren and his co-offender Charrington faced charges of importing shipments of cocaine with a combined worth of 500 million British pounds. All looked set for trial. However, two detectives revealed that Charrington was a police informer. The Customs agents knew nothing of this and it turned out that Charrington, with help of his informer status, had shipped a lot of drugs to Britain. The case was dropped and in 1993 Curtis Warren was acquitted of all charges. This lucky turn of events for Warren is a good example of entrepreneurial innovation by Charrington, in that, by playing the double role of a police informer, Charrington was able to, in effect, take out an 'insurance' policy against future enforcement action as had happened to him and fellow criminal. Warren was quick to learn this lesson.

Third capability: decision-making under uncertainty

As time went on the environment in Liverpool was undergoing significant changes in the criminal underworld. Gang wars started. Things were getting dangerous, several organized crime figures were found dead. Warren was also smart enough to realize that the English authorities were not going to take very kindly to the way the first attempt

Chapter 1: Entrepreneurialism of Organized Crime

to prosecute Warren had ended in disgrace for them, with an embarrassing collapsed trial. With such volatility and uncertainty in the wind Warren decided to move his headquarters to Holland in 1995. This is an interesting move as most drug traffickers would choose Amsterdam or Rotterdam as a good place to set up base. Warren decided on the quiet town of Sassenheim. He moved into a very nice villa from where he conducted his business and made his deals. By this time Curtis 'Cocky' Warren was a very, very rich man. He owned houses, mansions, and office blocks in Britain, casinos in Spain, discos in Turkey, a vineyard in Bulgaria, and his villa in Sassenheim. The rest of his money was stashed away in Swiss bank accounts. Warren could have easily retired to some tropical island but for reasons we can only speculate on he chose to come out of his semi-self imposed retirement and expand his criminal enterprise.

Fourth capability: people cooperation

As cocaine's popularity soared, Warren established further links with the notorious Cali cartel, a Colombian cocaine-supplying gang. The cartel was grateful to the Liverpool mafia, whose contacts and own distribution network allowed it to crack the European market. The Cali cartel, despite many high-profile arrests, has evolved into one of the most powerful crime syndicates in the world. But Warren also teamed up with officials to keep his business growing, corrupt detectives, port officials, and haulage contractors in order to ensure his status as an accomplished smuggler[2].

Fifth capability: profit maximization

Britain's cocaine market is estimated to a worth of £2 billion. The potential profit for those who control such a market is immense and this is what Curtis Warren wanted to achieve. To exploit such an opportunity Warren had to team up with the biggest sharks in the drug sea—most criminals would not risk going into business with one of the world's most fearsome crime syndicates. The risk of being eaten yourself, when dealing with such partners, is more than obvious. But if you succeed the potential profit is just as big as the risk—that's the way it works in any business. At the time, Warren was Interpol's most wanted man, who was nicknamed the 'Teflon criminal' (*Guardian*, 2009 [e]). Through his legitimate ventures, like his security company, and by keeping an extremely low personal profile, Curtis Warren was able to build up a massive fortune from his drug business. Estimates of Warren's fortune vary wildly, but a Dutch financial investigation has revealed an impressive list of real estate, including properties in Wales, Turkey, Spain, Gambia, a yacht, 200 houses in Liverpool, a brothel and a football club.

End game

Part of the game was up for Warren in 1997 when he was finally arrested, convicted, and jailed in the Netherlands for 13 years for drugs smuggling and possession of firearms (*Guardian*, 2009 [b]). His sentence was extended by four years in 1999 on a

---

[2] How Warren managed to co-opt such people into his criminal business enterprise will be the subject matter of later chapters when discussing 'corruption strategies' used by criminal groups.

manslaughter conviction after Warren got into a fight with a fellow prisoner and killed him. On June 14 2007 Warren was released early from prison.

However, Warren had only been out of prison for five weeks when he was arrested on 21 July 2007 by Jersey police and accused of being the ringleader of a crime gang trying to import 180kg of cannabis into the island from Holland via boat from France (*Guardian*, 2009 [d]). The Jersey police were tipped off about the planned drug importation, and Warren's involvement in it, by the UK's Serious Organised Crime Agency (SOCA) which had been gathering intelligence on him in 2006 while he was still in Nieuw Vosseveld prison in the Netherlands (*Guardian*, 2009 [e]). As the Director General of SOCA, Bill Hughes, said at the time:

> Serious organised criminals don't suddenly stop just because they're been caught once. That's why when a criminal comes onto SOCA's radar, they stay there for life. Curtis Warren was a career criminal for whom prison was a temporary setback. He was already planning his next operation from inside prison, and when he was released SOCA was waiting, watching and listening. Together with our partners in the States of Jersey police we've stopped Curtis Warren's plans in their tracks. Criminals need to know that this is a different world now – lifetime management is a reality (*Guardian*, 2009 [d]).

Warren was found guilty of conspiring to smuggle £1million worth of cannabis into Jersey. Warren was sentenced on 3 December 2009 to 13 years' imprisonment:

> Warren is currently held in the high security wing of London's Belmarsh prison, over concerns with regards his security. Jersey Police are also starting an investigation into his wealth, with the aim of confiscating his gains from drugs trafficking.

(<http://en.wikipedia.org/wiki/Curtis_Warren#Jersey_conviction>. Accessed on 4 April 2010.)

Summary

This initial chapter unpacked the central themes of this book, that of illegal businesses and entrepreneurial criminality, through discussion of the various capabilities of high-end, entrepreneurially-driven organized criminals.

One of the major implications for police and law enforcement agencies dealing with high-end criminal entrepreneurialism is the need to develop the capacity to identify the individuals within an organized crime network and/or syndicate that have such 'entrepreneurial flair'. The reason such capacity building is vital is because the typical characteristics of entrepreneurial criminals as outlined in this chapter make them more cunning and resourceful than other criminal types who may be engaged in illegal business activities. Such entrepreneurial criminals will not be easily deterred or stopped. They will be constantly thinking of, and planning ways, to outwit the police and their operational tactics. The lesson for policing is that operations against organized criminal entrepreneurialism will not be very successful if traditional policing methods and tactics only are used. It can be assumed that entrepreneurial criminals will know more about such policing methods, tactics, and technologies. Furthermore these types of criminals may well have infiltrated police ranks with their own informants and/or corrupted police officers who can tip off crime syndicates about planned police operations.

The chapter concluded with an analysis of a case study of a criminal entrepreneurship to illustrate the usefulness of the entrepreneurial capabilities framework. This capabilities framework is by no means exhaustive. Nor should this framework be seen as complete or sufficient. It is like all good research: a work-in-progress. This capabilities framework will be developed further in later chapters as an analytical policing tool to profile the core capabilities of individual criminal entrepreneurs and their illegal businesses as they develop over time. Such knowledge can assist police and law enforcement practitioners to conduct effective investigations to disrupt, dismantle, and prosecute criminal entrepreneurs and their illegal business activities. In essence, policing agencies dealing with high-end entrepreneurial criminality will require better police knowledge management. It is our mission in this book to assist policing and law enforcement to achieve that goal.

2

Criminal Enterprises, Markets, and Industries

Introduction

This chapter introduces a business development model as the operating framework for running a criminally-oriented business enterprise. It builds on the entrepreneurial capabilities framework presented in the previous chapter. The chapter explores the micro-economics of criminal market behaviour by discussing several business-related notions like competitive market forces, supply and demand graphs, market share, and size. This is followed by a macro understanding of how various global spheres of influence combine to shape market opportunities and global crime industries. These market-shaping mechanisms present both threats and opportunities for policing organized high-end entrepreneurial criminality. Two case studies are presented to illustrate the nature of profit-driven, market-oriented, and entrepreneurially-led criminal businesses.

Operating Framework: Model of Business Development

A business founded on crime will follow the same business phases in its development as any legal or legitimate business venture (Rubin, 1980; Moore, 1987). As Carter (1997: 137) notes 'any commodity for which a profit can be earned is open to organised crime'. The main difference between a legal and illegal business is one of legislation not one of development. Hence, the trajectory of a legal business can be charted or mapped out over time and used as an operating model for an illegal business. Modelling the development of a crime business provides policing agencies with a strategic vantage point to understanding its inherent strengths and weaknesses and so plan how best to combat its illegal

Chapter 2: Criminal Enterprises, Markets, and Industries

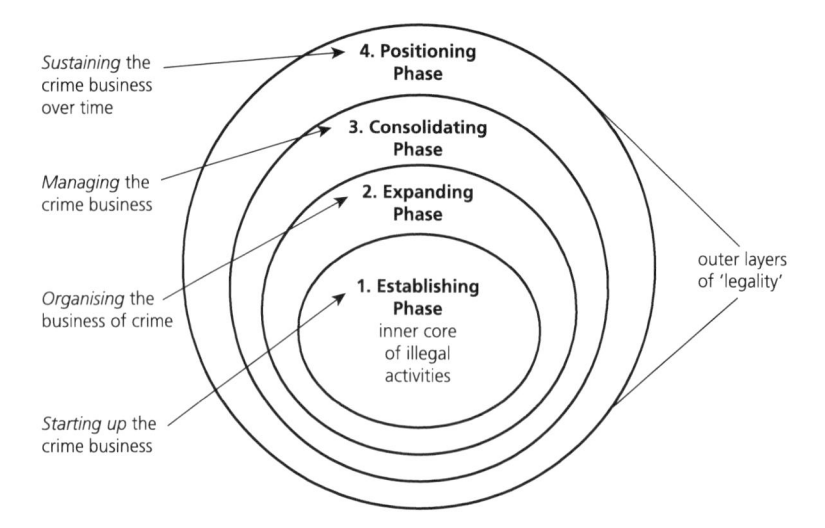

Figure 2.1 Model of business development applied to organized crime

activities. Figure 2.1 below, outlines our operating model of the key phases[1] or processes used in the building of an organized criminal business enterprise.

As can be seen, there are four phases/processes that any business, legal or illegal, follows as it develops and matures over time. Each phase has a key business task (*starting up, organizing, managing, sustaining*) that must be achieved to some functional level before moving onto the next business phase. Whilst, these phases are logically interdependent they don't have to occur in a linear or sequential manner. Sometimes various phases may occur in tandem. For instance, an established crime group involved in the drug market may expand into a new market like people smuggling. In doing so, they will bring their organizational and managerial skills learned in the drug trade to the new business venture of people smuggling.

The depiction of the four key business development phases as concentric circles shows their interrelatedness. Also, the business phases are numbered 1 to 4. This numbering denotes how one phase logically builds on the other but, as noted above, not necessarily in a sequential fashion. This numbering is for simplicity of discussion only and should not be interpreted as to

---

[1] A conceptual note is in order here. The use of the term business 'phases' is used interchangeably with the notion of business 'processes' in this book to indicate the fluid nature of how a business develops at a process level of phases and not necessarily through a set sequence of stages. Hence, the use of the term 'phases' should not be confused with a 'stage' model of business development in that, the term 'stage' implies a type of linear progression through each stage. A stage model is too reductionistic and does not capture the complexity of business development and its more erratic behaviour, especially with regard to the volatile environment in which criminal business enterprises operate. However, the notion of 'phase' is used in the physics/electronic sense of 'a point of advancement in a cycle' (Macquare Dictionary, 1981: 1276) whereby there is a 'phasing in' or gradual introduction and synchronization into a system by each phase.

how an organized crime business actually operates in reality by following such a neat linear sequence of phases. These four phases are more cyclical in nature and intermeshing in operation as depicted in Figure 2.1. This is because contemporary criminal business enterprises operate much more like fluid networks of both 'association' and 'transaction' (Ruggiero and Khan, 2007: 62) in their business dealings. This is the present day reality of organized crime rather than the picture described in traditional criminological literature of criminal organizations having a mafia-type hierarchical structure. Even such hierarchical depictions of the Italian Mafia are no longer an accurate contemporary picture of the current state of play of these criminal organizations. In fact, it is more precise to describe 'four' mafias (Nicaso and Lamothe, 2005)—the Sicilian Mafia, Calabrian ('Ndrangheta') Mafia, Camorra Mafia, and the Sacra Corona Unita (SCU) Mafia—that coexist in a set of uneasy relationships within the domain of the Italian underworld of organized crime.

Hence, the development of a criminal business enterprise may require a combination of these key business phases to occur simultaneously or close to real time, in order to maximize a business opportunity. For example, a business opportunity may arise quite suddenly for a crime group to expand its drug market because one of its criminal competitors is taken out of play by law enforcement action. This happened when police shot and killed Ramon Arellano Felix who headed the Tijuana cartel in Mexico in 2002. This police action dramatically changed the crime market context by creating an 'opening' for the rival Sinaloa cartel operated by Ismael Zambada-Garcia to increase his market share in the drug trade (Small and Taylor, 2006). To seize this business opportunity Zambada-Garcia needed to move swiftly to mobilize resources, money, and equipment to supply the extra demand before other rival crime gangs moved in to fill the gap. Hence, at one stroke, police intervention helped the Sinaloa cartel not only to *expand* its illegal drug business but also to *consolidate* and *position* the criminal enterprise quickly relative to other criminal competitors in the drug trade. Therefore, these four key developmental phases—*establishing, expanding, consolidation,* and *positioning*—of a crime business tend to jump around and overlap owing to different contextual factors that occur at various times, as in the above example of Mexican organized crime.

Establishing[2] a crime business (phase 1) requires 'start-up' resources like money, people, equipment, premises, materials, and so forth. Once up and

---

[2] With regard to the first phase of *establishing a business,* the difference between a legal business and a criminal one is the core activities of a crime business are illegal as shown in Figure 2.1. This difference draws attention to the fact that while a legal business may engage in illegal activities such illegality is not its core business. In that, where illegal activity by a legitimate business is peripheral to its main business, this type of business illegality is characteristically described as white collar crime, or corporate crime. This type of criminal activity has its own domain of academic study and will only be touched on where it falls within an entrepreneurial model of organized crime.

running the crime business has to be *organised to some degree*[3] in order for the business to 'grow' (phase 2). This organizing of the business will evolve over time into a loose or more tightly controlled organizational structure depending on a number of variables like how big the business becomes, the number of staff employed, and so forth. Furthermore, this process of organization requires some form of *management* to 'mature' (phase 3) into a viable business. Again there are a number of factors to consider in the organizational life cycle of a growing business. For example, questions arise about how good are the originating operators of the criminal enterprise at managing a business? Do they possess an adequate level of management ability and skills? What will happen as the business grows? Will they need to consider appointing a CEO-type leader with the necessary management skills to maximize their profit? Once some level of maturity is reached where the business is relatively stable and ongoing with a reasonable market share and a good profit margin then further questions (factors) of a 'strategic' nature arise. These questions revolve around the future longer term viability and *sustainability* (phase 4) of the criminal business. For instance, to grow the business more should a merger with a larger partner be considered? Or should a gangland style war be started to get rid of the competitors in order to increase market share? Or should a 'temporary' joint venture arrangement for a limited period be entered into with a market leader to increase profits for the crime business? Or does a crime business link up with a terrorist cell to sell weapons and bomb-making equipment to them because a particular terrorist network has big drug money to spend? Such questions go to the heart of the crime business and strategically will determine its future direction.

Finally, this business modelling assists police to track the evolution of particular crime groups in relation to each phase of their crime business development. Such tracking provides policing agencies with an empirically-grounded tool to predict what the next most likely moves or scenarios are in relation to a crime group's business development. The predictive value of our business development model is discussed in later chapters. Also, understanding the interrelated nature of these four key business phases stimulates insights into *where* and *how* and *when* to disrupt, disturb, and dismantle criminal business activities. Disruption strategies for combating entrepreneurial organized crime using this business model are also the subject of further chapters.

---

[3] The degree of organization is really a function of the 'entrepreneurialism' of the person or persons responsible for establishing the crime business. That is, a high level of entrepreneurial spirit by criminals starting up a business will want to 'push the envelope' as much as possible and as quickly as they can to establish a foothold in a crime market. Hence, 'entrepreneurialism' is a determining factor in the success or failure of any business.

Case Study: The Business of Organized Crime in Lithuania

The evolution of an economic basis for organized crime in Lithuania provides a clear picture of how the four business phases of *establishing, expanding, consolidating*, and *positioning* of a crime business unfold and interrelate over time. Lithuania is a particularly interesting example to study of the business development of organized crime because of its recent history since gaining independence in 1991. Lithuania after the collapse of the Soviet Union provides a clear demarcation line of the movement from a Soviet command economy to a Western-style free market economy.

Prior to the 1990s, organized crime in Lithuania according to Gutauskas, Juska, Johnstone, and Pozzuto (2004: 205) during the late Soviet period:

> ... grew because of unsatisfied demand in basic consumer goods such as clothes, shoes, furniture, housing and foodstuffs. This created the preconditions for the rise of a 'retail mafia', which was enriched by monopolising the trade and distribution of consumer goods.

However, by the early 1990s, which are considered as the 'founding years' for the vast majority of organized crime groups in Lithuania, the economic situation changed rapidly from an illegal manufacturing base of consumer goods '... to the supply of criminal consumables associates with privatization of state property and the development of a free market economy' (Gutauskas *et al.*, 2004: 206).

Thus, the *first business phase* of *establishing* a new crime business took root in Lithuania. Gutauskas *et al.* (*ibid*) summarize the situation succinctly:

> The introduction of competitive markets in Lithuania also led to the appearance of new types of crime characteristic of economies organised on the basis of free markets: economic crimes, organised professional crimes, white collar crimes, and the sale and export of nonferrous metals. Parallel to the new forms of criminal activities there continued to co-exist traditional criminal groups engaged in larceny, robbery and car theft.

This period of entrepreneurial establishment of criminal businesses was primarily driven by the opportunistic development of new criminal groupings. These new emerging crime groups were mainly formed by young individuals who saw they could get rich quick by banding together to engage in new forms of organized criminal enterprises. Such criminal business ventures went beyond the usual protection racket operations of the more traditional form of organized crime. This upsurge in newly formed criminal associations based on a business model quickly underwent an *expanding phase* with '... the embracement of a new economy model of exploring financial crimes, money laundering and the establishment of criminal enterprise links intra and inter Lithuania with other crime groups'. (Gutauskas *et al.*, 2004: 209).

As the expansion of criminal business activities of the types identified by Gutauskas *et al.* grew, so did the need to manage the booming crime business more efficiently and effectively. Hence, the next business phase involved a process of *consolidation*

Chapter 2: Criminal Enterprises, Markets, and Industries

by criminal entrepreneurs in order to maintain their market share and/or increase it. Often, associated with this consolidating push of a crime business is the employment of corruption strategies of police and other state officials to ensure the illegal business activities remain profitable. As Gutauskas *et al.* (*ibid*: 212) found in Lithuania a 'symbiosis between organised crime groups and state officials . . . can be suspected . . . when laws and regulations are being enacted favourable to the interests of criminal groups'.

It is interesting to note in this context that not only does bribery and corruption of public officials become a reality where organized crime groups operated but also several 'strategic mistakes', to use Gutauskas *et al.*'s term, were made by the law enforcement community. These strategic mistakes come down to a lack of an adequate appreciation by enforcement agencies of the new market dynamics of criminal behaviour that operates on a business model. For example, Gutauskas *et al.* (*ibid*: 210) point out that:

> The priority for police in response to organised crime was to arrest members of suspected groups rather than focusing on dismantling the financial infrastructure of such organisations or in arresting group leaders.

The fourth business development phase, that of strategically *positioning* the crime business for long-term sustainability, began to be seen in Lithuania in the mid-to-late 1990s when:

> '. . . former racketeers were becoming bankers and owners of legitimate companies and enterprises. . . . Organised crime was mutating into the qualitatively higher stage. It was becoming more professional, more sophisticated and more complex (Gutauskas *et al.*, 2004: 210).

This Lithuanian case study of entrepreneurially-driven criminal enterprises is but one possible scenario of how the businesses phases of *establishing, expanding, consolidating*, and *positioning* can develop over time in a country or state. Other business scenario trajectories for criminal entrepreneurs will be presented using the operating framework of our business development model in later chapters. Before looking at each business phase in detail in subsequent chapters, what remains to do in this chapter is to explore criminal markets in relation to the economics of market behaviour.

Market Mechanisms

There are two key business concepts that relate to business dynamics of markets. They are: the notion of 'competitive market forces' and the 'supply-demand' equation. These twin notions are central to running a successful business, be it a criminal or a legitimate legally-run business.

Competitive forces in legal and illegal markets

Competitive market forces exist in the underworld of criminal business enterprises just as they do in legal business markets. In legal markets the metaphor of the 'invisible hand' is often invoked to explain the way market economics work.

This notion of an *invisible hand* is an expression introduced by Adam Smith in his economic treatise on *The Wealth of Nations* (1776) as an analogy for the way in which 'the working of markets allows economic activity to be co-ordinated without any central organisation' (Dictionary of Economics, 2002). The key idea behind this concept of the *invisible hand* is that:

> Self-interest working through markets induces people to produce goods and services to meet the needs of other people whom they may never meet and for whom they need feel no goodwill. Equally, the market system allows people to satisfy their own wants from the produce of others who are similarly only connected with them through markets. The invisible hand is not a panacea, lacking the ability to deal with the provision of public goods, externalities, monopoly and problems of income distribution. *(ibid)*

This *invisible hand* thesis is not uncontested. For instance:

> Alfred Chandler (*Strategy and Structure*, 1962) has argued that the growth of large-scale corporations and monopolized markets has allowed greater social planning by the 'visible hand' of the corporate leadership (Dictionary of Sociology, 2005).

This *visible hand* view, of course, is not restricted to legal market manipulation by big multinational corporations. Researchers like Reuter (1983) and to some extent Chang, Lu, and Chen (2005) argue that illegal markets often engage in the 'economics of the visible hand' to exert their monopolistic control over certain sectors of criminal markets.

Hence, it is clear that both the *invisible* and *visible hands* are particularly involved in the way the economics of crime markets operate. However, whatever 'hands' are at work in legal and illegal markets, it is also apparent that a range of competitive market forces of a more discernable nature are at work in the economic behaviour of a market economy. For instance, a competitive market environment consists of a number of primary factors that interact in a range of predictable and sometimes unpredictable ways to create market forces or pressure on a business enterprise. These primary factors are: the business enterprise itself, its suppliers, and its customers, the various competing business enterprises offering the same or new products and/or services, as well as substitute products/services. These set of factors are illustrated below in Figure 2.2.

As can be seen, the business enterprise is placed at the centre of competitive action. The rationale for its existence is to make a profit from selling a product or providing a service in an environment where market demand, which is customers, for that product/service is deemed to exist. Hence, there must be some evidence of a relatively strong and consistent market demand to justify the expense of setting up the business enterprise in the first place.

The business enterprise, unless it is the manufacturer of a product, must also have a supplier that can guarantee a regular supply of the particular product, or in the case of a service, procure the necessary staff to provide such a service. In either case as product manufacturer, service provider, or 'go-between' company,

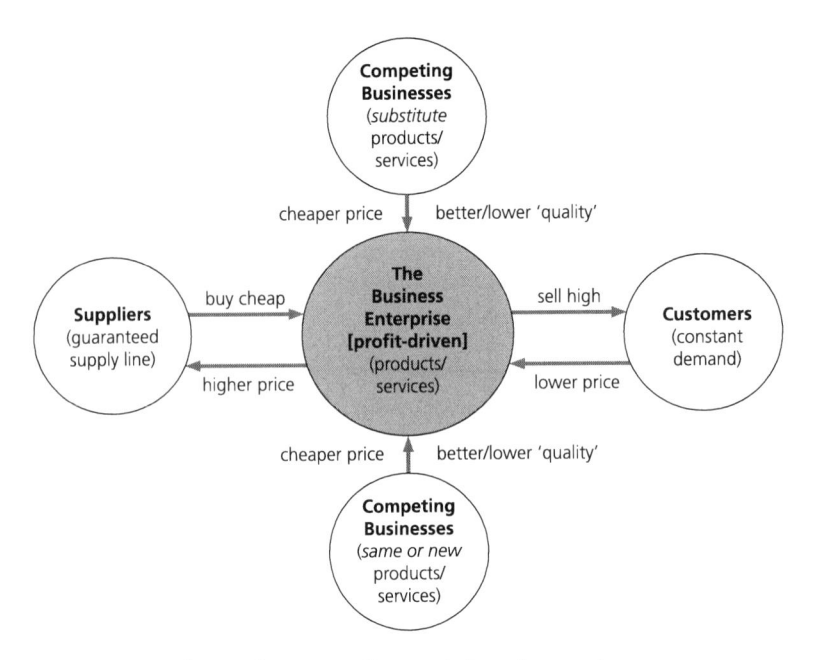

Chapter 2: Criminal Enterprises, Markets, and Industries

Figure 2.2 Key factors in a competing market environment

the business enterprise still has to procure the raw materials or talents of others to do business.

As is apparent from Figure 2.2 this market structure of suppliers-business enterprise-customers creates competitive forces on both sides of the equation. The business enterprise wants to buy the product/service as cheaply as it can from a supplier and sell the product/service to its customers for as high a price as it can in order to maximize its profit margin. Customers, on the other hand, only want to pay the lowest price they can for the product/service they desire, whilst the supplier will try to get the highest price for the product/service they can from the business enterprise that wants to procure their product/service.

Criminal markets are subjected to the same sort of competitive market forces that exist in the legal economy. For a long time it was assumed that organized criminals had a monopolistic hold on their markets (Chang, Lu and Chen, 2005); hence theories of monopoly were frequently cited in the study of organized crime. However, the reality is that this era of monopolistic all-powerful criminal organizations akin to the 'mafia mystique' has long since gone, if it ever really existed. Competitive market forces are the new agenda to study. For instance, a study showing some of the competing market forces operating in the drug markets of Italy, Germany, and Russia conducted by Paoli (2001: 31) found:

> The drug markets of the three environments we have investigated are open markets: the relationships between drug dealing enterprises usually more nearly resemble competition than collusion. There are virtually no barriers to entry. Although some suppliers (such as Italian mafia groups) may occasionally enjoy

considerable monopolistic power over local (usually small) markets, in most European and Russian cities drug enterprises seem to be price-takers rather than price-givers. This means that none of them are able to influence the commodity's price appreciably by varying the quantity of the output sold.

In a study by Kenney (2007: 235), of Colombia's drug trade, it is clear that competing market forces is the operating dynamic:

> Contrary to received wisdom, Colombia's drug trade has never been dominated by a price-fixing association. Even during the respective heydays of the Medellin and Cali 'cartels', cocaine production and exportation in Colombia was highly competitive as independent trafficking groups in more than a dozen cities smuggled substantial amounts of cocaine to American and European drug markets. While some of these enterprises transacted with Pablo Escobar, the Orchoa brothers and other prominent traffickers, their business relations more closely resembled informal producer-export syndicates than public or private cartels that controlled prices and monopolized markets. Although different groups occasionally pooled their resources to complete large-scale drug shipments, while reducing their exposure to government authorities, they steadfastly maintained their own sources of supply, financing and clientele.

It is also clear that when there are many customers and suppliers for a market, no single supplier or customer can determine the price. The price is determined on the market by what is called the *invisible hand* of the market. In this regard, Paoli (2001: 37) makes a valid point about the fluidity of criminal markets that police organizations do well to remember. Paoli argues it is precisely because of the 'invisible hand of the market' that it is so difficult for law enforcement to find evidence of what is actually going on in the realm of organized crime:

> Law enforcement agencies often resort to the spectre of large-scale criminal organizations to back their requests for extra funding. As a matter of fact, it is the 'invisible hand of the market' that reduces the effects of their repressive actions near to zero. At the retail level, the 'industrial reserve army' willing to sell drugs seems to have no end. As a Milanese drug user noted, 'for every five Moroccans who are arrested, there are at least fifty ready to do the same job even at less'.

While it is true that there are few criminal organizations that can completely dominate a market and have a monopoly situation, it is also equally true that there are few criminal groups who enter a market on their own. Most criminal groups will join forces with others in a network or hierarchy to gain strength in a competitive market. By joining forces with other criminals, there will be added value that is shared among participants (Pérez, 2007).

Of course, such a cause-effect depiction of 'supply and demand' forces as shown in Figure 2.2 is not the whole picture as any business, legal or illegal, must operate and remain financially viable in an environment where competitors exist to varying degrees and at different levels. For example, business competitors exist in any market and they exert considerable pressure on the original business enterprise to maintain its market share. Such pressures on the 'bottom line', or profit margin, of a business enterprise come about when a competitor is able to offer the *same* and/or substitute products/services at a cheaper price and/or better quality. In order to undercut the price of a product/service competing businesses may reduce the quality of a product or be prepared to discount it substantially. Some businesses offering discounts are prepared to take a financial loss in the short term, in order to 'flood the market' with their discounted product/service to get a foothold on market share. For example, in the electronics industry smaller players wanting to enter the personal computers market may substitute hardware parts of an inferior quality in order to offer bargain prices for their PCs so that they can compete with the big 'brand name' computer manufacturers. If this 'bargain prices' strategy of the smaller competing businesses has a significant impact on the big name brands' market share they in turn will be forced to consider substantially reducing their prices in order to maintain their market share.

This action-reaction cycle of price fluctuations by competing businesses in the same industry in response to each other's strategic manoeuvres complicates the simple linear 'supply-demand' equation. It introduces a deeper level of interactional complexity. Such complexity can be usefully understood in economic terms through a depiction of this fundamental market mechanism of 'supply and demand' as a graph.

Supply and demand graphs

The invisible hand of the market determines the market price of a product, that is, goods and/or services. For example, in the graph below in Figure 2.3 the market price of a particular product, be it goods or services, is determined at y with a quantity of x.

As can be seen, this 'market price' is where the demand curve meets the supply curve in Figure 2.3. Both demand and supply curves will change over time, causing change in price and the product in terms of the quantity of the goods or services available on the market. This is because suppliers will be willing to sell more products if the price is higher. Conversely, customers will be willing to buy more products (ie goods and/or services) if the price is lower.

It is in the 'interplay', therefore, between suppliers and customers that creates market dynamics, in that, an *increasing product price* leads to *rising* supply and *falling* demand. Or alternatively, a *decreasing product price* leads to *rising* demand and *falling* supply. For example, when law enforcement is successful in dismantling a criminal group that is dealing in drugs or sex trafficking for example, some of the supply will temporarily disappear from the market. Such market disruption through law enforcement activity will move the supply curve to the left as illustrated in Figure 2.4 below, causing a price increase and consequently a quantity (supply) decrease.

Market Mechanisms

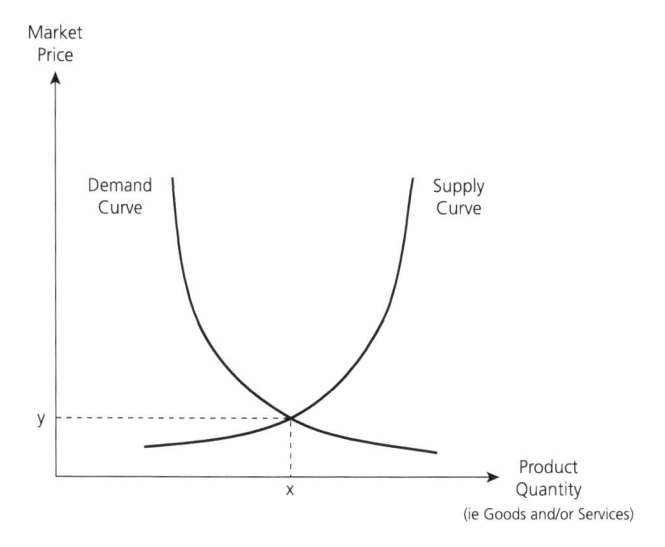

Figure 2.3 Market price determined by intersecting supply and demand curves

As can be seen the market price for a product (eg drugs, sex) increases from y to y', while the quantity decreases from x to x'. The formal business language for this type of market dynamic is referred to as 'elasticity' in economics. That is, the elasticity of demand and supply happens when price changes occur. For instance, if supply changes drastically by a minor price change, then this would be referred to in economic language as the price elasticity of demand is high.

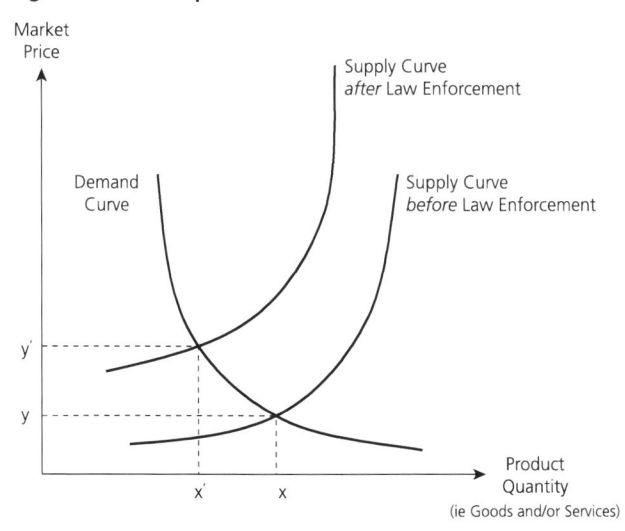

Figure 2.4 Market price fluctuations due to law enforcement

29

Chapter 2: Criminal Enterprises, Markets, and Industries

The business implications for organized crime of this notion of 'market elasticity' are profound. For instance, the disruptive effects on price fluctuations caused by strong law enforcement action will, ironically, assist some criminal businesses actually to increase their profits. This is because crime businesses in the drug market that are not targeted by police action and which have a supply stockpile of drugs, will be able to sell their drugs at a higher price due to the shortage of supply caused to competitors by successful enforcement operations.

Price elasticity of demand is an elasticity that measures the nature and degree of relationship between changes in quantity demanded of a good and changes in its price. So a price elasticity of 1.0 means that the demand will drop with the same percentage as that of the price increase. If, in response to a 10 per cent decline in the price of a product, the quantity demanded increases by 20 per cent, then the price elasticity of demand would be 2.0 (Dijck, 2007). The price elasticity in both demand and supply will vary from market to market. For example in a heavily-dependent drug market, where consumers are completely dependent on their daily dose, 'demand elasticity' may be very low, as indicated on Figure 2.5.

As can be seen, given a market condition like heavily-dependent drug users, then whatever the price, a low-varying quantity is 'in demand' to satisfy customer needs.

Another business implication of such 'elasticity' for organized crime groups, when law enforcement operations are successful, is that it makes the now higher market price for drugs more attractive to new or other competitive criminal groups to enter this market. If they do enter the market these new competitors will cause the market price to drop in the direction from y' towards y as shown in Figure 2.4

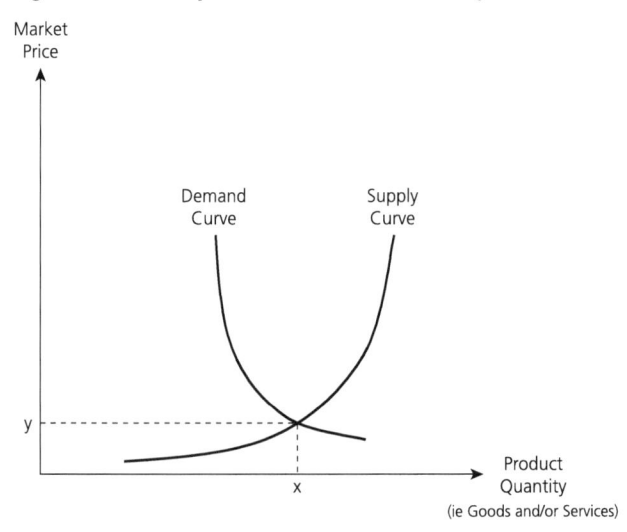

Figure 2.5 Market price when 'demand elasticity' is low

Hence, the unintended consequences of 'successful' law enforcement operations, either through the temporary disruption or significant dismantling of one criminal group, will serve only to establish a 'supply gap' in the market for another criminal group to fill. As noted previously, successful law enforcement will at the same time make other non-targeted criminal groups in the drug market more profits as they can demand higher prices due to the reduction in supply. This 'window of opportunity' to make more money for other crime groups through successful police actions will only last until the price drops again due to market elasticity since new competitors will increase the supply and therefore reduce the demand price over time. The Mexican drug trade scenario previously mentioned in this chapter is a good example of how 'supply' gaps in a market provide business opportunities for other competitors. As noted, after police shot and killed Ramon Arellano Felix, who headed the Tijuana cartel, in Mexico in 2002, the position of Ismael Zambada-Garcia's Sinaloa cartel was strengthened by increasing its market share in the drug trade (Small and Taylor, 2006).

Law enforcement actions are never neutral in their impact. It is always a question of degree or fuzziness—the 'grey area' between black and white enforcement options. When policing operations are very effective in removing a criminal player from the market then such law enforcement action acts as a 'competitive market force' which will influence how the other players in the market reorganize themselves. The issue of whether or not the other criminal players in the market, or a new emerging criminal group, are better or worse to deal with from a policing perspective only time will tell. What is of importance for the emerging criminal business is to get its share of the market.

Market share and size

Increasing market share is one of the most important goals in any business enterprise. Market share has the potential to increase profits. By increasing market share a criminal business enterprise can change the balance in the power structure in competitive markets. If a criminal business enterprise can significantly increase its market share, then it is in a position to reduce the financial impact from business rivals, customers, and new entrants in the marketplace as well as having more bargaining power with suppliers.

'Market share' can be defined as the percentage or proportion of the total available market or market segment that is being serviced by an organization. It can be expressed as an organization's sales revenue (from that market) divided by the total sales revenue available in that market. It can also be expressed as an organization's unit sales volume (in a market) divided by the total volume of units sold in that market.

An interesting example of market size and market share is the sex market in Norway. Norway has been criminalizing sex customers since 2008. This is similar to Sweden, where prostitute clients were criminalized some years earlier. While selling sex remains legal, both organizers and customers are

Chapter 2: Criminal Enterprises, Markets, and Industries

illegal actors. Criminal organizations that traffic women to the sex market in Norway are therefore illegal. How does this criminalization process change the market?

From a business economics view, firstly, the demand curve will change. Next, market shares will change. Also, a number of other effects can be seen. For instance, the prostitution market in Norway is shared among criminal organizations that offer a variety of women to cater to customer needs like Nigerian, East-European, and Asian women. It would be expected that some of these criminal organizations will pull out of the market owing to more enforcement activity, thus enabling other criminal businesses to increase their market share. While the total market size is expected to decline, some may increase their market share, thereby sustaining their sales volume.

Increasing market share is part of marketing management, which is a business discipline focused on the practical application of marketing techniques and the management of an organization's marketing resources and activities. Marketing managers are often responsible for influencing the level, timing, and composition of customer demand in a manner that will achieve the organization's objectives. Typical marketing techniques used by criminal business enterprises include threats, violence, and corruption.

In order to increase market share, businesses develop a marketing strategy based on an objective understanding of their own business and the market in which they operate. Traditionally, marketing analysis was structured into three areas: customer analysis, company analysis, and competitor analysis. More recently, collaborator analysis and industry context analysis have been added.

The focus of customer analysis is to develop a scheme for market segmentation, breaking down the market into various constituent groups of customers, which are called customer segments or market segments. Marketing managers work to develop detailed profiles of each segment, focusing on any number of variables that may differ among segments: demographic, psychographic, geographic, behavioural, needs-benefit, and other factors may all be examined.

Competitor analysis is the most important marketing activity to undertake as it directly influences the ability of a business to increase its market share. In competitor analysis, marketers build detailed profiles of each competitor in the market, focusing especially on their relative competitive strengths and weaknesses, opportunities and threats. Marketing managers will examine each competitor's cost structure, sources of profits, resources and competencies, competitive positioning, and product differentiation, degree of vertical integration, historical responses to industry developments, alliances, and relationships.

Hence, it is clear that the market share of a criminal business will only increase if the market shares of competing criminal businesses decrease. If the market is growing and sales are stable for a criminal business, then it means that the market share for the business is decreasing. Hence, again, the key market mechanism for increasing the market share of a criminal business revolves around the notion of competitive market forces.

So far in our analysis of criminal business enterprises we have discussed the dynamics of key economic market mechanisms involved in illegal business activity. Against this backdrop we will now turn our attention to the larger 'macro' frame in which criminal businesses operate—that of criminal markets.

Criminal Markets

A profit-driven business does not operate in a vacuum where all that matters is supply and demand curves and making sure your competitors don't undercut your profit margin or produce a better product or service. The notion of criminal markets introduces a larger context from which to view the operation of criminal business enterprises.

Global spheres of influence

There is a set of interlocking spheres operating in a global context that impact on business enterprises right down to the local level. A prime example of such ripple effects from the local to global and back to local is dramatically illustrated by the so-called 'sub-prime bad debt loans' that started the global economic meltdown in 2008. This global financial crisis was kicked off by numerous small financing agencies in America that sold houses to people who they knew could not possibly repay the loans. Such packaging of bad debt by small and large banks alike and then passing the 'hot potato' on for profit to another bank or financial institution became a vicious greed-driven virus. The net effect eventually resulted in a tsunami credit wave that hit the world economy and lead to the financial meltdown of the global banking system in the later months of 2008. Subsequently, governments around the world had to pump trillions of dollars into their local economies to keep their countries financially buoyant. It is the 'global interconnectivity' of various influential spheres (eg banking, property market, the Wall Street stock market, private hedge funds, government agencies, political, and so forth) that made this financial exposure in other spheres possible with such far-reaching ripple effects.

Criminal markets are not immune to such global financial viruses in their illegal pursuit of profit. For instance, a United Nations study (2002) on organized crime in 16 countries in Europe found that globalization and growing economic interdependence have encouraged and promoted the transformation of crime beyond borders in all parts of the world. Improved communications and information technologies, increased blurring of national borders, greater mobility of people, goods, and services across countries, and the emergence of a globalized economy have moved crime further away from its domestic base. Thus, the larger picture that criminal market activity takes place in and is subject to global spheres of influence on profit margins is depicted in Figure 2.6 below.

As shown, in so far as criminal markets are concerned, there are five key spheres (*environmental, economic, social, technological,* and *political*) that we have

Chapter 2: Criminal Enterprises, Markets, and Industries

Push – Pull Factors
- Environmental volatility
- Continuing social & economic inequalities
- Expansion of extremist ideologies
- Developments in market globalization
- Sophistication of criminal activities
- 'Invisible hand' of the market
- Fluctuations in world economy
- Increasing social polarization
- Media influence
- Development of digital technologies
- Corruption vulnerabilities

Spheres are interlinked, overlapping, dynamic entities that act like balloons by expanding and/or contracting in a constant flux under the influence of a variety of 'push-pull' factors at various levels of local/global connectivity

Spheres: Environmental Sphere (Business Opportunities); Economic Sphere (Opportunity Costs of business); Social Sphere (Supply/demand); Technological Sphere (Business Efficiencies); Political Sphere (Business Enablers) → Criminal Market Activity

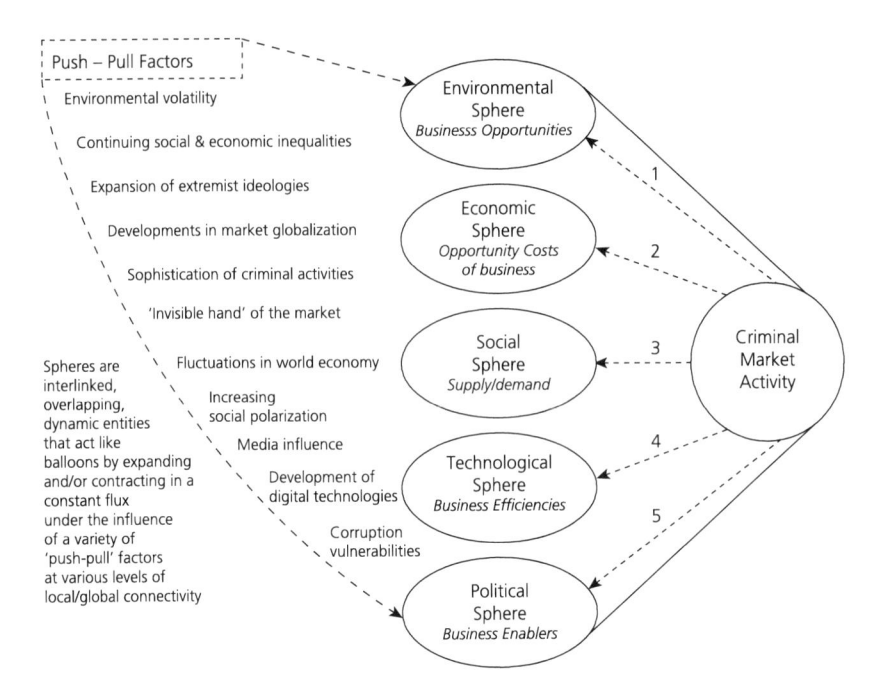

Figure 2.6 Global spheres of influence in criminal markets

identified from the organized crime research literature (Nelen and Huisman, 2008; Van Duyne, von Lampe, Van Dijck, and Newell, 2005; Reichel, 2005; Levi, 2003; Ruggiero, 2000; United Nations, 2002; Moore, 1987; Rubin, 1980; Carter, 1997; Fiorentini and Peltzman, 1995; Mack and Kerner, 1975).

These five spheres are fundamental to an entrepreneurially-run criminal business enterprise. The crucial point in this diagrammatic illustration is that these five key spheres are dynamic entities that are intrinsically and irreducibly interlinked. They overlap with each other in sometimes strange and interesting ways and are pulled and pushed in and out of shape and size, like balloons, by the various factors noted in Figure 2.6. It is this 'dynamic interconnectivity' of the spheres that is the essential element to be cognizant of in this depiction. Hence, the next Figure 2.7, tries to capture the dynamism by showing how under the influence of various 'push-pull' factors such ballooning out occurs. This in turn opens up new market opportunities for the alert criminal entrepreneur.

Figure 2.7 is but one suggestive depiction in which various spheres of influence intersect, overlap, and interact in a particular criminal market, like the drug market or human trafficking market. Many such potential depictions are possible. In reality, there are multiple ways to realize criminal business activity. It is the combination of a criminal entrepreneur's imagination and the range of push-pull factors operating in a market context at a particular point in time that sets the boundaries of where and how far this ballooning out occurs in different spheres.

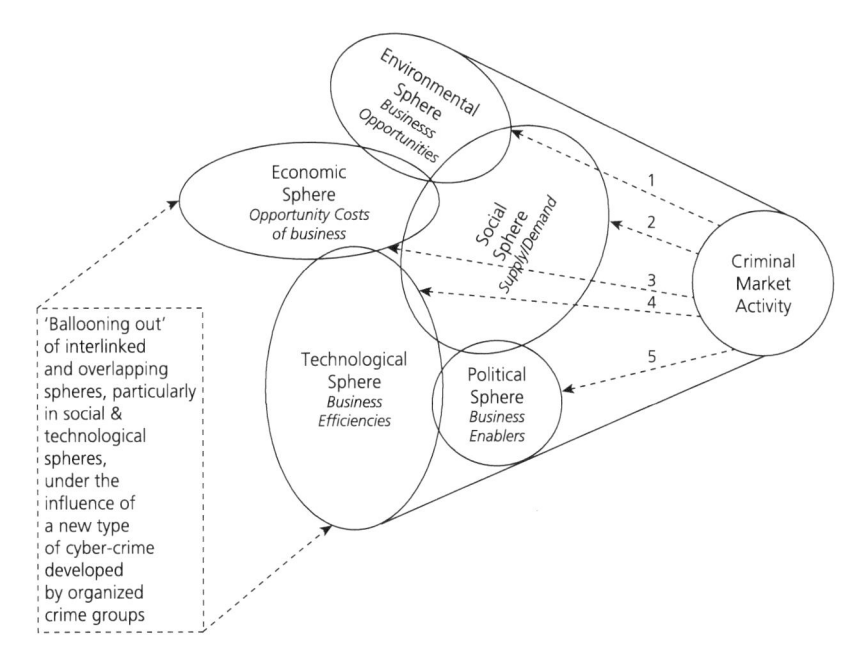

Figure 2.7 Dynamic interconnectivity in criminal market global spheres

Push-pull factors

The types of push-pull factors listed in Figure 2.6 can be regarded as intermediary factors that facilitate the ballooning out in and across various spheres. Of course, there are a multitude of factors operating at any given time in a particular crime market than this simple listing can show. The point to note is the very existence of a given range of push-pull factors that exert influence in any given sphere. What the precise push-pull factors are, at any given time and in any given sphere, in a specific crime market is where the hard investigative work of law enforcement agencies resides.

Therefore, policing organized crime means coming to grips with the analytical complexity of what law enforcement is dealing with from a market dynamics perspective—both locally and globally. This analytical complexity involves a market-by-market analysis of *which* push-pull factors are currently shaping these five key spheres (*environmental, economic, social, technological*, and *political*) across *what* particular crime businesses, *that are* operating or potentially could be operating. Such a crime business market analysis will involve several 'push-pull' factors interacting one with another, which in turn make some factors more important or influential in some markets and/or contexts than others at different periods of time. For example, consumers may be dependent on the goods supplied on the market, which is the case for many drug users. Also, customers in the sex trade may be more prone to explore various 'offerings' as a sex buyer. Moreover, there are cultural imperatives that must not be overlooked.

Chapter 2: Criminal Enterprises, Markets, and Industries

An interesting example of how not to transplant one culture's approach to business into a different culture and expect it to work is the case of Russia. According to Buss (2001: 95) when the American way of Western-style business was introduced to the legal economy in Russia, after the collapse of the Soviet Union, it failed. Buss argues that much of the failure resulted because American approaches to economic development could not work during Russia's transition from a command economy. Such things as promoting entrepreneurship, developing public-private partnerships, creating a market economy, accessing start-up capital, attracting foreign investment, overcoming bureaucratic corruption and high taxation, and working within the rule of law proved to be too big a jump to make for a centralist state.

The case study about the evolution of organized crime in Lithuania in the post-Soviet era presented previously is another clear case of a capitalist free market system actually stimulating (a push-pull factor), inadvertently, the growth of new organized crime businesses. Similarly, Tanev (2001) found that a Western-style market economy did not work in Bulgaria for many of the same reasons. One key reason was that the Bulgarian central government was not willing to lose power in favour of local democracy and market forces.

Furthermore, Europol (2006), as the premier crime analysis agency on organized crime for the EU, has identified a number of indicators (the international dimension; group structures; use of legitimate business structures; specialization; influence and corruption; use of violence; and countermeasures) which can be regarded as 'push-pull' business factors that facilitate the operation and expansion of criminal business enterprises. While such 'push-pull' factors assist crime businesses to survive and grow it is the fundamental economic conditions of supply and demand and how these are shaped by competing market forces which ultimately determine the success or failure of an entrepreneurial, profit-driven, crime business.

In sum, it is the very interconnectivity of these five key spheres of global influence (*environmental, economic, social, technological,* and *political*) and their associated 'push-pull' factors, that gives the strength to a criminal business but also its weakness. That is, a crime business, as it grows, pushes out and expands various spheres in both shape and size. As noted in the 2007 OCTA report by Europol, the issue of 'criminal structure' is of less conceptual importance now than how, at an operational level, 'criminal groups are self-organizing entities' that are engaging in strategic alliances and partnerships to form 'oriented clusters' of criminal activity (2007: 9). Through this mechanism of 'oriented clusters' the combined power of criminal groups working in unison, either as a hierarchy or a network, can thereby harness the 'economies of scale' and thus substantially increase their resource potential and inflict considerable harm on society.

However, just as case-hardened steel is incredibly strong, it is also very brittle. Ironically, its strength is also its weakness. Similarly, the strength that local and/or global interconnectivity gives to an organized crime group/hierarchy or network also exposes it to policing scrutiny, regulation, penetration, and enforcement. This issue of how to intervene operationally in disrupting and dismantling organized crime businesses will be returned to in later chapters.

Criminal Enterprises as Global Industries

In this final section crime business economics are connected to criminal markets in which they are embedded at the transnational level as 'global industries' of illegal business activity. A criminal industry is a collection of criminal enterprises that conduct business in the same or similar kind of business area and/or market. That is, crime businesses can be grouped according to the type of criminal industry in which they most participate. For example, in the commerce industry the types of criminal markets involved could range from trafficking in women and children, trading in illegal sporting drugs, narcotics commerce, prostitution, stolen cars, smuggling of liquor and cigarettes, and so forth. A 'criminal industry' frame is a useful point of reference for policing agencies and law enforcement organizations. It allows policing to develop macro insights into how various criminal enterprises will band together to 'do business' as 'criminal hubs' (Europol, 2007) and/or 'criminal networks' of association and transaction (Ruggiero and Khan, 2007).

In the 2007 OCTA report Europol introduced a simplified mid-range conceptual model to their regional typology of organized crime groups with the notion of 'criminal hubs' (2007: 23). A criminal hub, in Europol's definition is 'an entity that is generated by a combination of factors such as proximity to major destination markets, geographic location, infrastructures, criminal group types and migration processes concerning key criminals and OC groups in general' (2007: 25). In essence, criminal hubs act as 'routers' that receive and redirect the flow of illicit goods and services from one country or region to other countries/regions. This ability to connect diverse forms of organized criminality at central hubs of global business activity that transcend regional geographical boundaries makes organized criminality a potent economic force.

In keeping with its regional focus, Europol (2007) locates criminal hubs within each of the four EU regions: that is, the North-West, North-East, South-West, and South-East. In so far as the 'North-West' is concerned, this 'criminal hub' contains the major transport infrastructure that connects criminal business enterprises to worldwide markets. Hence, it is little surprise to find that the 'drug supermarket of the Netherlands' (Ruggiero and Khan, 2007: 66) is central to this criminal hub as a major distribution point for the illicit drug trade in cocaine, heroin, and cannabis to other European countries (2007: 25). The key point is that because of these 'criminal hubs' in the borderless countries that comprise the EU, it is no longer necessary for individual criminal business enterprises to build their own complicated supply networks from other far-flung continents like Latin America. This is because a wide variety of illicit goods and services are to some extent stockpiled or readily available from within their local regional criminal hubs.

The following case study of a global crime industry in illegal cigarette smuggling illustrates the interconnectedness of various criminal businesses and their use of criminal hubs as economic pathways to extend their global crime networks.

Case Study: Crime in the Commerce Industry

Illegal cigarette smuggling is a commercial crime that in relation to the EU is considered 'the single-biggest fraud against the community budget . . . .' when one considers that 'a single container or truckload of cigarettes is valued at €1 million in tax revenues to the EU and its member states' (*Griffiths*, 2004: 186). Hence, in Europe alone, the scale of this commercial crime in cigarette smuggling makes it a multi-billion Euro revenue problem (*op cit*).

The research literature makes it clear that several different European countries participate as industry players in the lucrative illegal cigarette smuggling market. For example, Dijck (2007) studied the illicit cigarette market in the Netherlands. He found the market to be relatively open in the sense of a low threshold to enter this market. Newcomers can easily set up a cigarette trafficking scheme. The Netherlands, being a nation of transit and transport, provide a setting for untaxed cigarettes. The market share of untaxed tobacco was estimated to be 3 per cent in 2003 and 5 per cent in 2005 while the total consumption of tobacco in the Netherlands was declining.

Furthermore, Dijck (2007) found that cigarette traffickers rely on limited networks, consisting of one or two suppliers and a dozen customers. The cigarette black market provides ample opportunity to make a good profit. The profit opportunities exceed the low risk involved. Hence, in this type of cigarette smuggling crime market there are substantial opportunities for small-scale organized crime groups to network and link up with several criminal businesses to form a crime industry.

Even when law enforcement efforts are successful in disrupting some of the supply lines involved in illegal cigarette smuggling there are still many players in this crime market to come to the rescue of local dealers. As Dijck (2007: 165) notes:

> In one case, for example, offenders discussed over the phone the question whether they would accept a substitute shipment of counterfeit Marlboro cigarettes instead of the original brand cigarettes they bought at previous occasions. The supplier of the original brand cigarettes could not continue his delivery because the police had raided one of the main warehouses and confiscated all cigarettes. Though there is a market for counterfeit cigarettes in the Netherlands as well, these offenders were afraid that their customers particularly favoured brand cigarettes, more precisely Marlboro and that they would not be able to get rid of other brands than Marlboro cigarettes.

In a similar study conducted in Estonia into cigarette smuggling Markina (2007) found that ironically it was the prospect of Estonia joining the EU that provided a significant impetus (push-pull factor) for the huge growth in the illegal cigarette crime market in that country. To join the European Union, Estonia had to harmonize taxes on cigarettes and other tobacco goods quite quickly. For an ordinary smoker the harmonization of taxes meant nothing else than a shocking increase in cigarette prices within a relatively short period of time. As a consequence, many smokers looked for alternative supplies of tobacco, and they found it on the black market. A survey in Estonia found that 60 per cent of the respondents were ready to purchase illegal cigarettes as a reaction to the price increase. Hence, the market share of untaxed tobacco in Estonia is estimated to be much higher than in the Netherlands. This is not because legal tobacco prices are higher in Estonia. It is because neighbouring countries such as Russia have much cheaper tobacco and because tobacco prices have risen much faster in Estonia as compared to the Netherlands. For example, a package of legal cigarettes had the price of €2.05, whereas an illegal package only cost €0.57 in Estonia in 2007.

Furthermore, the places were illegal cigarettes are sold are quite well known to the public in Estonia. According to Markina (2007: 204) customers buy illegal cigarettes either directly from retailers on the street (53 per cent) or at the trader's home (35 per cent). Thus, cigarette smuggling in Estonia becomes a very attractive option for a crime entrepreneur in a situation where there is high demand and wide distribution networks available. Moreover, on the supply side there is easy access to a cheaper product in neighbouring countries. The only real cost factor is transportation. This problem is also easily solved since most of the illegal cigarettes sold in Estonia come from bootlegging. This particular type of smuggling strategy involves the purchase of low-priced cigarettes in one country and transporting them either for personal consumption or resale to a high-priced country in quantities exceeding limits set by custom regulation. For instance, shipments of inexpensive Russian brands like 'Prima', 'Prima Nevo', 'North Star', or 'Arktika' are regularly bootlegged to Estonia (Markina, 2007: 204).

Thus, bootlegging is a low-risk crime business strategy that offers good profit at low cost by transporting cigarettes over relatively short distances, usually between neighbouring countries. So long as a secure transport route can be arranged then any criminal group can get involved. Therefore, for a new start-up criminal business entrepreneur the key to success lies in knowing the 'criminal hubs' to relate to arrange the logistics for the supply and deliver of bootlegged cigarettes.

At a conceptual level what is going on in the cigarette-trafficking crime market is not too dissimilar or structurally different from what goes on in other crime markets. For instance, the drug trafficking crime market is a criminal industry where economic partnership arrangements are established and networks of suppliers, distributors, retailers, and wholesalers are forged between multi-ethnic criminal businesses, both locally and globally. Research on the drug economy documents that where ethnic competition and/or violence is found to exist it was usually 'only at the low level' as large drug dealing networks are 'more multiethnic' and will do '. . . . business with all sorts of people, irrespective of their ethnic background' (Ruggiero and Khan, 2007: 64). It is the colour of money that counts for a criminal entrepreneur not one's skin.

Chapter 2: Criminal Enterprises, Markets, and Industries

Summary

This chapter introduced a 'business model' of organized crime composed of four logically interdependent and cyclically intermeshing business phases, that of *establishing, expanding, consolidating,* and *positioning,* which assist entrepreneurially-oriented criminals to build their illegal business activities into a viable crime business.

This type of business modelling assists policing agencies by providing a strategic vantage point from which to track and assess the business strengths and weakness of a crime business and therefore to be able to plan the policing of illegal business activities. Further, in order to make a realistic analysis of a crime business's current and future potential for societal harm, the economics of market mechanisms have been explained and discussed in relation to organized crime. Specifically, the key notions of competitive market forces, supply and demand graphs, market share, and size, have been presented.

The chapter then moved from a micro view of the inner workings of market behaviour to a more macro perspective of how global criminal markets are comprised of various layers or spheres of influence. Five spheres (ie *environmental, economic, social, technological,* and *political*) of influence that shape market opportunities and global crime industries were outlined. Implications were drawn for policing the dynamic interconnectivity of various push-pull factors operating in and through these global spheres for entrepreneurially-run criminal business enterprises.

Two case studies and other examples were presented throughout the chapter to illuminate the operation of profit-driven, market-oriented, and entrepreneurially-led crime businesses. These case studies demonstrated not only how individual and/or corporate entities operate but also how such criminal entities can be usefully viewed as 'collectives' that exist as global crime industries. Such criminal industries have the economies of scale to forge global alliances and working partnerships to transact both legal and illegal 'business'.

Finally, this chapter on market dynamics made it clear that there is a symbiotic relationship between organized crime and policing where the actions of one assists the other in different ways. For instance, police and law enforcement agencies get the 'credit' for busting a major drug group by taking out one crime player but also their actions 'increase profit' for the remaining crime players and 'open up' the market to new crime players. Ironically, from the perspective of market dynamics, organized crime 'need' police to be effective, every now and then, to rid themselves of players when the drug market gets too congested and to make more money. The flip side for organized crime is that it is sometimes worth their while to 'help' police by tipping them off about a competitor. Not only does the 'informing' crime group get rid of a rival but it also creates the opportunity to make more profit for a limited period of time until the market vacuum gets filled. Thus, there is a mutually-reinforcing and never-ending dance between entrepreneurial criminality and the 'effectiveness' of policing it.

PART TWO

Crime Business Phases

The development of a crime business requires the combination of four key business phases—*establishing, expanding, consolidating,* and *positioning*—to maximize business opportunities. These four business phases are cyclical in nature and intermeshing in operation. Hence, this second section comprises four interlocking chapters (3, 4, 5, and 6). Each chapter provides an in-depth examination of a particular business phase and the specific business factors used to develop illegal businesses.

Chapter 3 looks at the first business development phase of *establishing* the crime business, whilst Chapter 4 examines the second business phase of *expansion*. Similarly, Chapter 5 deals with the third business phase of *consolidation* and Chapter 6 is devoted to the fourth and final business phase of *positioning* the crime business. A wide and varied range of case examples are presented in each chapter. These cases show how criminal entrepreneurs use various business factors to develop their criminal enterprises. Finally, each chapter concludes with a practical application of an analytical tool, based on fuzzy logic, which maps the business dynamics of crime groups at a particular phase in their development of a criminal business.

3

Establishing the Crime Business

Introduction

This chapter examines the first phase of *establishing* a crime business in relation to three considerations. Firstly, the entrepreneurial capabilities associated with starting up a crime business. Secondly, specific business factors which give practical expression to these entrepreneurial capabilities. Case examples are presented on these business factors to illustrate how they develop a crime business within the context of criminal markets. The third and final consideration involves a 'fuzzy' mapping tool based on a matrix analysis of the entrepreneurial capabilities and their associated business development factors. The usefulness of this analytical mapping tool is demonstrated through 'hypothetical' case scenarios of crime groups at this establishing phase of a criminal business enterprise.

Criminal Business Modelling: Establishment Phase

The development of a crime business requires the combination of four key business phases—*establishing, expanding, consolidating,* and *positioning*—to maximize a business opportunity. These four phases are cyclical in nature and intermeshing in operation. From an analytical perspective such interconnectedness can be represented as a logical sequence of business phases. However, one must never lose sight of the inherent cyclical complexity of these intermeshing phases in running a business. Figure 3.1 below builds on our operating model of a crime business by incorporating key business factors associated with developing this first phase of 'establishing' a crime business.

Chapter 3: Establishing the Crime Business

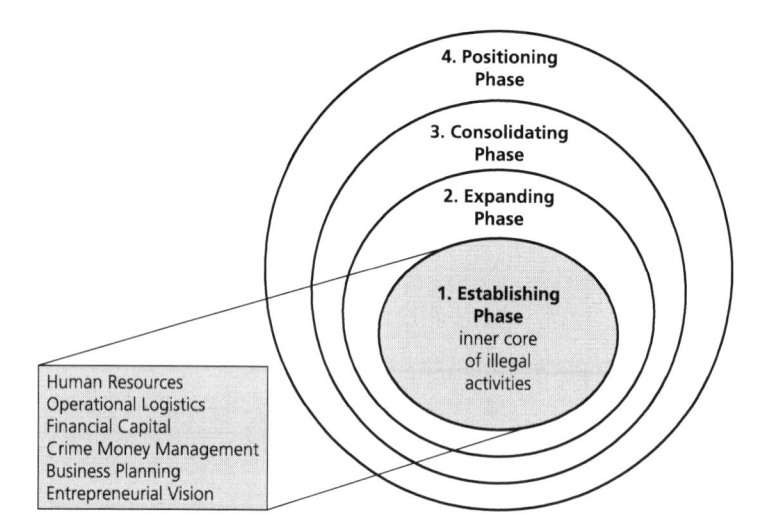

Figure 3.1 Crime business model: Phase 1—'establishment' business factors

Concentric circles labeled:
4. Positioning Phase
3. Consolidating Phase
2. Expanding Phase
1. Establishing Phase — inner core of illegal activities

Callout box:
- Human Resources
- Operational Logistics
- Financial Capital
- Crime Money Management
- Business Planning
- Entrepreneurial Vision

As can be seen, there are six main factors involved in starting up a viable business. These factors are identified in the organized crime literature[1] as having the potential to enable a crime business to become established. Also, these factors are 'developmental' in the sense that one builds on the other so that collectively they assist a business to reach a maturity level where profits can be maximized. As the business grows these factors will need to be revisited and reconceptualized. This is because contextual elements in the larger crime market will impact on these micro business development factors. Hence, from time to time, some of these business factors will need to be re-aligned.[2]

No business can develop without some individual showing entrepreneurial initiative to start it up. Our research of the business management/organizational studies literature[3] identified five entrepreneurial capabilities (*opportunity*

---

[1] This list is of 'necessary' business factors involved in giving practical expression to and development of a start-up crime business. There is no claim being made, nor can there be, that the list is an exhaustive one. There are numerous factors, small and large, potentially involved in establishing a crime business. What the list reflects is the key or main factors involved in developing a crime business at phase 1.

[2] It should be borne in mind that the larger context in which a crime business operates is crime markets and the spheres of influence within various crime market sectors that, as noted in Chapter 2, contain a wide variety of 'push-pull' factors. Hence, these larger 'macro' crime market factors, under the influence of the dynamic interconnectivity associated with the ballooning out and contracting in of the various multi-layered spheres (*economic, social, technological, political,* and *environmental*) in crime markets, will influence to varying degrees each of these more 'micro' business development factors.

[3] There are areas of overlap in the research literature between our core set of five entrepreneurial capabilities and various entrepreneurial characteristics. Some of these entrepreneurial characteristics can be regarded in our crime business model as operating more like 'business development factors'. Readers interested in this aspect may wish to review the material in Chapter 1 to appreciate

Entrepreneurial Capability: Opportunity Perspective

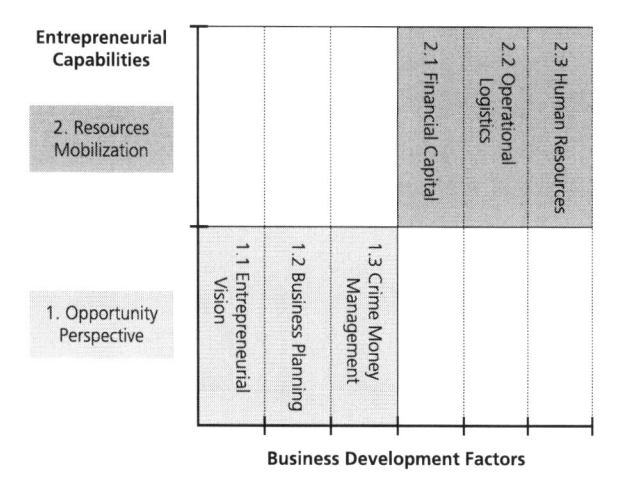

Figure 3.2 Entrepreneurial capability by business factors at 'establishing' phase

perspective, resources mobilization, decision-making under uncertainty, people cooperation, and *profit maximization*) to be core components of individual entrepreneurialism. Operationally, each of these five entrepreneurial capabilities translates into a range of business development factors. This means there are specific business factors associated with each entrepreneurial capability which can assist criminal entrepreneurs in developing their crime business at each phase of our business modelling framework.

At the 'establishment' phase there are two entrepreneurial capabilities of particular relevance that a 'would-be' criminal entrepreneur must attend to: they are, firstly, discovering a business opportunity to exploit and, secondly, getting the resources to make it happen. Therefore, by cross-matching these two entrepreneurial capabilities with their related business development factors a 'matrix' results as shown in Figure 3.2.

In practice, the set of business factors associated with each entrepreneurial capability as shown in Figure 3.2 provide the combined impetus for starting up a criminal business venture. These two entrepreneurial capabilities and their related business factors will be discussed in turn and illustrated with case examples.

Entrepreneurial Capability: Opportunity Perspective

The first entrepreneurial capability involves being on the lookout for opportunities to turn into a business. This usually occurs in one of two ways—either through identifying new business opportunities and/or discovering new directions in

---

fully how various business factors and/or entrepreneurial characteristics relate to each entrepreneurial capability.

which to expand or grow an existing business. There are at least three necessary business factors associated with this capability as shown in Figure 3.2. They are: *entrepreneurial vision, business planning,* and *crime money management*.

Entrepreneurial Vision

Having an *entrepreneurial vision* involves not only perceiving business opportunities but also having the self-confidence and a strong sense of conviction to carry the vision out. This business factor is often a mix of one's cultural upbringing, such as exposure to a familial entrepreneurial culture, as well as individual personality dynamics.

Entrepreneurial vision is all about searching for and identifying criminal business opportunities. There is research evidence (Witt, 2007; Grennan and Britz, 2006) to support the view that criminal entrepreneurs are more likely to grow out of a life of crime where exposure to a criminal sub-culture through family, ethnicity, or simply gangs, provides the context for developing entrepreneurial vision and talent. But this is not always the case. As noted in Chapter 1, there are a range of factors that motivate individuals to engage in setting up a crime business. Such factors can be out of 'necessity' due to a sudden loss of a job, as in times of global economic downturn and recession. Or alternatively, there may be a more 'opportunistic' motivation to make easy money quickly. For others it can come down to simply the thrill of being 'innovative' enough to outwit the legal system (Markovski and Hall, 2007). The following example illustrates how an organized crime group can start up quite 'opportunistically'. This was the case when an entrepreneur running a legitimate enterprise in the Netherlands saw more financial reward was possible through establishing an illegal business alongside his legitimate activities.

Case example 3.1 Verhagen Group (Dutch)

An entrepreneur whose legal business involved traded cars in Europe and the United States initiated a parallel crime business in drug trafficking that became known as the 'Verhagen group' in the Netherlands. The group imported hashish by sea from Morocco, Lebanon, and Pakistan and then distributed it to the Dutch, mainly in the cities of Amsterdam, The Hague, and Rotterdam, as well as to Danish, British, Belgian, and Swiss markets.

The legitimate entrepreneur who started this crime group had extensive contacts to small-scale business activities in other countries and this resource provided ready-made opportunities to establish a supply and distribution network for illicit drug markets.

continued

> The Verhagen group was a loosely organized network of associates that made extensive use of trans-border smuggling operations and the occasional use of violence and corruption. The core group consisted of five members, surrounded by approximately 45 associates. Within the core group, two individuals took a leading role. Associate members comprised couriers, persons taking care of storage and distribution, and captains and crew members of the ships that transport drugs. The core members were exclusively Dutch, other members being German, British Asian, African, and American. All members were male. The leading persons in the group interacted on the basis of friendship. The group had no strict code of conduct. However, a clear ban existed on incriminating other members. Internally the group did not use any violence at all. Even if members did not comply with the standards or the ban on incrimination, they were not physically punished but simply put out of work. The members possessed a small number of firearms.
>
> This crime group was formed to concentrate solely on illegal business enterprises hence they had no strong overlap with legitimate economic activities. Most of the group members were employed in the car dealing industry or received unemployment benefits. Apart from their main drug smuggling business enterprise, the group engaged in a diversity of other illegal activities, like large-scale fraud/embezzlement, theft of large quantities of electronic goods, fraud involving precious materials, trafficking in expensive jewellery, as well as fraudulent real estate transactions, according to the United Nations (2002).

The next case example of 'entrepreneurial vision' demonstrates a crime group's capacity to search for opportunistic openings for criminal exploitation in various market sectors. In this case the technology market was the target of a Vietnamese crime group. Robinson (2000) recounts the event.

Case Example 3.2 Computer Chips (Vietnamese)

'Not long ago, a Vietnamese gang spotted a real opportunity – computer chips – and alighted on California's Silicon Valley exactly like a plague of locusts. They forced their way into factories and warehouses at gunpoint and stole millions of dollars' worth of chips and motherboards, which were soon flooding discount electronics markets across the country. It took a joint task force of police from California, Oregon and Washington to break up the gang of some fifty people. Working with them were other Asian gang members, pointing up yet again the Vietnamese tendency to cooperate with anyone who can help get a job done. In this case, it was a $75-million-a-year job' (Robinson, 2000: 303).

Another recent case example that also involves technology clearly shows the innovative edge of criminal entrepreneurs who are always on the lookout to make money. For instance, a story that came to light in Australia in 2009 involved hijacking GPS technology.

> **Case Example 3.3 Hijacking Technology (Australia)**
>
> A recent trend that entrepreneurially-oriented criminals are doing is attending sporting events, especially those taking several hours and in the evenings. The gang scouts around the sporting grounds looking for up-market vehicles with GPS devices in them. They break into the vehicle and hotwire it and then press HOME on the GPS. The navigation device then directs the vehicle to the victim's house.
>
> The criminals will also ascertain at this point that the vehicle's owner has left the remote door controller of the house's garage door in the vehicle as well, as most people do. Hence the gang is then able to open up the garage and start ransacking the house with about two hours' headstart on the unsuspecting victim.
>
> The best bit is that none of the neighbours will take any notice of the victim's vehicle coming home and driving straight into the garage and then the lights coming on in the house (Queensland Retired Police Association, 2009).

In a similar vein, enterprising street criminals doing handbag snatches will not only be content with stealing credit cards, driver's licences, and so forth to access money and identity theft. They have added an interesting new twist. They will check the mobile phone contents. The criminals are looking for any sort of term that indicates a spouse, partner, or lover relationship, like words of endearment such as 'sexy beast', 'wild one', 'honey', or a partner's surname identified on a stolen credit card, driver's licence, etc. Having found the spouse/partner's name in the mobile, the criminal will text a message that 'the loved one' is at the bank or shopping and needs the PIN number and has forgotten it. Again, if the spouse/partner is unsuspecting then they text back the PIN and literally the keys to their bank account (Queensland Retired Police Association, 2009).

Business Planning

This second business factor involves developing the perceived entrepreneurial opportunities into a business. Therefore, some sort of *business planning* or strategy is needed to take the vision from an idea to reality. Clearly there is an overlap here with the self-conviction and can-do mentality associated with having an entrepreneurial vision.

The primary focus of planning is working out how best to exploit the business opportunity. Crime groups, like individuals, will vary in the extent to which they devote time, effort, and talent to planning the establishment and running of their crime business. For instance, some criminal groups may have a more 'ad hoc' opportunistic outlook and not bother too much about planning their illegal business activities. For example, if extortion and protection rackets are the 'thing' that makes them money then some crimes group will be content to just keep doing the same old thing without too much thought about how to develop their business. However, other crime groups will spend considerable time and resources in researching and planning their illegal business ventures. A case in point is the famous Russian organized crime initiative known as the 'Red Daisy' investigation. This criminal business venture is regarded as one of the most successful scams in the organized crime genre to do with the more sophisticated 'thinking man's crimes' (Nicaso and Lamothe, 2005).

Case Example 3.4 Thinking Man's 'Red Daisy' Fraud (Russian)

The 'Red Daisy' scam involved setting up a complex daisy chain of companies by Russian organized crime figures to exploit a weakness in the American motor fuel excise tax law. Through this web of companies the Russian crime syndicate was able to defraud the American government of hundreds of millions of dollars in fuel taxes. Nicaso and Lamothe (2005: 147) note that:

> The scheme was so lucrative that La Cosa Nostra went into business in partnership with Russian crime bosses. In a single 18-month period, law enforcement arrested 136 suspects who had milked American and federal governments of an astounding US $363 million.

This next example demonstrates a similar level of criminal sophistication for business planning by a Chinese gang that 'value-added' to their already lucrative illegal immigration business. Robinson (2000) reports.

Case Example 3.5 Value-Added Illegal Immigration (Chinese)

'In one recent case, eighty illegal aliens from China – each paying $45,000 for their passage – posed as rich businessmen on a junket to Canada. The criminal gang leader had duped a businessman in Toronto into setting up a tour for these 'investors'. Paid US $2,500 per visitor, the Canadian businessman arranged flights, visas and a weeklong program to show the Chinese what Canada and Toronto had to offer. But shortly after the group arrived, its members disappeared.

Only two were found by the RCMP and returned to China. The others made their way into the United States through Akwesasne, with the help of the certain St. Regis Mohawk and the Toronto-based members of the Chinese gang' (Robinson, 2000: 311).

Another example of 'innovative' business planning by a career criminal entrepreneur is provided in the person of Giovanni Bandolo. Bandolo was a 64–year–old

Chapter 3: Establishing the Crime Business

member of the Secondiglianao group associated with the 'Camorra' when he was investigated by the Canadian police. The Camorra is one of the big four Italian organized crime mafia groupings that operate out of Naples. Bandolo had an entrepreneurial talent for spotting what would make a good business scam. Bandolo was cooling his heels in Canada after fleeing Italy when an arrest warrant of Camorra members was issued by the Italian government. The warrant was for Bandolo's alleged involvement in a homicidal gangland war that had been raging since 2002 over a breakaway gang's attempt to corner a stake in the lucrative drug trade controlled by the Camorra. This drug business reportedly bought in for the Camorra more than $650,000 a day (Nicaso and Lamothe, 2005: 69).

Case Example 3.6 Fake 'Versace Jackets' (Italian Camorra in Canada)

Bandolo's scam was simple yet elegant in its business plan. Bandolo imported thousands of cheap plastic jackets at a cost of US $20 to $30. Included in the shipment were also thousands of counterfeit logos and tags of the Versace design label. The counterfeit 'Versace' jackets were repacked on fancy hangers or in designer boxes then shipped to criminal associates throughout Canada, the States, and even Australia. Gullible victims paid hundreds of dollars for these fake jackets.

While it would seem a low-grade business activity for an organized crime group to be involved in the selling of fake leather jackets in parking lots, on street corners, and at street markets, the Canadian investigation revealed that the profit margin was substantial (Nicaso and Lamothe, 2005: 70).

Police traced the profits back to Italy where they were used to fund the Secondiglianao group's gang war. Bandolo was deported under police guard back to Italy to face the outstanding warrant charges against him.

What we see in this 'fake leather jacket' scam is a business plan that was simple to operate. Bandolo with his long-standing criminal connections and the entire infrastructure necessary was able to run the new crime business venture. It is estimated that he had up to 20 'salesmen' (criminal associates) every week in cities all across Canada, the United States, and in Australia selling his fake product for up to 10 or even 20 times the cost price per jacket (*op cit*). With this economy of scale the 'fake leather jacket' business raked in tens of thousands of dollars per week. What this case example shows is a very simple and effective business plan capable of generating huge profits for a crime group prepared to 'think-out-of-the-box' of its usual criminal activities like drugs, prostitution, protection rackets, etc.

There are two sides to a business plan—the cost side and the profit side. Thus, a criminal entrepreneur must factor in both 'transaction costs' and 'opportunity costs' into their 'business planning'. A transaction cost is simply 'the cost associated with the process of buying and selling' (Bannock, Davis, Trott, and

Uncles, 2002: 370) whereas an 'opportunity cost' is 'the value of something that has to be given up—a lost opportunity—as a result of a decision' (Bannock, Davis, Trott, and Uncles, 2002: 257).

Therefore, the notion of 'opportunity cost' is a more ubiquitous concept than simply adding up transaction costs to establish the financial outlay for an activity. However, opportunity costs are useful to consider in terms of gaining a better understanding of the true costs and benefits of engaging in an activity. Hence, the value of assessing opportunity costs when planning a new business venture. For instance, a criminal entrepreneur with some capital to invest in a new business should not simply look at what profit they can make from it but rather what other opportunities are foreclosed by tying up their capital in this one particular activity.

With regard to transaction and opportunity costs, the business planning perspective which sophisticated criminal entrepreneurs adopt is one of 'risk assessment'. For instance, Wright (2006) contends that mafia groups consider the costs of each transaction by estimating the risk involved. For example, there are risks associated with betrayal of the group by informers leading to disruption of operations, seizure of drugs, and arrest of group members. There are significant transaction costs and hence the profit available must be worth such financial risks. Hence, crime groups must plan for such eventualities and be prepared to 'write off' a certain percentage of their profit margin due to things like drug shipments being captured by police and law enforcement activity.

Other transaction costs are things like the cost of conflicts and misunderstandings between criminal associates that can lead to delays, to breakdowns, and to other malfunctions. Depending on the crime market sector being exploited, there will be other types of transaction costs incurred, such as asset specificity, transaction frequency, and uncertainty. 'Asset specificity' is the degree to which an asset can be redeployed to alternative uses and by alternative users without sacrifice of productive value (Hancox and Hackney, 2000). 'Transaction frequency' distinguishes occasional from recurrent transactions and hence the cost involved for each type of transaction (Williamson, 1979) while 'uncertainty' is always present in illegal markets and costs can suddenly escalate due to unforeseen circumstances like 'unknown' costs.

In relation to 'unknown' costs, the ever-present danger of self-interest, opportunism, or lack of candour or honesty in transactions (Hancox and Hackney, 2000) is a key concept. 'Opportunism', while present in legal markets, is a substantial business risk factor in criminal markets where the profits to be made can be so astronomical as to tempt many a criminal to engage in opportunistic behaviour, like ripping off some profit from their boss. In a criminal network context, opportunism often involves misrepresentations, unresponsiveness, unreasonable demands, and lying. The notion of opportunism is what differentiates transaction cost theory from alternative conceptualizations of the organization, such as agency theory, relational exchange theory, or resource view. The presumption in 'transaction cost economics' is that business actors attempt to forecast the potential for opportunism as a function of unfolding circumstances, and then they take preventive actions in transactions where opportunism is likely to be high. Therefore, 'opportunism' is an explanatory mechanism. But it is not readily observable because of its very nature and so is typically empirically untested. However, it is important because it has potential for enormous impact on economic performance, especially in criminal markets where there are few moral barriers to engaging in opportunistic self-interest.

Opportunism, therefore, is likely to increase if there are only a small number of owners of strategic resources in a particular organized crime market. Transaction costs appear to be difficult to avoid and may be unavoidably greater in some settings than in others. For example, in transnational and global crime, contract creation and monitoring are more difficult because of the complexity and need for secrecy, security, and above all trustworthiness of crime partners or criminal alliances. Hence, there are costs associated with varying ethnic backgrounds and distances, which are hard to allocate and quantify for specific functions.

Crime Money Management

This business factor involves the other side of business planning—the profit margin. Whilst managing crime money is integral to all phases of a business operation, it is the 'establishment' phase where the pattern for planning how to hide money gained though illegal activates is set in motion.

The notion of 'Crime Money Management' (CMM)[4] is used in this book rather than the more commonly used term of 'money-laundering'. CMM, naturally includes money-laundering, but is conceptually a wider and more accurate description of what is involved in organized crime, in that crime groups not only wish to 'clean' their money but also seek to invest it and manage it. High-end criminal entrepreneurs make use of complex financial accounting practices and often use sophisticated investment strategies for their criminal money management.

The management of money for criminal purposes generally involves a 'money cycle' of production/supply, distribution, concealment, and/or disguising. For instance, money is used to make illegal goods (production side) and/or to buy illegal products or services (supply side). These illicit products/services are then sold on to a 'demand' market (distribution side). The illegally-derived profits are hidden (concealment side) from government agencies like taxation, customs, police, and other regulatory bodies. At some point such criminal profits are

---

[4] The term 'Criminal Money Management' (CMM) is used in the EDGE project on criminal financing (2005) that was commissioned by the EU to research the link between Profit Oriented Crime and Terrorism. The EDGE project defined 'Profit Oriented Crime' as any money derived from the various activities of what has academically been considered as related, yet different fields of study, into organized crime, white collar, and gang crime (EDGE, 2005: 29). The link with terrorism and CMM relates to the extent to which legal and/or crime money is used to finance terrorist attacks and activities.

generally cleaned through various money-laundering schemes (disguising side). Tracking the 'money cycle' of crime groups is no easy task owing to the secrecy, security and indeed, invisibility of much of what goes on in criminal markets.

Clearly, a big part of a CMM cycle is money-laundering, which itself consists primarily of three stages—placement, layering, and integration (Dietz and Buttle, 2008; Sheetz, 2004; McCusker, 2005: Jost and Sandhu, 2000).

- Placement—is the starting cycle of any money-laundering scheme. It involves working out how to get large sums of money into the legitimate financial and economic markets. For instance, cash businesses like bars, restaurants, and pizza shops are prime places for placement as they allow crime-derived money to be deposited as income produced by the 'legitimate' business
- Layering—is the cleaning cycle and acts much like a washing machine does. It separates the illegal activity from the money by moving the money around. This often involves numerous bank accounts both onshore and offshore with several levels or layers of corporate structure. The key to layering is its 'opacity'. That is, the obscuring of the original money source through use of multiple accounts, multiple businesses, and in multiple countries. Obscuring the money source works best in countries with lax or unregulated banking laws for declaring income sources
- Integration—is the spin-dry cycle whereby access is now possible to the money since it has been 'cleaned' for legitimate use. In other words, integration mimics legitimate business transactions. As noted in the 'placement' cycle cash intensive businesses, bars/cafes/pizza shops, work well for integrating or mixing up crime money with legitimately-earned money, as does invoice manipulation in import/export businesses or construction companies and so forth

Another common feature of CMM is the use of Informal Banking Systems (IBS). IBSs are of critical importance to organized crime groups as they can be used to do 'back-door laundering' as oppose to 'front-door laundering' where money is laundered through established legitimate systems (Zdanowicz, 2004). Informal banking schemes are also known as Alternative Money Remittance Systems (AMRS). AMRSs act as 'informal' funds transfer systems with the same structure and operational characteristics as the formal banking sector but without any of its bureaucratic rules or external regulatory requirements. Examples are the 'Hawala' money remittance scheme that is prominent in India (Van de Bunt, 2008), the 'Hundi' funds transfer scheme in Pakistan, and the 'fe ich'ien' system in China. Informal Banking Systems like these are culturally based and are hundreds of years old (Stamp and Walker, 2007).

In regard to CMM, Duyne (2007: 87) undertook an interesting study of what wealthy criminals do with their illegal-acquired money. He found that:

> The criminal money-management (or laundering in common parlance) was carried out with a sophistication geared to the available acumen as well as what

was required in the given circumstances. In general the sophistication hardly mirrored the imagery of criminals-getting-smarter and always 'ahead-of-us'. Ethnic minority crime-entrepreneurs with a social-economic home elsewhere used to take their money cash out of the country, while indigenous entrepreneurs faced always the requirement of justifying the acquired registered assets, like cars, boats, real estate and of course well-filled bank accounts. Apart from a few complicated and well thought-out exceptions, extensive chains of financial cross-border transactions had a low frequency.

Furthermore, according to Duyne (2007), in many cases the crime money was handled in cash and carried around personally by criminals, in clothes, suitcases, on and/or in the body, in the boot of a car, or some other hiding place. Banking transactions are much less frequent. Thus, the picture painted by Duyne of CMM is hardly one of financial sophistication for many criminal entrepreneurs although the extent and degree of criminal finances is far from clear.

Another important component of CMM, especially in starting up a crime business, is that of corruption. For instance, to get into a market, corruption is often required.

Case Example 3.7 Systemic Corruption in Pharmaceutical Industry (Ukraine)

In a study of the systemic nature of corruption in Ukraine, Markovska (2007) relates how legal western firms were able to start up in the Ukraine through offering bribes at different levels and in different sectors.

For instance, to get involved in the medical sector, the following actors need to be bribed by pharmaceutical companies—the pharmaceutical committee in Kiev, which engaged in the most corrupt practice, that of tender purchase (the main absorbent of bribes, the first contact of western pharmaceutical companies with Ukrainian reality); major hospitals (paid for clinical trials); specialized hospitals (paid for research results and general publication); local surgeries (basic equipment, torches, pens and paper).

Markovska's (2007) study underscores how the transition from Soviet rule and communism to independence and capitalism enabled many successful criminal enterprises to start up. Financing criminal enterprises became easy under such transitional circumstances as illegal privatization enabled criminals to gain control over enormous wealth quickly.

While corruption strategies like those above can be part and parcel of the set-up costs for 'legitimate' businesses, especially in post-Soviet satellite countries in the Eastern Bloc, corruption is also part of the business tool kit in all phases of crime business development. A more in-depth examination of corruption strategies is undertaken in the next business phase of 'expanding' a criminal enterprise. This is because 'expanding' a crime business is where the use of corruption as a market control mechanism is most evident.

This next example of CMM involves a money-laundering method which is becoming very prominent, that of 'smurfing'. The term 'smurfing' was first used in the United States according to Madinger (2006) but originates from cartoon figures in the Belgian cartoon. Smurfing is commonly used to refer to a money-laundering methodology that involves structuring or layering of crime money by moving it through multiple accounts in multiple banks using low-level and expendable associates to place amounts under a required limit before banks are required by law to file a suspicious transaction report. At the time of writing, bank deposits of over a AUS $10,000 limit in Australia require banks to file a suspicious transaction report.

Case Example 3.8 Variations on Smurfing: 'Cuckoo' Fraud (Europe and Australia)

This 'smurfing' methodology has been refined in recent years into other forms like 'cuckoo' smurfing. The term 'cuckoo smurfing' developed in Europe when similarities between this money-laundering method and the activities of the cuckoo bird were noticed, in that cuckoo birds lay eggs in the nest of other species of birds which then unwittingly take care of the eggs believing them to be their own (AUSTRAC, 2008). In a similar manner, entrepreneurial criminals seek to transfer their crime money 'nest eggs', so to speak, through the bank accounts of innocent third parties.

The real benefit to organized crime groups in using this type of 'cuckoo smurfing' method to clean their crime money is that they can remain completely anonymous. Currently, at the time of writing, there is no legislative basis in Australia that requires persons who deposit money into third party accounts to identify themselves.

In sum, the case examples presented in this section highlight numerous and innovative ways criminal groups seek to identify potential areas of vulnerability for criminal exploitation. They do this through using their entrepreneurial capability of 'opportunity perspective' and its associated business factors—*entrepreneurial vision, business planning,* and *crime money management.*

Entrepreneurial Capability: Resources Mobilization

The second entrepreneurial capability, resources mobilization, has three necessary business factors associated with establishing a crime business. These are *financial capital, operational logistics,* and *human resources.*

Financial Capital

Starting up a new crime business requires *financial capital* and often lots of it. For instance, to enter the illicit drug trade requires financial capital to buy drugs from suppliers. Legitimate options to source capital, like bank loans and short-term bank funding for working capital by extending a line of credit, are not available to a criminal entrepreneur.

Typically, a criminal entrepreneur will need to search for funding from crime money. Crime money will be available if the potential profit is high and the potential risk is low. As Nicaso and Lamothe (2005: 2) note, 'The territory of the underworld is no longer geographic: it's financial'. In other words, it's the profit that matters to organized crime not where a crime business is geographically located. We live in a global village and the reach of organized crime is such that 'every organised crime group in the world is now active *everywhere* in the world' (*ibid*). Organized crime is a globalized and deregulated market with a free trade zone policy where any crime group can enter, do deals, make alliances, form partnerships, and generally do as they please so long as they have the financial capital to get started.

There are, in general, three options for acquiring capital from crime money to start an illegal business venture—working oneself up in the criminal underworld; being bankrolled by a bigger criminal; or pooling finances and/or resources through alliances and partnerships to establish a larger working capital for a syndicated business enterprise.

The first option involves direct participation in small-scale but lucrative illegal activities that yield enough profit to build up over time the necessary working capital to establish a new or bigger crime business for oneself. This is the route many an aspiring criminal takes in setting themselves up through bank robberies, running brothels, dealing in drugs, extortion, kidnappings, and various fraudulent scams to get their 'big break' into the major crime league with their own business and market share.

The second option for acquiring financial capital is by being 'bankrolled' by a bigger, more successful criminal entrepreneur. Such a big shot may be someone the want-to-be criminal entrepreneur looks up to, like a mentor to the inexperienced criminal. Also, there are criminal financiers who can provide the working capital to get a new crime business idea going. Typically, financial backers of other criminals will extend a loan after some cost/benefit analysis where the potential profit is seen as high and the potential risk is low. It is up to the individual want-to-be criminal entrepreneur to convince the financial backer that the balance of profit to risk is worth taking. However, in some crime markets the initial working capital may only require a minor outlay of money. For instance, it is relatively easy for a newcomer to set up a cigarette trafficking scheme as shown in the case example below.

Case Example 3.9 Financing Backing for Cigarette Trafficking (Europe)

A small time criminal would only need a modest amount of capital to buy a large quantity of cigarettes like cheap Russian brands with the support of a financial backer and then to 'on sell' the untaxed cigarettes in places like Estonia.

While a small time trafficker of smuggled cigarettes may experience difficulties in linking supply and demand, research by Dijck (2007: 165) also found that cigarette traffickers rely on limited networks, consisting of one or two suppliers and a dozen customers.

Once a trusted network is established the want-to-be criminal entrepreneur is well on their way to having a successful crime business where the profit opportunities exceed the low risks involved. For, according to Dijck (2007), the cigarette black market provides ample opportunity to make a good profit.

The third option for acquiring financial capital is by pooling finances and/or resources with other criminal groups to build up a larger working capital for a new crime business enterprise. Research by Ruggiero and Khan (2007) on the drug trade in the UK provides a clear picture of how criminal groups will often work together in loose partnership arrangements to reduce costs and maximize profits.

Case Example 3.10 Pooling Resources in Drug Trade (United Kingdom)

Interestingly, criminal groups are seen as interacting among themselves and with society at large like entrepreneurs. Whereas traditionally, organized crime was constituted by a relatively narrow membership based on kinship or other common ground, entrepreneurial crime appears to be characterized by a small core of permanent members who establish contingent partnerships as required by specific tasks. This interpretation suggests that a criminal enterprise is similar to an 'adhocracy', led by a 'task force management' (Carter, 1997) that we often find in ordinary business (Ruggiero and Khan, 2007: 63).

Operational Logistics

This business development factor revolves around working out in detail the operational aspects of how a crime business is going to function. For instance, developing the *logistics* to operationalize an illicit drugs business could involve renting out a warehouse to store drug shipments, arranging transport routes, buying equipment to set up a drug factory, contacting suppliers and establishing a distribution network, and so on. Such logistics can also involve, to varying degrees, a level of entrepreneurial innovation as crime groups come up with new ways to do business. For example, such innovation could involve smuggling drugs in lead containers to avoid scanners and similar innovative operations.

There are as many combinations of operational logistics as there are crimes. Hence, the following set of case examples illustrate some of the operational possibilities used by criminal entrepreneurs in different types of crimes, namely cyber crime, human smuggling, and firearms trafficking.

This first case example concerns the risk of damaging criminal attacks from cyberspace on corporate networks. Enterprise networks contain the most precious assets of a corporation for cyber crime. Essentially, everything a company creates or does manifests itself within the corporate network. Consequently, corporate networks have become fertile ground for abuse and theft (Ortega, 2007).

Case Example 3.11 Cyber Crime: Electronic Gambling Machines (Canada)

A special case of cyber crime was discovered in Canada, where a cyber crime scheme was applied that defrauded electronic gambling machines by a criminal group. Three criminals would travel to a business with video lottery machines (VLTs). First person would stay in the vehicle with a lap top computer, radio equipment, and relevant software. Second and third criminals would enter the business. The player would be outfitted with a video camera, communication equipment, an earpiece and a power source. This person would focus the camera on a terminal screen and relay the playing/spinning of the screen to the operator in the vehicle enabling the computer guru to determine where the screen was in the random mode. From here the person with the computer using high speed equipment could tell how far away the terminal was from paying out. When the device was close to paying out, the person inside the business would be told to increase the bet from 5 credits to 50 credits (McMullan and Perrier, 2007).

Another technique deployed by the same cybercriminal group involved accessing the machines' back-up memory boards from the main logic boards to observe random access memories in the computers. By using a machine code monitor, an operation known as boot-tracing, the crime group was able to locate the bonus meter in the memory. They then inserted new instructions that modified the back-up memory board. In so doing they could manipulate the contents of the bonus meter memory logic so that they could trigger a cash payout at will (McMullan and Perrier, 2007).

The second case example relates to human smuggling and trafficking in Belgium. This case highlights the involvement of multiple crime groups in one country in one crime market sector and the operational routes and *modus operandi* used by different crime groups.

Case Example 3.12 Human Smuggling and Trafficking (Belgium)

In a study of irregular migration in Belgium, Kaizen and Nonneman (2007) found that human smuggling and migrant trafficking is related to criminal organizations in Belgium. Mainly four criminal groups are involved in irregular migration in Belgium.

The first crime grouping revolves around Pakistani criminal organizations who are mainly involved in heroin smuggling and human trafficking, often with traffic in identity documents and marriages of convenience.

The second crime grouping involves West African criminal groups and they tend to specialize in organizing irregular airport entry and women trafficking, although one smuggling route chosen by organized criminals in Africa for human trafficking is between Libya and Lampedusa. The sea route takes illegal immigrants from Libya to the Italian island of Lampedusa, 180 miles north of the Libyan coast. In 2006, almost 19,000 illegal migrants arrived in this small island (Coluccello and Massey, 2007).

The third criminal grouping centres in the Albanians who are deeply involved in the sexual exploitation of mainly Eastern European women in Belgium.

Finally, the fourth criminal grouping found in Belgium was Chinese criminals who used forged documents such as false Chinese notaries' deeds or false attestations from consulates to traffic humans.

As is evident in the example above, there are minor variations in *modus operandi* between different crime groupings, particularly with regard to organized crime in Asia and especially human trafficking. The next case example is the trafficking in illicit firearms for criminal purposes. Illicit arms trafficking is often associated with weapons being shipped to combatants in divergent irregular conflicts all over the world.

Case Example 3.13 Trafficking in Illegal Weapons (Europe)

In Europe, the buyers of illegal weapons are mostly criminals and to a lesser extent separatist movements in, for instance, Northern Ireland, the Basque regions, and Corsica. Most of the illicit arms trade is based on legally produced weapons.

Of the firearms that were seized by Dutch police, more than 95 per cent of the weapons were originally legally manufactured. The transfer from the licit to the illicit domain occurs on different routes: leakage directly from the factory, fake exports, recycling of discarded weapons, and theft from dealers and authorities (Spapens, 2007).

When it comes to operational logistics, organized crime has made a home of this business factor in Canada. As Nicaso and Lamothe (2005: 261–262) explain:

> It's often said that if organized crime were to create a country, it would look a lot like Canada. . . . Canada holds a special place in the underworld. . . . There are several reasons why Canada is a triple threat - haven, transit, and source - from organized crime. The same values, fairness, and emphasis on personal and human rights that makes Canada a desirable destination for the world's refugees and honest immigrants also makes it desirable for gangsters, terrorists and war criminals.

The case example presented below demonstrates the operational advantages of doing crime business in Canada, especially in the 'home-grown' illegal drug trade of high-grade marijuana production and distribution.

Case Example 3.14 'Criminal Heaven' for Organized Crime (Canada)

'Canada's prime service to the underworld is in drug trafficking. Always a transit country and a staging area, Canada has become a source country for both high-grade marijuana and precursor chemicals needed to process synthetic drugs.

. . . the growth of Canada's marijuana industry - the famed "B.C. Bud". B.C. Bud is a potent and now legendary product of Canada, grown mostly on the West Coast. But motorcycle gangs and Vietnamese criminal organizations have increasingly set up sophisticated and massive "grow-ops" in several locations along the top border of the U.S. Literally millions of plants are grown in Canada each year, and much of the marijuana is shipped through pipelines into the U.S.

The crossover between criminal initiatives is manifestly clear in the marijuana grow-op trade. Several indoor "farms" have been uncovered in which illegal migrants in transit pay off their fees by babysitting plants. Basically indentured slaves, the migrants are usually the first and only suspects picked up by police during raids. And seldom do the investigations reach much beyond these front-line workers serving out their debt bondage: financiers, lawyers, real estate agents - all usually walk away and set up another operation. And even when the back-end players are caught, their sentences are relatively light: drug trafficking in Canada is seen as a non-violent offence, resulting in early release from custody after a very short sentence' (Nicaso and Lamothe, 2005: 265–266).

Human resources

All businesses need staff and criminal businesses are no different. Getting the right staff to run a crime business and retaining them involves the business factor of *human resources*. It is a major consideration for a criminal entrepreneur to employ people who will fit into the type of illegal operation to be established without drawing unwanted attention to themselves and hence the 'business'.

Issues of security, secrecy, and trust are of primary significance. For instance, the issue of trust may be such that only family members are involved in the business or criminals of a certain ethnic origin. This is also the reason known gang members already present in a criminal group or other trusted criminal contacts are often employed as staff for a new crime business. Whatever shape the staffing requirements may take it is a matter of fundamental importance to ensure the secrecy of the new crime venture in order to avoid penetration by law enforcement.

Traditionally, it is a common practice in the criminal underworld to employ only 'family', mainly along kinship or ethnicity lines, and certainly as core members of a criminal business enterprise. As Ruggiero and Khan (2007: 63) point out, 'Even among scholars who see organised crime as entrepreneurial, the importance of membership amalgamation through ethnicity, cultural and geographic proximity is highlighted. However, Ruggiero and Khan (2007: 65) also found that 'while users and small dealers are often engaged in the strenuous affirmation of ethnic identity, those above them conduct business in total multi-ethnic harmony'. Hence, while the ethnic element is often important at the street level of business operation, 'market dynamics may overshadow such an element' (*op cit*). In other words, when it comes to making a profit the considerations are economic rather than ethnic.

Another factor that comes into play when hiring staff is that 'groups amalgamate on the basis of a sense of common bonds related to lifestyles and social characteristics' (Carter, 1997: 140); hence, employing associates already in the criminal underworld and other gang members is also a common policy.

Case Example 3.15 Employment Pool: Criminal Lifestyle (Global)

A criminal career in a gang often emerges out of something else, such as a playgroup, a clique of friends, or a loose sub-culture. Entry factors in relation to criminal gangs might include attraction to join because of ideology and politics, provocation and anger, protection, thrill-seeking, violence, and weapons.

Exit factors might include negative social sanctions, disillusionment with activities of the group and losing position within the group (White, 2007). While a young entrepreneur is often the common hub initially in a gang, groups that persist over different generations of young people would appear to involve a transfer of some type of commonality within communities. The persistence of a gang identity can be explained in terms of sharing the same ethnic background or social experiences (White, 2007).

It is a well-known reality that everyone involved in any business wants maximum profit and minimum risk. This profit-risk ratio is clearly apparent when entrepreneurial criminal groups seek to recruit staff. Crime groups need staff they can trust to remain loyal as well as keep their mouths shut about the nature and operation of the crime business. This is especially the case for an illegal drug business where the staff requirements for loyalty, secrecy, and security are particularly acute. Perhaps the most risky side of the drug trade is the actual smuggling of the illegal drugs from the production place to the market place. To get around these challenges criminal entrepreneurs often show an impressive creativity in the cat-and-mouse game with police and customs.

In terms of risk reduction strategies one such method criminal groups may use is entrapment. The case presented in Chapter 1 involving the recruitment of innocent 'clean skins' is a good example of an elaborate ploy developed by drug trafficking criminal groups. This case involved an entrapment method that has recently been employed in Norway by South-American drug dealers. The target group for entrapment is young white Norwegian women who get caught up in a recruitment scam and end up doing the dirty and highly risky job of being an unsuspecting drug mule for the criminal business.

In the final analysis, employing staff for a new start-up crime business venture is about getting the balance right between people who can be trusted and the type of skill-set needed to do the job of making money for the business. In this regard, there is potentially a wide pool to draw from because of the perception that easy money can be made quickly through crime. According to Andreano and Siegfried (1980: 4) individuals that become involved in the crime sector of the economy are 'consciously or subconsciously weighing the costs and benefits of their actions and making explicit choices among alternatives'. In other words, people involved in illegal business activity try to maximize their self-interest rationally as a trade-off against the constraints they may face in the criminal marketplace. Rubin (1980: 13) underscores this perspective of a rational cost/benefit analysis when he states that 'the decision to become a criminal is in principle no different from the decision to become a bricklayer or a carpenter, or indeed, an economist'. However, it can be argued that such a choice is much more risky and is often not one that is less rationally calculated than being a bricklayer. Involvement in criminal activities is often due to contextual factors like one's peer group and social environment, where belonging to a street gang meets personal and emotional needs for a sense of identity. The problem of recruitment is often a major challenge for legitimate entrepreneurial businesses, and is even more challenging for criminal business entrepreneurs where it is crucial to be able to trust staff.

In sum, the case examples presented make it clear that crime entrepreneurs have a range of business factors to consider when starting up an illegal business venture. Each business factor offers both opportunities and pitfalls for 'would-be' criminal entrepreneurs. In the next section an analytical tool is outlined to assist police and law enforcement agencies to develop a more detailed picture of how these business factors combine and interact under different crime group conditions. This analytical tool is based on a fuzzy modelling of the set of business factors associated with the two entrepreneurial capabilities of 'opportunity perspective' and 'resources mobilization' as discussed so far with regard to the 'establishment' phase of a crime business.

'Fuzzy' Mapping of *Establishing* Crime Business

The notion of a 'fuzzy' map is based on the mathematics of fuzzy logic.[5] The formal name in science for fuzzy logic is 'multivalence' (Kosko, 1993). The opposite of fuzzy logic is binary logic known formally as 'bivalence' or two-valuedness. Binary logic states that there are two ways to answer a question—true or false, 1 or 0, right or wrong, black or white. By contrast, fuzzy logic recognizes that human reasoning is based on knowledge that is often inexact, incomplete, or not totally reliable (Zadeh, 1990).

Human reasoning can rarely be put in neat little right or wrong boxes of bivalent machine logic. In other words, human reasoning is multi-valued and full of vagueness and therefore 'truth' can only be approximated or arrived at to varying degrees of value. Therefore, in essence, fuzzy logic models human reasoning which by extension is 'reasoning with vague concepts' (Kosko, 1993: 8).

It is in the 'vagueness' of human reasoning that fuzzy logic comes into its own. Such thinking in vague terms can be given a 'fuzziness factor' which equates to the varied shades of grey between the two extremes of black and white, true or false, right or wrong thinking. Fuzzy logic uses multivalence mathematics or 'computing with words' to express the shades of grey humans think in and reason with rather than the algebraic equations of binary logic. This human ability to 'compute with words' is the distinct advantage of multivalence mathematics that allows the construction of the *fuzzy mapping* tool presented in this section.

This fuzzy mapping tool provides a graphical 'Business Profile' about what police and law enforcement agencies know, to an inexact degree (*fuzziness* factor), about the current state of business development at various phases for a particular criminal group or groupings.[6] The data needed to construct a Fuzzy Crime Business Profile (FCBP) is compiled in the usual way through a combination of police intelligence, open sources information, and law enforcement knowledge gleaned from other agencies and trusted sources. What is new about this type of fuzzy matrix mapping of a specific crime group is how this diverse information is combined into a single analytical model.

The outcome of this modelling process is matrix-type holistic visualization of the crime group under analysis. This matrix has the capability of assigning, on the basis of policing knowledge, a fuzziness rating for each business factor associated with the constituent parts of a particular business phase, be it *establishing*, *expanding*, *consolidating*, and/or *positioning* a crime business. Moreover, the matrix model provides the value-added advantage of not only being able to make

---

[5] Readers unfamiliar with fuzzy logic and especially how it relates to policing are referred to our previous work of *Knowledge Management in Policing and Law Enforcement* published by Oxford University Press in 2007 (see Chapter 7, pages 136–142).

[6] The term 'crime group' is used as shorthand for what in effect can be a range of criminal groups working in some sort of association network as an alliance or partnership or even part of a larger crime syndicate either on a semi-permanent basis or as 'one off' projects. In other words, the notion of a crime group is not a fixed entity but rather reflects the fluid nature of contemporary criminal groupings.

Chapter 3: Establishing the Crime Business

a fuzzy quantifiable assessment of a crime group's business profile at each phase of development but also the potentiality of their entrepreneurial capabilities.

Hypothetical scenarios

The following Figure 3.3 is a fuzzy map of a series of 'hypothetical scenarios' in which various crime groups are seeking to 'establish' a crime business. As can be seen the fuzzy scaling for each scenario is indicated by connecting lines on the graph in Figure 3.3. It is also evident from the above figure that the different crime groups, A, B, and C go about establishing their illegal business activities through employing, to varying degrees (fuzziness factor), each of the business factors associated with the entrepreneurial capabilities of 'opportunity perspective' and 'resources mobilization'.

With regard to the *first scenario*, for *Crime Group (A)*, at first glance it is apparent that its crime business profile contains a lot of uneven development in relation to the business factors at this *establishing* phase. For instance, the level of this crime group's 'entrepreneurial vision' is given a fuzziness factor rating of between 'low to medium' on the *opportunity perspective* entrepreneurial capability scale.

Therefore, it would be reasonable to assume that this 'hypothetical' crime group possesses a less than medium level of vision to seek out new entrepreneurial business ventures. Given this fuzzy assessment it is unlikely that having

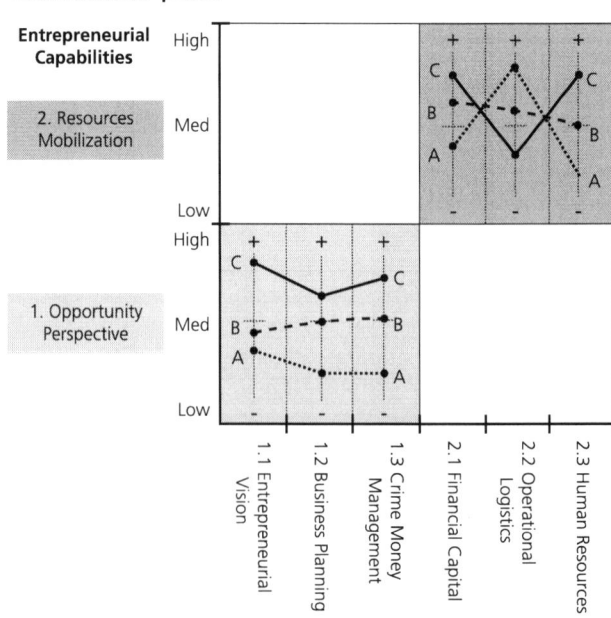

Figure 3.3 Fuzzy scenarios of entrepreneurial capability at 'establishment' phase

a strong entrepreneurial vision will be the driving force behind this crime group's subsequent business activities and operational actions. In other words, this crime group is more likely to wait for business opportunities to fall into its lap rather than aggressively pursue any opportunities. Unless something changes in this dimension of their entrepreneurial vision, such as a change of leadership in the group or the entry of more entrepreneurially-oriented members, then it is unlikely that this crime group will pose much of a threat in terms of business growth.

However, it is also clear from Figure 3.3 that this group of criminals is also not very strong on developing a 'business plan' for its entrepreneurial activities. Such a 'perceived' business planning weakness means that this crime group probably favours action over considered thought about its business direction. Hence, one would expect an 'ad hoc' opportunistic development to be the model for this crime group's business growth, if any, in the future—assuming, of course, it continues to give little importance to business planning. However, again, if the dynamics of the group membership change, with new more business-oriented members joining, then this hypothetical scenario may well change. Hence, the importance of monitoring developments in criminal groups so as to keep up with changes on which to base a 'fuzzy assessment'. Organized crime group data needs to be as accurate, reliable, and up-to-date as possible.

As for the third business development factor, that of 'crime money management' (CMM), this is, as to be expected, closely related to business planning and hence has a similarly low fuzzy rating. This is not surprising because any crime group that has little interest in planning its business, apart from the operational logistics required to get it up and running, is unlikely to have the mindset to devote much time to thinking through how it is going to manage its crime money, other than make as much profit as possible.

In so far as the second entrepreneurial capability, *resources mobilization,* is concerned it is apparent that this crime group has access to enough 'financial capital' to kick-start its business. It is also quite strong on the 'operational logistics' side of the business. By contrast, with regard to 'staffing requirements' it has a relatively low fuzzy rating. This could mean it is a small-scale business operation at this stage that relies on other criminal friends, or an ethnic community-type arrangement, or even a loose association of similar criminals. Again, police intelligence and surveillance should be able to clarify the staffing situation in a real crime group profile. Depending on what is found with regard to the type of staff this crime business employs the potential for police infiltration through informants or undercover agents is then a decision that can be more accurately judged.

In sum, Crime Group (A) has a mix of relative strengths and weaknesses in its crime business profile in relation to the extent of its entrepreneurial capabilities to start up a new business venture.

In the *second scenario, Crime Group (B)* has a slightly higher level or vision to perceive business opportunities than Crime Group (A). This crime group also has a better understanding of the need to plan one's crime business. However, while stronger than Crime Group (A) in thinking about how to manage its crime money, such thought is mainly devoted to 'cleaning' its ill-gotten money. In so far as its entrepreneurial capability to mobilize resources is concerned, Crime Group (B) appears to have ready access to other crime money to finance new business ventures. However, as indicated in Figure 3.3, apart from that high spot, this crime group's attention to the operational side of carrying out its illegal business and the human resources it needs are all rated as going downhill. This fuzzy assessment indicates that for Crime Group (B) once it has done some planning about how to do a scam or conduct an operation and has found the working capital to get it done, then in all likelihood it will tend to take its hands off the rudder. It prefers to hire in the staff it needs and let them work out how to do a job. In a manner of speaking, this crime group opts more for a 'contracting out' type of arrangement for running its crime business. So long as sufficient money comes in then it is happy to leave it to others to make it happen. Hence, Crime Group (B) is good at spotting money-making business opportunities but does not really want to get involved much beyond this point, once it has secured the finance to pay for a new business venture.

For the *third scenario*, it is evident that *Crime Group (C)* is very entrepreneurially-driven. It has a strong sense of vision for business opportunities and is constantly on the lookout for new ways to make money through criminal means. In fact, so strong is Crime Group (C) on searching for new business opportunities that it devotes only a limited amount of its energy to other business factors. For instance, once it plans a new business venture and ways to hide and manage its crime money, it does not give much attention to the operational side of the business. This may in part be because it has substantial capital funds to mobilize the necessary resources to operationalize the business by hiring in criminal professionals to run it. The high fuzzy rating on human resources is evidence of this staff quality control dimension. There is a type of insurance logic to this 'contracting out' strategy of business operations to other criminals. If effective law enforcement does make inroads to the crime business then Crime Group (C) is sufficiently removed from daily operations that only the hired criminals are likely to be caught. In this regard, the business profile of Crime Group (A) on the 'operational logistics' factor is its high point. So much so, that Crime Group (A) is the sort of criminal group with which Crime Group (C) might want to form a strategic partnership or alliance in order to utilize its operational strength to look after Group (C)'s new business venture.

An alternative explanation for Crime Group (C)'s high rating on human resources could be that this crime group has learnt from experience that people are the 'weak link' in any criminal business. Therefore, it will only employ family and trusted friends to run key sections of its crime business. This explanation is also consistent with a low focus on the operational logistics factor. Because trusted family/friends are running the business other group members can devote their energy to seeking out new business opportunities.

To conclude, a comparison of the emergent Fuzzy Criminal Business Profiles of the 'hypothetical scenarios' for Crime Groups (A), (B), and (C) provides some useful insights for policing each of these groups. For example, Group (A) presents as a small-scale crime group strong on carrying out the operational side of opportunistic business ventures. Whilst it can find enough capital to put into its pursuit of illicit profits it has a distinct lack of business planning and crime money management expertise. Another potential problem for Crime Group (A) is insufficient vetting of the staff it is likely to employ. As for Crime Groups (B) and (C) it is evident that each has areas of business strength yet also areas of business vulnerability that can be exploited by well-conceived targeted police and law enforcement actions. Later chapters will explore these policing and law enforcement options.

Summary

This chapter examined the first business phase of *establishing* a crime business. Two entrepreneurial capabilities—*opportunity perspective* and *resources mobilization*—are closely related in this establishment phase. The first entrepreneurial capability, *opportunity perspective*, translates into three business factors—'entrepreneurial vision', 'business planning', and 'crime money management'. The second entrepreneurial capability, *resources mobilization*, is associated with three other business factors: 'financial capital', 'operational logistics', and 'human resources' or staffing requirements to run the crime business. How each of these six business factors can be used to entrepreneurially establish and develop an illegal business was illustrated through a variety of case examples. Finally, the chapter presented a 'fuzzy' analytical mapping tool that graphically depicted the crime business profiles for three distinct crime groups through a set of hypothetical scenarios. These 'fuzzy' maps showed the various pathways different crime groups can take in how they choose to establish their illegal business operations at this phase of their entrepreneurially-oriented business model. Such a fuzzy mapping matrix is capable of showing potential areas of strength and weakness for different crime groups depending on the business choices they make, which police and law enforcement agencies can usefully exploit.

4

Expanding the Crime Business

Introduction

The second phase of *expanding* a crime business is examined in this chapter. First, the entrepreneurial capability of 'making decisions under conditions of uncertainty', which is associated with this expanding phase, is considered. Second, specific business factors related to this entrepreneurial capability are discussed and illustrated with case examples of their operation within criminal markets. The third section demonstrates the use of the 'fuzzy' mapping analytical tool, introduced in the previous chapter, through 'hypothetical' case scenarios of crime groups at this expanding phase of a crime business.

Criminal Business Modelling: Expansion Phase

This phase of expansion in our operating framework of business development requires the 'organizing' of an established crime business in order to grow its market share. Business organization is based on an understanding of the business factors needed to foster growth. Figure 4.1 below lists key business factors associated with developing this second phase of 'expanding' a crime business.

At the 'expansion' phase of a crime business the key entrepreneurial capability that criminal entrepreneurs need is the ability to make wise business decisions under conditions of uncertainty and risk. Cross-matching this entrepreneurial capability with the four associated business factors noted above produces a 'matrix' as shown in Figure 4.2.

As can be seen, there are three entrepreneurial capabilities represented on this matrix. Only the entrepreneurial capability of 'decision-making under uncertainty' (middle box) associated with 'expanding' a criminal business in our model is discussed in this chapter. This expansion phase is highlighted by its larger size and bolded text. The other entrepreneurial capabilities—'resource

Criminal Business Modelling: Expansion Phase

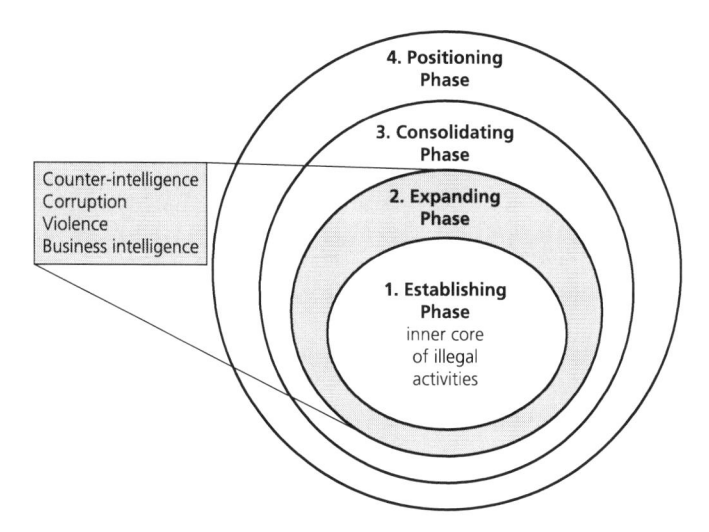

Figure 4.1 Crime business model: Phase 2—'expansion' business factors

mobilization' and 'people cooperation'—are included on the matrix above in order to show how each capability builds on the other in a developmental sequence. The 'resource mobilization' capability was discussed in the previous chapter in relation to the *establishment* phase, whilst, 'people cooperation' will

Figure 4.2 Entrepreneurial capability by business factors at 'expansion' phase

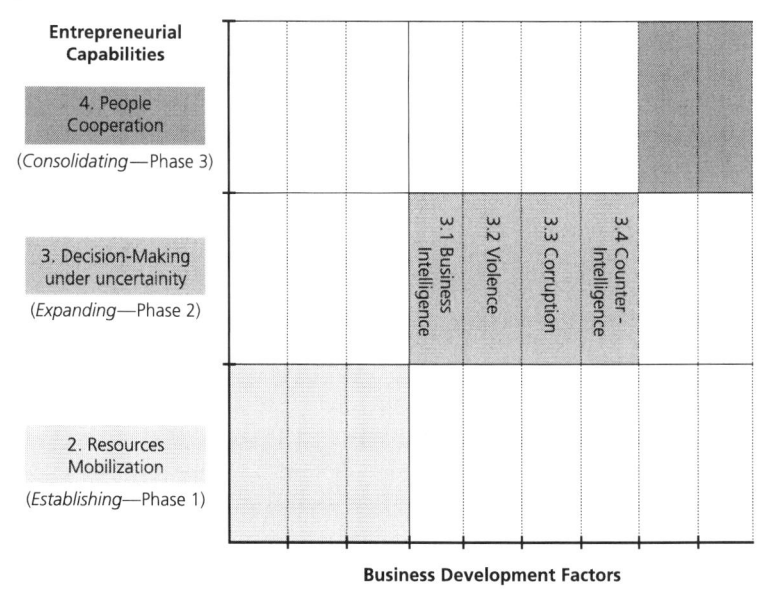

be discussed in the next chapter to do with *consolidating* a criminal business. At a very practical level, the four business factors as shown in the above figure associated with criminal entrepreneurial decision-making carry high risk not only for making or losing profits but also to the criminal entrepreneur's life expectancy. Crime markets are dangerous places.

Entrepreneurial Capability: Decision-Making under Uncertainty

A criminal entrepreneur's capability to make business decisions under conditions of uncertainty involves higher risk factors than in legitimate enterprises. Illegal businesses operate in a hostile environment both from law enforcement and other crime competitors in the underworld market. Duyne (2000: 370) succinctly sums up the operating conditions in the volatile crime business environment for the would-be criminal entrepreneur, when he states:

> Criminal entrepreneurship is enterprising in an *enduring hostile* landscape, which means a constant jeopardy of the continuity of the crime-enterprise. For the crime-entrepreneurs it means that the daily organisation of their trade is not only focussed on money, but at the same time on a highly elaborate risk avoidance strategy. A good crime-entrepreneur is an expert risk manager, facing the two-fold close-down by law enforcement as well by his criminal competitors.

For criminal entrepreneurs 'risk management' is the name of the game. They must manage their illicit business in an *uncertain* and *highly risky environment* by having a *tight control structure* to ensure secrecy and security as well as exercising *entrepreneurial judgment*. This is especially important in terms of resource acquisition and allocation to prosper from criminal business opportunities. Also they need *strategic knowledge* to ensure the survival of their criminal business enterprise. All of these issues require a 'risk-to-reward trade off' mindset for a criminal entrepreneur. This risk/reward mindset involves balancing out at least four necessary business factors associated with this entrepreneurial decision-making capability as shown in Figure 4.2. They are: *business intelligence, violence, corruption*, and *counter-intelligence*.

Business Intelligence

This business development factor, *business intelligence,* involves two dimensions—market potential and market rivals. The first dimension relates to the market potential for an illicit product and/or service. A criminal entrepreneur has to decide that there is enough of a market for their product/service not only to start up their crime business in the first place but also to 'expand' their business.

Business intelligence planning and analysis requires similar information as gathered at the 'establishing phase' of a crime business, but it also requires constant updating to ensure that threats to and opportunities for the business are not missed. Manitoba Hells Angels Chapter President, Ernie Dew, highlights this change to business-oriented market thinking. Dew reportedly commented that:

> Back in the old days, nobody worked. Get out of the sixties guys: we're not in the sixties anymore. Everybody's well dressed. You don't see hair down to your arse anymore. There's a big change. We all get older and we all get wiser (New Zealand Police Association (2006a: 67).

Sophisticated Outlaw Motorcycle Gangs (OMCGs) are now more like 'businessmen in biker attire' (Nicaso and Lamothe, 2005: 217).

There are various ways to assess market potential, such as a 'barriers-to-entry' analysis, a 'risk-to-reward' analysis, a 'SWOT' (Strengths-Weaknesses-Opportunities-Threats) analysis, an 'environmental scan' analysis, and so forth. The following case example of how OMCGs use a strategy of 'patching over' smaller biker clubs to expand their market reach illustrates the effectiveness of this business strategy. In particular, Interpol identified a trio of American gangs—the Hells Angels, Bandidos, and the Outlaws as being the 'big international movers and shakers in the illicit drug trade' (New Zealand Police Association, 2006c: 71).

Case Example 4.1 'Patching Over' Business Strategy (OMCGs)

As a business expansion strategy 'patching over' is a very successful technique. For example:

> the Hells Angels have 1,800 patched members and several thousand associates spread across 22 countries. This trio have begun to patch over and take control of the smaller clubs in return for the sought-after Hells Angels, Bandidos, or Outlaws patches. The smaller clubs then become known as 'puppet' clubs (*op cit*).

These patched over 'puppet' clubs are often used to do the dirty work of the larger OMCGs such as their intimidation, bombings, and retribution (New Zealand Police Association (2006a:66).

The second dimension to *business intelligence* relates directly to other crime competitors. A sophisticated criminal entrepreneur will want to know what their rivals in the crime market are up to in order to work out how best to counter or capture the business share of their competitors. Also, at the very least, business intelligence is needed to 'neutralize' any inroads to their own market share by rival crime groups.

Competition is the very nature of markets and there is often fierce competition amongst competitors in the same market for commercial success. For instance, in relation to the drug trade in the UK as Ruggiero and Khan (2007: 64) report in their face-to-face interview research project with drug traffickers and distributors held in custody:

> *'There is ethnic competition in the market, but only at a low level'* one respondent remarked. Large dealers (middle level) do go outside their area of residence, doing business with all sorts of people, irrespective of their ethnic background. South Asian cocaine dealers, for example, *'buy supplies from black people, while black people buy quantities of heroin from South Asians'*. Large dealing networks tend therefore to be more multiethnic or *'anyway more fluid'*.

This research interview makes it clear that even where ethnic background is a consideration for doing business it is restricted to low or street level contacts. It is economic competition for commercial success that drives middle and upper level drug dealing in the UK rather than ethnic pressure. Hence, for a criminal entrepreneur there is a strong competitive drive to make money by expanding into other markets or a rival's territory. Such expansion plans can lead to turf wars and gangland-style killings. Therefore, good business intelligence is required before a crime entrepreneur embarks on a particular road that could end up very rocky and unwise in hindsight. For instance, a local turf war between rival biker gangs in New Zealand that had been going on for years came to a sudden end when the Mongrel Mob and the Black Power gangs held a meeting in Wellington in 2005 in order to '. . . extend common "business" interests' (New Zealand Police Association, 2006b: 69). The same sort of strategic business mindset by entrepreneurially-oriented crime groups to make money is often considered more important than infighting and rivalry between gangs. This mindset is evident in a reported case about a 'street war' that had erupted in Vancouver, Canada.

Case Example 4.2 Brokering 'Street War' (Canada)

There'd been a street war in Vancouver between Gum Wa, known as the Golden Boys, and the Lotus Family, two fairly historical groups from the late 1960s and early 1970s. Their combat peaked when a boy was beaten to death with a steel bar on the main street of Chinatown at four o'clock in the afternoon. At that hour of the day, and on that one block, there were probably eight hundred to one thousand people, most of whom saw what happened. But when the police asked for cooperation, nobody would say anything. Nobody would come forward.

Within seven months, the two group leaders were working together robbing jewellery stores under the control of a Dai Huen Jai group. In fact, the two were arrested together in the same house. The police later learned that someone from the Dai Huen Jai group said to them, there is enough money to be made here, we don't need to fight, when you fight, the police gain more information which makes it difficult for all of us. So they simply stopped fighting and started making money together (Robinson, 2000: 315).

Violence

Criminal entrepreneurs use *violence* as a business development factor. Its use has both instrumental and expressive purposes. For instance, organized crime groups often use violence that is instrumental in nature to achieve some defined aim like intimidating someone rather than simply expressing violence for the sake of it. The controlled use of instrumental violence by a crime group is the purest form of a 'business option'. On the other hand, expressive violence is often a way of life for some criminal groups. They use violence purely for its own sake, to meet their personal needs for power, control, and aggression, rather than as a well-planned 'business option' to advance their crime business. Hence, expressive violence is rarely a sophisticated way to run a crime business. It attracts too much police attention for a crime group that wants to fly under the radar of law enforcement.

Therefore, how a crime group uses violence provides insight into the business sophistication of the group as well as a reflection of its cultural antecedents. For instance, Russian crime groups will not hesitate to kill a police officer who gets in the way of their business, whereas, Asian crime groups in general, and Chinese criminal entrepreneurs in particular, understand that killing a police officer is not a smart thing to do unless the circumstances are exceptional. Robinson (2000: 309) makes this point in relation to Chinese organized crime gangs when he states that:

> they are extremely patient—the culture lends itself to that—and therefore more insidious. They go after the one area where the officer will have real trouble defending himself: his reputation. They make allegations about his honesty that tie him up for years in investigations.

It is not that Chinese organized criminals are averse to using extreme and brutal violence but rather the point is that when they do so it is usually more indirect and is intended to send a signal to others. Hence, the use of extreme violence for Chinese gangs is a question of how it is used and for what reason. The following case example illustrates in a rather macabre way this cultural disposition to violence by a Chinese drug trafficking group.

Case Example 4.3 'Baby's Bonnet': Indirect Brutal Violence (Chinese)

A North American gang member named How was trafficking heroin for a man in China. A fifty-kilo shipment was late in arriving. How complained to his boss that he was being severely pressured by his own investors. The boss didn't seem to respond. How told the man that he was losing face with is own investors and that they would evoke revenge. And still the man did not respond. How threatened that if the heroin didn't get to him soon, something might happen to the man's family.

continued

Chapter 4: Expanding the Crime Business

> The drugs never arrived.
> How invited the boss's mistress out to lunch. She arrived with her two children – both fathered by the man in China – including their five-month-old son. He told the woman that he'd been drinking and asked her to drive. He suggested a restaurant, let her four-year-old daughter sit in the front sear, climbed into the backseat, where her son was strapped into a car seat, facing backward.
> On the way, How kept repeating what a lovely baby she had. And as he did so, he took revenge on the man in China by wrapping the strings of the baby's bonnet around his throat and strangling the child (Robinson, 2000: 309).

This sort of indirect brutal violence against a gang member's family, rather than against the man himself, is typical of the way Asian crime gangs use violence. Violence is used in a very calculated and cruel manner against their own who fail to deliver on agreements. It has the effect of ensuring compliance in future and avoids having to replace a gang member. If this gang member is simply killed, as the Russian or Italian crime groups would most likely do, then getting a suitable replacement becomes another problem.

However, Asian crime gangs do not just restrict brutal violence to their own. Where they see a way to make money out of violence then some Asian crime groups are not averse to using it. A particularly gruesome example can be found in 'Operation Kronos', an investigation by the British police into illegal human smuggling in 1998.

Case Example 4.4 'Operation Kronos': Human Smuggling Twist (United Kingdom)

A Triad gang was bringing Chinese nationals form Fujian into Britain. The routing took them across various staging points in Thailand and Burma, into the Czech Republic, then to Holland, and into the UK. At each staging point, the gang phoned back to China demanding of the alien's families that another payment be made. But once the gang smuggled the people into Britain, the case took a brutal turn. The illegal aliens were now held in ransom.

Six hostages in one house were told that if their families didn't pay, they would be killed. And the method the gang intended to use was horrible. The six would draw lots, and the one with the short straw would be allowed to live as long as he murdered the other five. The gang explained that by letting the sixth man live, he could never testify against them because by doing so he would have to confess to five murders. If the chosen hostage refused to kill the others, his hand would be cut off. And just to make certain the gang could do that effectively, they tied tourniquets around their victims' arms for a couple of days so that when a hand was cut off, the person wouldn't bleed to death. Tourniquets were still in place when the police arrived to save the hostages (Robinson, 2000: 313).

Furthermore, excessive violence can serve both instrumental and expressive purposes for some crime groups.

Case Example 4.5 'Reputational Violence': Branding Strategy (Sicilian Mafia)

Gambetta (1993) argues that the Sicilian Mafia use what he terms 'reputational violence' as both a means to an end and a resource or 'brand name' to enhance their protection status and credentials in the criminal underworld. In fact, Gambetta (1993) posits that the Sicilian Mafia are not entrepreneurs in the traditional sense of dealing in the production and distribution of illegal products and services as their primary focus and criminal specialization has always been the protection racket, in that, they license and sell illegal protection to the provider of illicit goods and services.

Clearly the Sicilian Mafia, in particular, demonstrate a certain level of criminal entrepreneurialism in the way they go about their 'protection' speciality. However, such branding of violence, in a reputational sense, is not the exclusive domain of the Sicilian Mafia. Wa (2007: 219) notes that historically, '... the triad societies in HK (Hong Kong) were profit-oriented gangs and financed primarily by franchising their brand of violence in the form of protection service to other legitimate and illegitimate businesses'. In this regard, when it comes to marketing violence, the Asian-style 'brand' of violence is noteworthy. In particular, the Vietnamese are up there with the Mafia, both the Sicilian and Russian[1] brands, as this next case example very clearly demonstrates.

Case Example 4.6 Violence 'Asian-style' (Vietnamese)

In the violent world of Asian organized crime, Vietnamese violence is notorious. So much so that other gangs also famous for violence sit up and take notice. Even the Hells Angels motorcycle gang has made accommodations with Vietnamese gangs to head off confrontation. British Columbia is the home turf of the richest Hells Angels club in the world. An organized criminal gang known for manipulating shares on the stock market, running all sorts of lottery scams, prostitutes, and drugs ... A few years ago, one of the chapter presidents in B.C. went missing and

continued

---

[1] 'We Italians will kill you, but the Russians are crazy. They'll kill your whole family'. Attributed to John Gotti (Mafioso) in Robinson (2000: 83).

> the story was quickly passed around that the last place he was seen was entering a house of a Vietnamese drug dealer. The Vietnamese denied having anything to do with his disappearance. It was later learned that he'd owed $400,000 to some California bikers and they'd simply grown tired of waiting for him to pay up.
> But his disappearance spurred a meeting between a Chinese gang member and the Hells Angels. The Chinese fellow was trying to work his way into the middle of an alliance. He assured the Hells Angels that he could control the local Vietnamese groups, warning that as long as they authorized him to go ahead and make a deal, there would be peace. If not, there would be war.
> When the bikers didn't seem particularly intimidated by the prospect of a gang war, he reminded them that with the Vietnamese, war is eternal. He told the bikers, there are perhaps fifty of you in this whole province, there are perhaps fifty of them in that apartment building down the block. If you start to kill them, then you must accept that, for the rest of your life, you will be at war with them.
> The Hells Angels have since come to a 'coexistence' accommodation with the Vietnamese (Robinson, 2000: 304–305).

Corruption

The use of corruption is a 'signature' characteristic of organized criminality. There is an astounding variety of corruption strategies practised by particular organized crime groups as part of their trade mark art and craft. Corruption, as a business option, from a criminal entrepreneur's perspective, is primarily useful as a market control mechanism, in that, corruption strategies, like bribes and/or kick-backs to police, politicians, government officials, 'honey-traps', and blackmail, assist criminal entrepreneurs to facilitate their business opportunities as well as increase their market share. For example, the Organized Crime Threat Assessment (OCTA) 2006 report by Europol concluded that professional, well-established organized crime groups were making significant inroads through high-level targeting of officials within the public sector in the EU, and especially in the construction sector through corrupt practices in public tendering for contracts. The 2007 OCTA report found a further corruption threat was emerging from the way criminal groups originating from outside the EU (referred to in OCTA as 'non-indigenous' OC groups) are beginning to penetrate the EU with the corrupt practices they have refined in their own country of origin. In the recent past, most 'non-indigenous' criminal groups lacked the interest or ability to influence and/or corrupt legal structures in the Member States that make up the EU. However, times are changing rapidly in this regard. 'The increased capability of these second generation (non-indigenous) OC groups to corrupt their environment in the EU is identified as a threat' (OCTA, 2007: 12).

Corruption starts with individuals and can end up with whole communities and states being overrun with corrupt police, military, politicians, and government ministers. Examples of failed states, bent politicians, and corrupt businessmen abound in the daily news. Of particular concern is the use of corruption to target law enforcement officials, especially police and customs officers, as these are the front line personnel in the fight against organized crime. The enormous wealth amassed by successful crime groups make it possible to buy almost anyone. The FBI estimates the annual income of the Hells Angels' drug trade worldwide is US $1 billion (New Zealand Police Association, 2006a: 67). Thus, corrupting police and other law enforcement officers is not a question of money but of opportunity. 'Police corruption' and similar terms like police crime, misconduct, and deviance is a significant research area in its own right. The following Figure 4.3 presents a matrix to illustrate the conceptual links between this 'police crime' research area and its interconnectedness to the 'organized crime' focus on this work.

It is apparent from the above figure that the opportunities for criminal entrepreneurs to target and co-opt police officers in positions of influence and strategic advantage to their criminal businesses are many and varied. The figure clearly indicates that once police officers engage in even relatively minor unethical behaviours (misconduct) that can start a 'slippery' slide into a range of corrupt practices. There is considerable research to support this 'slippery slope' theory of police deviance (O'Connor, 2005) whereby there is a gradual deterioration of social-moral inhibitions accompanied by a perceived sense of permissibility for deviant conduct amongst police.

As can be seen, on the left-hand side is 'police misconduct' and on the right-hand side 'predatory policing' while 'police corruption' is located in the middle. Thus, the matrix shows the development of 'police crime' in terms of the categories of *misconduct* through to *corruption* proper and in some cases into a more *predatory* type of police crime. The matrix also shows how police crime progresses down from the level of individuals, to groups and finally, if left unchecked, through to organizational 'pockets' of systemic corruption. Once a policing organization becomes systemically corrupted the context is ripe for 'failed' states and 'corruption-prone' countries to appear and, as a consequence, organized crime is at its zenith. A case in point is the level of corruption in post-Soviet Russia. Robinson (2000: 17) asserts that:

Case Example 4.7 Perfecting a Criminal State: Systemic Corruption (Post-Soviet Russia)

Today, organized criminal groups are the only effective government in Russia. They control 40 per cent of all private businesses, 60 per cent of state-owned businesses and 80 to 90 per cent of the banks.

They exert executive control over key economic sectors, such as consumer products—including two thirds of all alcohol sales, estimated to be worth $1.5 billion

continued

Chapter 4: Expanding the Crime Business

Matrix of Police Crime

Categories ↑

Police Misconduct
Violations of departmental rules, policies, procedures (eg gratuity [free meals, discounts etc.], improper use of police resources for personal use [favours for friends, relatives, etc.], aggressive stop & search, security breach, obscene & profane language and so forth.) [O'Connor, 2005]

'Slippery Slope' of Police Deviance
(behaviour inconsistent with norms, values, or ethics)

Police Corruption
Key element is the *misuse* of police authority for gain (eg taking bribes, 'fixing' a criminal prosecution by leaving out relevant information, drug dealing, police brutality (use of excessive force), and so forth. Moreover, police corruption can also involve criminal collusion with organized crime and/or politicians. [Punch, 2003]

Predatory Policing
Police *proactively* engage in predatory behaviour (eg extorting money from the public or from criminals by providing protection and other 'services' to them. [Gerber and Mendelson, 2008]

Individual
'rotten apple' theory (individualistic model of human failure)

Group
'rotten barrel' theory (occupational socialization model of police culture failure)

Organization
'rotten orchards' theory of systemic corruption (institutionalized model of systemic failure)

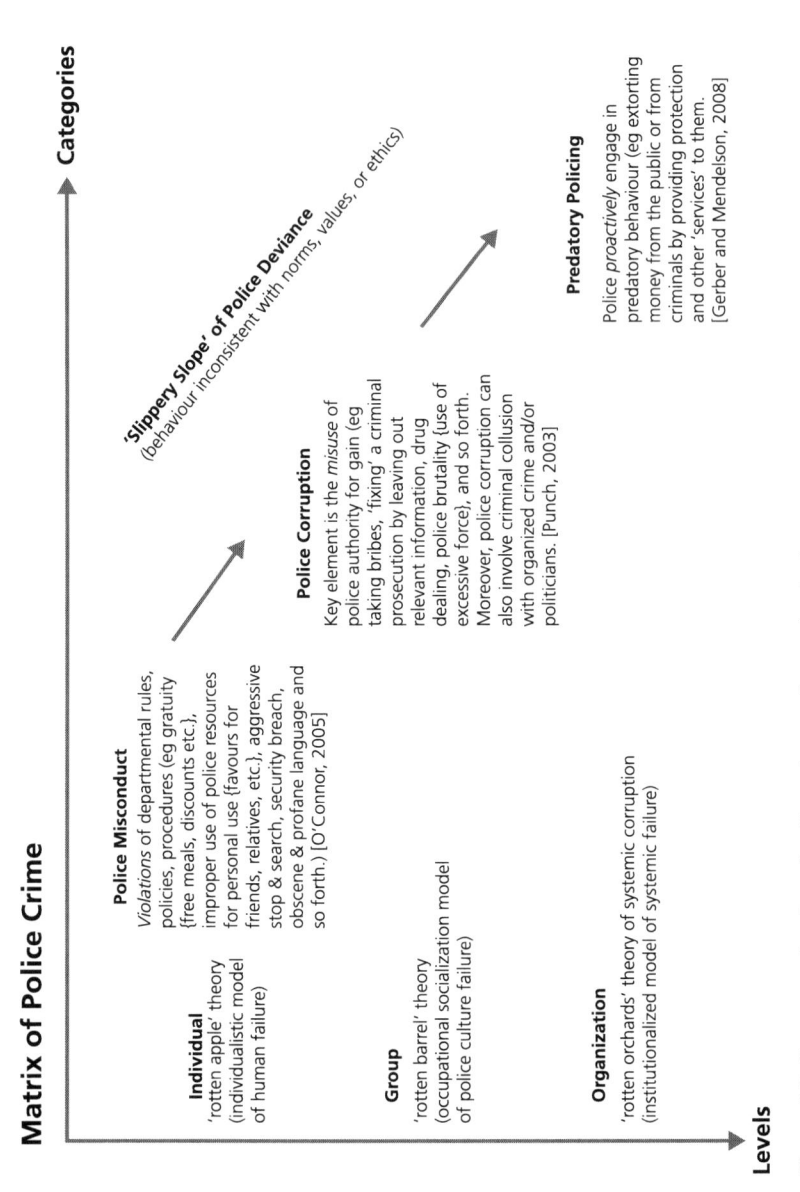

Levels →

Figure 4.3 Conceptualization of police crime and organized crime

78

> a year—petroleum distribution, and pharmaceuticals. By its own estimate, the Russian Interior Ministry believes the annual black market revenues of these groups have now topped $18 billion, about the same amount that Russia was expected to reimburse its creditors in 1999. (Robinson, 2000: 17)

As Serio (2008: 234) succinctly puts it, 'Russia has not been marching towards democracy since the dismantling of the Soviet Union but rather closer to perfecting the notion of a criminal state'. There has been a steady blurring of the lines between business, bureaucracy, and crime groups in Russia in the 1990s to the point that it is '. . . difficult to differentiate between the upper world and the underworld' (*ibid*: 233). Furthermore, Serio (2008) reports the following case example of Vladimir 'The Poodle' Podatiev of Khabarovsk, where the blurring of lines between businessmen, bureaucracy, and criminals became an art form.

Case Example 4.8 Vladimir 'The Poodle' Podatiev (Russia)

After spending 17 years in prison camps for theft, armed robbery, and rape, Podatiev emerged as one of the top crime bosses in the Russian Far East and was believed to control much of Khabarovsk's trade. More than that, he formed his own political party, owned a local television station, and reportedly obtained a letter from the Patriarch of the Orthodox Church blessing his charity work.

Among the numerous companies he founded, one was a security firm called Svoboda, the Russian word meaning 'freedom'. He even placed an ad in the local newspaper advertising Svoboda's services:

> Svoboda is a leading firm in the organization of security and detective services in the Russian Far East. We help you to collect confidential information about a person or firm of interest to you. We will settle disputes in a fully civilized manner in any region in Russia.

He was reportedly a member of the Commission of Human Rights of the Public Chamber of the President of Russia.

Such cases of systemic corruption within a country's business community, political parties, and governmental institutions and organs cannot happen to such an extent unless there is also widespread police misconduct, corruption, and predatory policing.

The value of relating police crime research to organized crime in the manner shown on the matrix is to highlight for police organizations how seriously diligent they need to be in rooting out police crime at all levels. This wider conceptualization provides a different vantage point than the traditional individualistic 'rotten apple' police perspective on misconduct and deviance within their ranks. For example, Punch (2003: 172) makes the point that:

Chapter 4: Expanding the Crime Business

The police themselves often employ the 'rotten apple' metaphor—the deviant cop who slips into bad ways and contaminates the other essentially good officers—which is an individualistic, human failure model of deviance.' One explanation for favouring this individualistic model of police deviance (Perry, 2001) is provided by O'Connor (2005: 2) when he states, 'Police departments tend to use the rotten apple theory . . . to minimize the public backlash against policing after every exposed act of corruption.'

Hence, following this 'individualistic' view of police criminality, anti-corruption strategies are generally targeted at finding the 'rotten apples' through measures like 'integrity testing' (Commission on Police Integrity, 1999). This 'rotten apple' view of police crime is a comfortable perspective to adopt for police organizations as it allows them to look no further than suspect 'individuals'. It is only when other forms of 'group' (O'Connor, 2005) and/or 'systemic' (Punch, 2003) corruption erupts upon a police service that a more critical look is taken of police criminality. Usually, it is only then that police agencies are provoked into putting policies and procedures in place to reduce the opportunity for engaging in misconduct and/or corrupt practices.

Organizations with a wider conceptualization of police crime than just 'rotten apples' will find the corrupting influence of criminal entrepreneurs on law enforcement, in general and policing in particular, more abundant and innovative. For example, smart criminal entrepreneurs will target and 'test out' particular police officers, customs officials, prison and/or immigration officers, and others who are strategically placed in their crime area of illegal business activity, much as police organizations now do with 'integrity testing', to see which particular officers respond positively to a request for some low-level misconduct. For instance, criminal entrepreneurs may ask a junior officer to search a police database for a car that was reported missing as a 'favour' for a friend. In Auckland, New Zealand, in 2005 a Police Communications Officer was charged after it was discovered that she had passed on information to a senior member of the Head Hunters (OMCG), David Dunn, that helped him to avoid arrest (New Zealand Police Association, 2006c: 72). In the final analysis, it is absolutely clear that organized crime wields corruption as a powerful and corrosive business tool.

Case Example 4.9 Corruption as a 'Corrosive Agent' (Global)

Corruption operates as a strong corrosive agent not only on police but, as Zhang and Pineda (2008) note, across whole sections of law enforcement agencies, as well as countries, especially in the big money business of human trafficking.

> Human trafficking . . . is now considered the third-largest criminal industry in the world as of 2006 after the arms and drug trades, with profits reaching billions each year' (Siobhan, 2006).

continued

> According to FBI estimates, human trafficking generates US $9.5 billion annually in the US alone (Siobhan, 2006) (Zhang and Pineda, 2008: 41).
>
> These authors further note:
>
>> In a report from the *Program against Corruption and Organized Crime in South Eastern Europe* (PACO), the list of corruption officials extends to include intelligence and security services, armed forces, and private businesses such as travel agencies, airlines, and financial institutions (PACO, 2002). The PACO report found that almost all countries in south eastern Europe had corruption problems directly linked to human trafficking and asserted 'trafficking cannot take place without the involvement of corrupt officials' (PACO, 2002: 9).
>>
>> These corrupt acts range 'from passivity (ignoring or tolerating), or actively participating in or even organizing trafficking in human beings, that is, From a violation of duties, to corruption or organized crime' (PACO, 2002: 7). In many countries, local police officers frequent brothels where trafficked victims are kept as customers (Cockburn, 2003). Visa and immigration officials receive free sexual services in exchange for overlooking fraudulent documents presented by human traffickers (Agbu, 2003).
>>
>> It is no surprise that countries accused of high levels of corruption are also those exerting little effort against human trafficking, whereas states low in official corruption mostly strive to combat human trafficking (PACO, 2002). (*ibid*: 46)

Counter-intelligence

Organized crime groups use this business factor, *counter-intelligence,* to expand their criminal activities in much the same way as the *business intelligence* factor discussed earlier in this chapter. Counter-intelligence is all about risk-avoidance. Organized criminals want to avoid detection and prosecution by police and other law enforcement agencies. Thus, a counter-intelligence system involves any action undertaken by an organized crime group to avoid law enforcement interest. Generally, this involves counter-surveillance and use of high-tech equipment to spy on police or interfere with police communications. Using counter-intelligence measures like this against police and other officials is a viable business option given the hostile, uncertain, and highly risky landscape in which criminal entrepreneurs operate.

Counter-intelligence involves both reactive and proactive measures. For example, reactive countermeasures generally take the form of trying to shield a crime group's communications from law enforcement agencies through actions like frequent changes of mobile phones and pre-paid cards, using coded language, spoofing and encryption of emails, using false identities, and holding face-to-face meetings (OCTA, 2007: 13). By contrast, proactive measures involve more of a strategic orientation that are designed to infiltrate law enforcement agencies through actions like hacking into police communications, placing 'informants' in policing agencies, counter-surveillance on specific police officers, and so forth.

Chapter 4: Expanding the Crime Business

Case Example 4.10 'Criminal Intelligence Service' by Hash-Smuggler (Netherlands)

Duyne (2000: 370) reports a case example of such counter-intelligence by a relatively sophisticated criminal entrepreneur:

> One of the smarter top hash-smugglers in Holland realised that this [risk] management was not only important for the tactical operations but had a strategic value of its own. So he elaborated his version of a 'criminal intelligence service' and hired outside professionals to undertake surveillance on police detectives and police cars, tapping communication lines and infiltrating the police with 'criminal' informants who worked for him. Most crime-entrepreneurs do not display such strategic feeling for information, but they are all aware that in the criminal society there is no such thing as a free flow of information.

Another example of counter-intelligence measures by criminal entrepreneurs involves the Outlaw Motorcycle Gang (OMCG), the Hells Angels in Canada, specifically in Montreal, when law enforcement agencies began a crackdown on their criminal drug trade, according to the New Zealand Police Association (2006a: 67).

Case Example 4.11 Hells Angels' Surveillance Programme on Police (Canada)

The Angels' started a surveillance programme of prison guards and police officers. They stole police laptops and the Rockers intercepted and recorded police radio 'traffic'. The gang obtained a list of police radio frequencies and built up a dossier of police officers' names, addresses, car registrations and videoed and photographed individual officers.

In yet another twist, the Angels in Montreal and further afield, employed ex-police officers as private investigators. Police discovered one ex-cop was now working for the Rockers and was employed as the chief emissary to a Columbian drug cartel. (New Zealand Police Association, 2006a: 67)

Whilst this Hells Angels case demonstrates a proactive approach to counter-intelligence by not only targeting police but also employing ex-police, such pro-activity does not stop there. The more sophisticated crime groups take a long-term view of their business ventures. They send members or associates to educational institutions like universities to specialize in areas of interest to their crime business such as IT, business, accountancy, law, and so forth. Education gives access to government positions and legitimate jobs in police, prisons, customs, taxation, defence, and other occupational roles that can assist organized crime groups to stay ahead of law enforcement. Moreover, such crime groups will also send 'clean skins' to police academies in order to ensure a long-term infiltration of police ranks (New Zealand Police Association, 2006d: 72).

These case examples make it clear that counter-intelligence (reactive and proactive forms) by crime entrepreneurs must be factored in to police thinking about organized crime. Smart criminal entrepreneurs see counter-intelligence as a necessary strategy to sustain as well as expand their business ventures.

'Fuzzy' Mapping of *Expanding* Crime Business

The decision-making capability of criminal entrepreneurs seeking to expand their business opportunities relies on four business factors (*business intelligence, violence, corruption*, and *counter-intelligence*) as discussed. In this section, a similar analysis using the fuzzy mapping tool, outlined in the previous chapter, is used to chart the business profiles of crime groups at this 'expanding' phase of their criminal business enterprises.

Hypothetical scenarios

The following matrix in Figure 4.4 offers a fuzzy map of three hypothetical scenarios at this expansion phase for crime groups involved in the drug trade.

In the first scenario, for *Crime Group (A)* it is apparent from the fuzzy map above that this crime group, which is involved in the illegal drug trafficking market, is relatively unsophisticated in its entrepreneurial capability to make 'good business decisions'. For instance, in relation to the *business intelligence* and *criminal intelligence* factors, it is rated at essentially the same 'low' level on the fuzzy scale. Members of this crime group show little interest in doing any 'intelligence' on the crime market they are in nor on their drug dealing competitors, or indeed the police. This crime group is simply interested in making lots of easy money and it knows from experience that drug dealing is where lots of money can be made quickly. This is certainly the case with 'Ecstasy', the street name for MDMA (N-methl-3-4-methylenedioxyamphetetamine), a designer illegal substance. According to Nicaso and Lamothe (2005: 93):

> Ecstasy is in great demand as a party drug and is used across classes, which makes for an enormous marketplace. Costing literally pennies to produce, Ecstasy tablets can sell for up to $25. For criminal syndicates, Ecstasy has become what heroin was for traditional Triads: a high-profit illegal product generating tens of millions of dollars from a relatively small investment. And having access to a market and a supply of product is at the heart of any successful criminal operation.

Chapter 4: Expanding the Crime Business

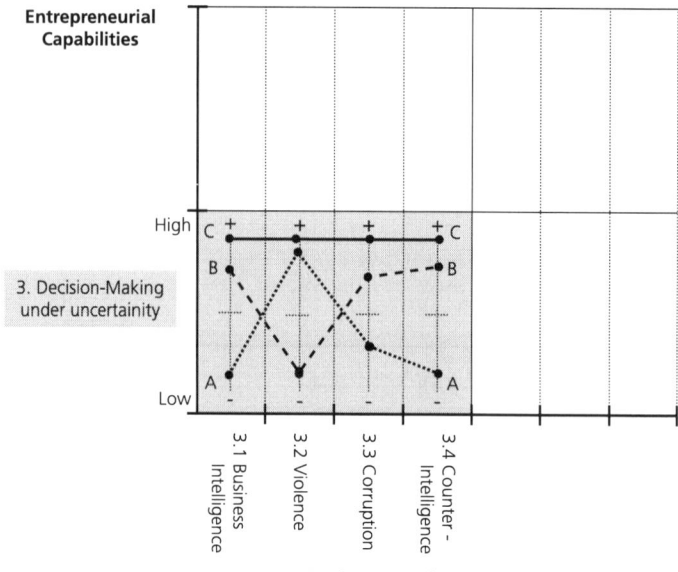

Figure 4.4 Fuzzy scenarios of entrepreneurial capability at 'expansion' phase

Moreover, as Klerks (2003: 101) reports, '. . . . The drug trade especially allows for relatively small operators to expand dramatically on the basis of a few successful drug imports and thus become criminal 'top dogs' almost overnight'.

As the fuzzy scaling indicates Crime Group (A) has little concern to 'know' the market or the 'players' in it, apart from the network contacts it already knows though criminal association. Moreover, as the high rating on the violence factor implies, this crime group takes the view if the police get wind of its operation and give it any trouble then a few well placed threats to kill a few cops or their families will take care of such law enforcement interference.

With regard to the corruption factor as a business option, this crime group is scaled at a relatively 'low' level. This crime group restricts its use of corruption to buying off or bribing a few customs officers to ensure supply imports are kept up. The reasoning is that why waste money and time corrupting others when only a few people are needed on the inside of law enforcement agencies to keep the money rolling in? Besides, if this crime group needs any extra help from a businessman or a politician then, again, a bit of violence is all that is generally needed for such people to change their attitude. Violence is cheap compared to bribes, and very effective in this crime group's experience.

What this crime group excels at is the excessive use of violence. Clearly, this group's use of violence has both strong instrumental and expressive functions. It 'enjoys' inflicting violence and it works for its business. In fact, violence is the only business factor it really needs to use in its experience.

In the second scenario, it is apparent that for *Crime Group (B)*, its fuzzy scale is a reverse image of that of Crime Group (A), in that the defining difference between these two scenarios is the excessive use of violence by Crime Group (A) and the limited use of violence by Crime Group (B). Furthermore, *business* and *criminal intelligence* for Crime Group (A) were scaled as 'low' whilst for Crime Group (B) these factors are rated as relatively 'high'. In other words, Crime Group (A) has little interest in using business factors other than violence, whereas Crime Group (B) has a much stronger sense of the value of business intelligence, criminal intelligence, and corruption as business tools to expand its illegal drug trade. Clearly, Crime Group (B) is more attuned to taking an entrepreneurially-oriented business approach to growing its criminal enterprise.

For the third scenario, it is evident that *Crime Group (C)* uses all business factors to their fullest extent, as shown by the fuzzy scaling. It seeks business intelligence and counter-intelligence to use against rivals and law enforcement efforts. Also, it is not averse to using extreme and brutal violence to enhance its 'reputational violence' trade mark as this helps to expand its share of the drugs market. Moreover, this crime group will use corruption frequently and to great effect to expand its market share. While it might appear that using all business factors to their fullest potential, like Crime Group (C), is the most profitable pathway for a crime business to expand, this is not necessarily the case. In fact, a 'high' fuzzy score on some of these business factors, notably violence and corruption, may actually work against the profitability of a crime group since the excessive use of violence and, to some extent corruption, will focus the public's unwanted attention on such a group. This will then put pressure on governments and politicians to commit more resources to fighting a 'war on crime' by police and law enforcement agencies. Therefore, the safest pathway for a crime group to pursue its expansion plans may well be as shown for Crime Group (B).

To conclude, there are two quite distinct 'mirror opposite' crime business profiles that emerge from the scenarios for Crime Groups (A) and (B), while Crime Group (C) shows little variation in its extensive use of all business factors at this second phase of business expansion. These different routes to business growth reflect the level of business sophistication each crime group possesses. Crime Group (A) has little business appreciation and relies almost exclusively on using extreme violence to advance its drug trafficking business. It presents as a local gang of thugs who got lucky with dealing in illicit drugs and found themselves getting rich quickly. They see little reason to change or add to what works for them. Their limited entrepreneurial capability to 'make good business decisions' in the hostile, uncertain, and risky business of the criminal underworld will work against them as the violence they extol will inevitably get noticed by the police and law enforcement agencies. Whether or not such excessive violence will be their undoing remains to be seen—the police always have competing priorities. However, if the spotlight of policing does eventually shine strong enough and long enough on this type of crime group, then as our fuzzy mapping shows, there are several business 'weak spots' for police to exploit. On the other hand, Crime Group (B) is evidently more business-attuned and 'looks' more impregnable to law enforcement intervention. But looks can be deceiving. Certainly, it will be harder to crack and more sustained effort will be required by police but there are still weak points even within this crime group. Its entrepreneurial capability to 'make better business decisions' is based on the accuracy of its business and criminal intelligence. Intelligence is a probability game and its accuracy is always open to bad information, misinformation, and manipulation. The American military machine found that out with the non-existent WMDs in Iraq. Finally, Crime Group (C)'s extensive use of all business factors may well be its undoing by bringing unwanted police and law enforcement crackdowns of its illegal drug dealing operations.

Summary

This chapter examined the second business phase of *expanding* the crime business. The entrepreneurial capability of *decision-making under uncertainty* is primarily related to this second phase of growing a crime business through a combination of business factors. These factors are: 'business intelligence' on criminal markets and rival crime competitors; the selective use of 'violence' for instrumental and expressive goals; the targeted use of 'corruption'; and a range of 'counter-intelligence' measures. How each of these business factors can be used entrepreneurially to grow an illegal business was illustrated through a variety of case examples. Finally, the chapter presented three hypothetical scenarios using the 'fuzzy' mapping tool employed in the previous chapter. The various pathways drug trafficking crime groups can take in how they choose to expand their illegal business operations, as well as their areas of strength and weakness, were analysed and discussed through the fuzzy mapping scenarios.

5

Consolidating the Crime Business

Introduction

This chapter examines the third phase of *consolidating* a crime business. Firstly, the main entrepreneurial capability of 'people cooperation', which is associated with developing a criminal enterprise at this consolidation phase, is discussed. Secondly, the business factors related to this entrepreneurial capability are examined and illustrated with case examples of their operation in criminal markets. The third and final section, as in the previous two chapters, demonstrates the 'fuzzy' mapping analytical tool with 'hypothetical' case scenarios for consolidating a crime business.

Criminal Business Modelling: Consolidation Phase

This phase of consolidation in our operating framework of business development focuses on 'managing' a crime business. Entrepreneurial management exists at every business phase, but is especially necessary at this consolidation phase in order to maintain one's market share. The following Figure 5.1 lists the key business factors associated with this third phase of 'consolidating' a crime business.

As can be seen the main entrepreneurial capability needed to manage this 'consolidation' phase is getting people to cooperate in running and developing the crime business. The business factors specifically related to this capability are: *criminal business connections, legitimate business connections*, and *influential people connections*. Figure 5.2, below, contains the matrix that results from the cross-matching of this 'people cooperation' entrepreneurial capability with these business factors.

Chapter 5: Consolidating the Crime Business

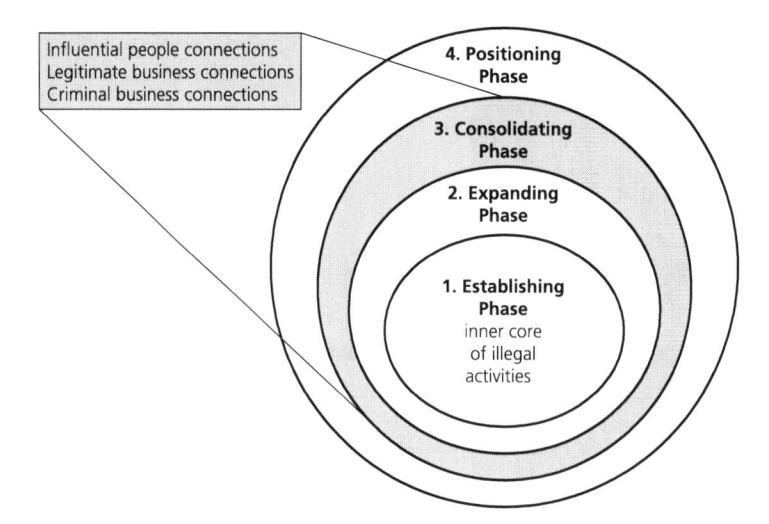

Figure 5.1 Crime business model: Phase 3—'consolidation' business factors

As shown, the three business factors related to the 'people cooperation' entrepreneurial capability are represented on this matrix in the middle section. Again, as in the previous chapters, adjacent entrepreneurial capabilities (*'decision-making*

Figure 5.2 Entrepreneurial capability by business factors at 'consolidation' phase

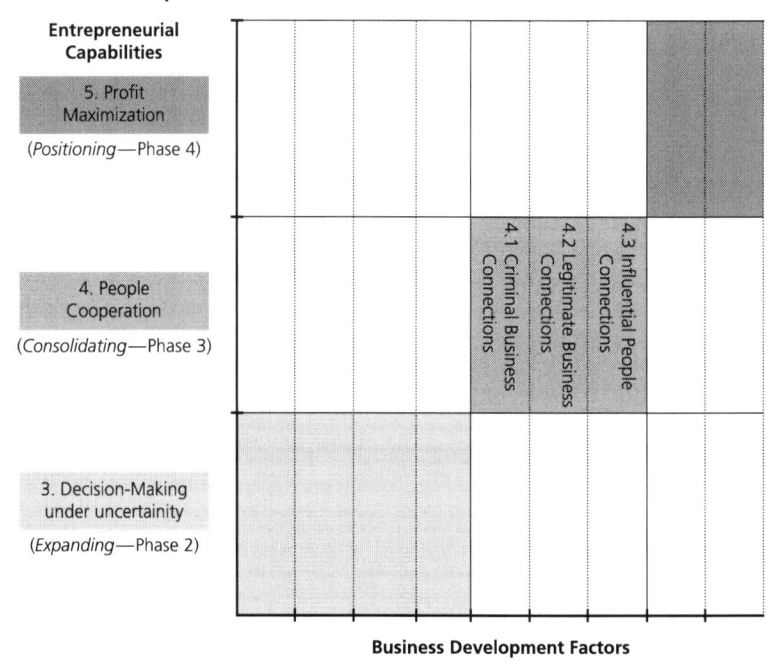

88

under uncertainty' and *'profit maximization'*) are also included in Figure 5.2 as developmental points of reference for a crime business.

Entrepreneurial Capability: People Cooperation

A criminal's capability to manage people entrepreneurially to cooperate with their illegal business activities involves both a direct active role and a more indirect, passive role. A direct 'hands on' management role requires a criminal entrepreneur to seek assistance from various kinds of people. This can range from criminal associates to 'legitimate'[1] business persons like bank managers, lawyers, accountants, and influential people in politics, government, industry, and certainly underworld kingpins.

At a more indirect or passive management level, a criminal entrepreneur requires the cooperation of people who have the power to get in the way of their profit-making business ventures. For instance, government officials in customs, taxation, immigration, policing, and related law enforcement agencies can obstruct their illegal business activities. Such people have to be 'managed' either through co-opting them, corrupting them, or in some other way neutralizing their power or influence.

There is debate in the literature about the extent to which a criminal entrepreneur needs to have 'good communication skills' or at least the ability to persuade others to be involved with an illegal enterprise. Lampe (2007) uses the term 'social microcosm' in relation to criminal entrepreneurs to include all those individuals they encounter in the course of their criminal activities that are in a position to influence the success or failure of their particular criminal enterprise. Having the ability to relate and communicate well with a diverse range of people would most certainly be an advantage. As to whether or not it is necessary is a moot point. Money is a powerful motivator for cooperation. If a crime business generates lots of money then being good at communicating becomes less important. As Kugler, Verdier, and Zenou, (2005) note bribery and corruption, combined with violence and threats of violence, is an effective strategy for many criminal organizations. Whilst 'money talks' all languages, we argue for someone to be considered 'entrepreneurial', as defined in our operating framework, does imply some degree of communicative ability. Criminals with poor communication skills who run successful illegal businesses are at the low end of entrepreneurial behaviour, for instance, 'thugs' that happened to be in the right place at the right time to capitalize on a business opportunity through violence and/or corruption to achieve business success.

---

[1] It is a moot point as to how 'legitimate' someone who knowingly deals with organized criminals in their professional capacity as a banker, lawyer, accountant, and so on, can be considered 'legitimate' in a moral sense. Hence, the term 'legitimate' in this context is restricted to a legal definition of not having been convicted on any related criminal activity—so far!

The key point is there are three main business factors—*criminal business connections, legitimate business connections,* and *influential people connections*—as shown on the matrix in Figure 5.2, which give form and substance to the entrepreneurial capability of people cooperation.

Criminal Business Connections

The main game of this 'people cooperation' capability is to make 'connections'. Chinese organized crime groups believe the key to their business success is *'guanxi'*. It means 'connections'. The power of the cell is the cell leader's networking' (Robinson, 2000: 306). Of course, such cooperative networking is not restricted to Asian organized crime groups. In fact, the 'networking paradigm', as Klerks (2003: 97) terms it, is currently the dominant perspective from which to view how organized crime operates. According to Klerks (*ibid*: 100) 'the paradigm of organized crime as social networks has become widely accepted among Dutch criminologists within just a few years'. It is also widely used in the UK and the US. In fact, in a Ministry of Justice Research Centre (the WODC) in the Netherlands a study of over a hundred organized crime cases and confidential investigations emphasized:

> ... the need to look at 'criminal co-operatives' (the term they propose instead of 'organisation', 'group' or 'structure') in terms of fluid network relations with occasional 'nodes' representing the more successful and enterprising operators (*ibid*: 101).

Criminal connectedness is a specific and special 'microcosm' (Lampe, 2007) within larger society and is the social milieu out of which criminality is born and bred. This social milieu is composed of 'criminal co-operatives' (Klerks, 2003); underworld *guanxi* (connections) in Chinese (Robinson, 2000); social networks formed by career criminals through gangs (Gambetta, 1993); cultural antecedents (Chu, 2000); and/or in prisons (Serio, 2008). A typical example of the need for criminal connectedness and cooperation is the case of the Hells Angels in Canada. The Canadian Hells Angels chapter is so powerful in the drug trafficking business that its only serious rival is the Italian Mafia.

Case Example 5.1 Avoiding Turf War: Hells Angels and Italian Mafia (Canada)

To avoid a turf war the Hells Angels:

> ... decided on a different, more business-like approach by setting up joint-interest business alliances with the Mafia. The Angels decided to consolidate their operations by implementing a price control system. In 2000 they formed La

continued

> Table (or the Company) for the purpose of fixing the price of cocaine at $50,000 a kilogram. They tried to strike a deal with the Mafia, the other major importer of hard drugs in Canada. At the height of their operations the Angels were importing 250 kilograms of cocaine a week into Montreal alone. . . . The FBI estimates that the annual income of the Hells Angels worldwide operations is $1 billion (New Zealand Police Association, 2006a: 67).

Entrepreneurially-oriented crime groups, like the Hells Angels, place high value on criminal business connections that facilitate profit-making even when it involves rival competitors. This is not uncommon where old rivals are replaced with new alliances in crime markets when huge profits are available for all. For example, the case example noted in the previous chapter about Asian-style violence and the accommodation the Hells Angels reached with the Vietnamese in Canada.

Another structural arrangement where criminal entrepreneurs work together is in syndicated criminal networks. This is a particularly evident in Asian organized crime where Triads[2] operate. More precisely, in current usage the term 'Triad' is really an umbrella notion (Robinson, 2000: 307). In a contemporary context, a Triad is not a gang as such but rather a collection or society of gangs, in that being a Triad member allows access to all other gangs. In other words, Triad members in one gang can trust members of another and ask for favours and assistance with their criminal businesses. Robinson (2003: 308) quotes an Asian-crime coordinator with the Criminal Intelligence Service of Canada as saying 'the best description I ever heard (*of the meaning of Triad*)[3] came from a fellow in Hong Kong who told me, Triad is the water that allows the fish to survive. His advice was, always focus on the fish'.

The Triads in Hong Kong according to Chu (2000) operate much like how Gambetta (1993: 155) characterized the Italian Mafia as a set of firms active in the protection industry that operate under a common trade mark and use of violence to enhance their reputation as a credible protector. The primary role of Hong Kong Triads is:

> . . . to provide strong-arm services to illegal entrepreneurs so that they are able to run their businesses smoothly in a risky environment. Although they may get directly involved in the operation of illegal businesses, triad members are mainly responsible for security (Chu, 2000: 8).

With regard to syndicated criminal forms, the Asian crime group known as Dai Huen Jai, or more colloquially as the Big Circle Boys[4] (BCB), is a leading

---

[2] The name 'Triad' is a term that was coined by the British in Hong Kong. It refers to the triangular shape of the Chinese character for 'secret society'. The three points represent the relationship between heaven, earth, and man. Originally, Triads emerged around the seventeenth century and were resistance groups fighting to overthrow the non-Chinese Manchu Qing Dynasty.

[3] Words in *italics* are those of the current authors.

[4] The name BCB comes from China's Cultural Revolution in the 1960s when Mao's Red Guard was purged and many of its members were put in prison. The prisons around Canton City were

exponent of this organizational method. The following case example expands on this method.

> ### Case Example 5.2 Syndicated Criminal Networks: Big Circle Boys (Chinese)
>
> Although the BCB are regarded as a separate entity to Triads (Nicaso and Lamothe, 2005: 92) they still have varying degrees of attachment to Triads as 'business' syndicates for illegal operations. The BCB are a very fluid organization that are able to engage in diverse criminal activities at different times and in different places. As Nicaso and Lamothe (*op cit*) point out with regard to the BCB,
>
> > The makeup of the organization changes often, with new participants entering a particular conspiracy for sometimes brief periods of time, then branching off into another enterprise. Sometimes the syndicate shifts entirely out of one activity and into another, retaining the same core leaders but drawing an entirely new set of players.

Also, most Asian crime groups will cooperate with any other group to make money—most notably the Dai Huen Jai or BCB. As Robinson (2003: 306) notes:

> It doesn't matter to them (BCB) whether they're Vietnamese, Laotian, Funienese, Taiwanese, Hells Angels or even the LCN (*La Cosa Nostra – American incarnation of Italian Mafia*)[5] – with whom they have invested in shipments, done importations together and cooperated with distribution projects – it's the deal that matters, not the dealers.

This example of the BCB raises an important issue about the role that ethnicity plays in criminal enterprises. Clearly, there are ethnic and cultural components to organized crime. However, research on the drugs trade in the UK by Ruggiero and Khan (2007) found that one's ethnic background may be a consideration for doing business for street level contacts but at the middle and upper levels of drug dealing it is economic competition that drives the trade not ethnicity. As Klerks (2003: 101) observes, '. . . the supposed ethnic homogeneity of criminal groups that supposedly caused the participating individuals to co-operate and obey is, in fact, now largely a thing of the past'. Similarly, Nicaso and Lamothe (2005: 4) note that:

> There is an undeniable ethnic or national component to the *culture* of crime groups; you don't have to be Italian, for example, to *work* with the Italian mafia; you do, however, *have* to be Italian to be part of the culture. Similarly, with Chinese Triads; only Chinese people can be members of the Triad; however, everyone may be *permitted* to be involved in their criminal operations.

---

laid out in a circle. The ones that survived the prisons joined up on the outside and organized themselves into small working crime cells. They named their criminal organization after the circle of prisons (Robinson, 2003: 304).

[5] Words in *italics* are those of the current authors.

An observation by Duyne (2000: 377) sums up the essence of making 'criminal business connections' when he states:

> Successful crime-enterprises do not only owe their success to marketing skills, but more important to criminal 'human engineering', including 'human risk assessment'. Translated into simple mobster language: 'I only trade with whom I know and trust'.

These cases about making and maintaining 'criminal business connections' show what a powerful business factor this is for consolidating a crime business for all criminal groupings, regardless of national identity and cultural constraints. Making money is the name of the organized crime game.

Legitimate Business Connections

Criminals use legitimate business connections to go 'legal' in one of more aspects of their illegal business activities. Often a crime group will need someone with specialist skills or know-how such as accountants, financial experts, IT specialists, bankers, stock exchange brokers, or chemists. Profit-oriented criminal entrepreneurs regard this business factor of developing their criminal connections with legitimate businesses to be of fundamental importance. Siegel and Nelen (2008: 2) note:

> Many scholars have pointed out that there is a strong symbiotic relationship between organized crime and the legitimate environment in which it flourishes. . . . criminological research indicates that lawyers, notaries, real estate agents, tax consultants, accountants, bankers, and other professionals sometimes play a delicate role in shielding crimes and criminal proceeds from the authorities.

In this regard, Duyne (2000: 374) refers to the 'social infrastructure' that is necessarily involved in organized criminality and such an infrastructure hypothesis '. . . implies the availability of financial experts, haulers etc'. Criminal entrepreneurs could not operate as successfully as they do without the involvement at some level of a host of 'legitimate' professionals smoothing the way forward for their crime businesses. The Russian 'Mafiya'[6] is a case in point.

Case Example 5.3 Banking Scam: 'Mafiya' [*vory v zakone*] (Russian)

Historically, the Russian Mafiya were known as *vory v zakone* or 'Thieves Within the Code' that consisted of small groups of clannish outsiders—pickpockets, shoplifters, and in some cases beggars, the poor and needy—who lived outside the margins of

continued

---

[6] 'Russian Mafiya' is a catch-all label for various criminal gangs from several countries other than Russia within Eastern European organized crime. The only common denominator is that all such crime groupings speak Russian (Nicaso and Lamothe, 2005: 138).

> society. Over time, the *vory v zakone* have evolved into variant groups of ruthless and violent gangs as well as criminal entrepreneurs capable of perpetrating sophisticated criminal scams with the aid of 'legitimate' professionals. Nicaso and Lamothe (2005: 144) report a case where '. . . in 1993 Russian entrepreneurial criminals had made $12 billion vanish from the banking system'. Such a scam could not happen unless there was a massive criminal conspiracy '. . . operated by Soviet businessmen, politicians, spies, and the *vory v zakone*'. (*ibid*: 144)

However, the nature of this symbiotic relationship between illegal and legitimate business practitioners is by no means clear-cut. In some cases, legitimate business people like lawyers, accountants, bankers, and so forth are fully aware of the illegal nature of their dealings with criminal entrepreneurs. They are prepared to enter into a criminal conspiracy for financial enrichment and mutual benefit. In other situations, there is a more subtle moving in and eventual taking over by a criminal group of some legitimate business structure or entity. It is only much later that the full realization of the criminal intent behind such manoeuvrings may become clear, even to the professional they have employed. A case in point in this regard are the 'Tongs' or benevolent family and/or business associations that have long been considered as necessary components in the financial and cultural life of Chinatowns around the world. Thus a new immigrant could go to a Tong to get assistance with accommodation, a job, or a small loan in order to set up and adjust to a new life overseas. Furthermore, Tongs arranged a new immigrant's social life with dances, parades, fundraisers, cultural events, and so on. However, there can be a darker side to Tongs. The following case example reports on how some Tongs become ensnared in illegal gambling and prostitution rackets for mostly male new immigrants (Nicaso and Lamothe, 2005: 86).

Case Example 5.4 Triad Infiltration of 'Tongs' (Chinese)

The existence of legitimate and influential cultural vehicles like Tongs throughout the world for Chinese immigrants make it only a matter of time before such benevolent business associations became targets for infiltration for Chinese criminal gangs and Triad groups. In the 1980s an FBI report on Asian organized crime found '. . . that although many Tong leaders were legitimate businessmen, others had come under the influence of Triads and criminal syndicates' (Nicaso and Lamothe, 2005: 87). Moreover, in recent years police in the US and Canada have found other cases '. . . where criminal elements have either set up their own Tong-like associations or have infiltrated and taken over existing Tongs' (*ibid*).

The next case example is about how criminal entrepreneurs use legitimate business structures to further consolidate their crime business. The case involves a more enterprising narcotics trafficker who was able to take control of a publicly traded company through an elaborate scam whereby shares were traded for drugs. How this 'shares scam'[7] worked is elaborated in the following case box.

Case Example 5.5 Publicly Traded Company 'Shares Scam' (Australia)

A drug dealer (Mr. D), a resident of Country A acquired the vast majority of freely tradable shares of ABC Ltd, a public company with its head office in Country A. ABC Ltd was a speculative stock that traded on the over the counter market in Country B.

Mr. D sold drugs to Buyer A. He did not receive money. Instead, he instructed Buyer A to buy ABC Ltd through the stock market. Buyer A had previously set up an account in a non-cooperative jurisdiction and instructed his agent to purchase ABC Ltd. The agent contacted his broker in Country B and instructed him to purchase the shares. Mr. D instructed his agent in Country D to sell ABC Ltd. His agent instructed his broker in Country A to sell the securities.

Because the stock was thinly traded there were no competing bids for the securities. The transaction was cleared through the clearing corporations with the end result being that Mr. D received the money and Buyer A received the drugs and the shares. Their cost was a few hundred dollars in commissions.

This transaction was repeated several times through several countries and brokers. It had the added benefit of providing liquidity to the market and the public was led to believe that there was actual interest in the securities. The public then got involved in the trading and with the heightened awareness the stock increased in value. This meant that Mr. D and Buyer A's shares were now worth more and they were able to generate additional profits. Mr. D was able to legitimize the source of funds as being 'market' profits.

Just as criminal connections provide the social milieu for illegal businesses to consolidate their market share, likewise legitimate business connections give access to other consolidation options for a crime business. Money can be laundered, markets can be expanded, and the risk of law enforcement detection reduced.

---

[7] This typology was developed by the Financial Action Task Force (FATF), to assist members of industries at risk of being used for money-laundering/terrorism financing (ML/TF) purposes to recognize ML/TF activities and techniques. This FATF typology was originally used within AUSTRAC's 'Securities and Derivatives' presentation delivered to members of the Australian financial markets sector in June 2008.

Chapter 5: Consolidating the Crime Business

Influential People Connections

This business factor involves making and maintaining connections with an array of 'influential people' in both the legal world and the criminal underworld. Nelen and Lankhorst (2008) found that the types of services and roles that lawyers, in particular, can play for entrepreneurially-oriented criminal groups are many and varied. For instance, lawyers are used as:

- 'Mailboxes' or 'errand boys' for organized crime
- Intimidation or manipulation of witnesses
- Providing assistance to human traffickers
- Abusing their access to facilities of the law firm
- Conflicting representation
- Money-laundering
- Using third party accounts as 'safe-havens' for crime money
- Mortgage and investment frauds

The cases reported below involve lawyers who acted as 'messengers' or 'mailboxes' to pass confidential information onto their criminal clients and other criminal parties.

Case Example 5.6 Lawyers as Go-betweens for Organized Criminals (Italy)

In this context, the Italian national report refers to one of the mafia-style maxi trials in Turin, in which the public prosecutor started an investigation and found evidence that a lawyer was acting as a go-between for several members of the organized criminal group in custody and other suspects and wanted accomplices.

The Dutch report refers to a situation in which a criminal defence lawyer had several clients, simultaneously, in the same case. During the process whereby suspect A was being put in police custody, the lawyer passed information to suspect B, who had not yet been arrested at that time. Moreover, the lawyer also allowed suspect A, who was subject to restrictions, to read the statements of other suspects (Nelen and Lankhorst (2008: 132).

More serious examples of lawyer involvement in organized crime can be found in the human trafficking domain. In fact, the legal profession is very useful in this area for entrepreneurial criminal groups. Again, research by Nelen and Lankhorst (2008) indicates that corrupt lawyers often supply false identity papers and other legal documentation to assist human traffickers in carrying out their illegal trade in humans.

Influential People Connections

> **Case Example 5.7 Lawyers as Enablers of Human Trafficking (Italy)**
>
> The Italian national report refers to the arrest and conviction of a lawyer accused of forgery, slander and breaking immigration laws. He had counterfeited documentation, allowing several non-EU citizens to obtain residence permits to which they had no rights. Through forced labour contracts, the lawyer attested the presence of the non-EU citizens in Italy before January 1998, a requirement necessary to benefit by the deed of indemnity. The lawyer was also convicted of the slander of several policemen, declaring with written statements and during an interrogation that they had abused their powers and slandered him and his clients.
>
> In February 2000, an Italian lawyer was sentenced to 5 years and 6 months imprisonment for having organized clandestine immigration. In November of the same year, a criminal lawyer was arrested in Modena. The lawyer laundered the proceeds of trafficking in women. The trafficking was organized by a band of Albanians who were connected to local criminal organizations. They imported women from Albania and forced them into prostitution with threats and violence, in effect reducing them to slavery. The Albanian group, with the aid of the lawyer, reinvested the proceeds in economic activities, above all in Albania. The lawyer was accused of money-laundering and external participation in a criminal association with the aim of forging public documents (*ibid*: 133).

Post-Soviet Russia is a prime example of criminal involvement by politicians and other influential government officials. The extent of such influential criminal connectedness in the political life of a country is illustrated in the following case example.

> **Case Example 5.8 'Mafiaocracy' (Post-Soviet Russia)**
>
> With regard to Russia Serio (2008: 260) states 'There is no way to beat organized crime because it was in the interest of various elements of the state and business to maintain it'. Serio (*op cit*) goes on to quote a former Moscow criminal investigator, Alexander Gorkin, as evidence for his assertion:
>
>> Organized crime was heavily politicized and there was no way we could get a handle on those 'goodfellas' who were supported by the regime – which needed organized crime to exist as a special tool in the 'real world' to cover up governmental wrongdoing and other nefarious activities . . . in order to give the world the impression that all bad things happened because of organized crime.

Clearly, as is evident in the previous business factor of 'legitimate business connections', the more some of these 'legitimate' connections also include 'influential people' in government and business, the better for the 'business' of organized crime. It is a relationship of mutual benefit for both parties. However, making criminal 'connections' in the political, governmental, and legitimate business realms is

Chapter 5: Consolidating the Crime Business

only half of a two-sided coin for co-opting 'influential people'. The other side of the coin is making 'influential connections' in the criminal underworld itself.

Knowing 'who' to 'connect' one's crime business to in the lethal world of criminality can make all the difference to surviving or dying. Triads are a leading example of this type of criminal connectedness.

Case Example 5.9 'Triads as Water': Triads in Czech Republic (Chinese)

The Chinese Triads control the criminal underworld in whole countries like the Czech Republic. As mentioned previously, Triads are the 'water' in which 'fish' swim. So if a crime group wants to operate somewhere like in the Czech Republic then they will have to ask permission from the Triads to be allowed, as 'new fish', to swim in those criminal waters. Robinson (2000: 314) underscores this point of having to make the right influential criminal connections if a newbie crime group wants to enter this particular country:

> Today, Vietnamese gangs in the Czech Republic control the marijuana and hashish markets, supplied by Arab and Balkan state distributors, and are the main client of Kosovar traffickers. They also deal in small amounts of heroin, supplied by two Triad groups—Red sun and 14K—who likewise see Prague as a revolving door into Western Europe. Triad money is being laundered in Prague through local real estate deals and restaurants. It is a certainty that any alien smuggling ring staging in the Czech Republic does so with the knowledge of the Triads already there . . .

The stock market is another area where this business factor of connecting with 'influential people' finds a ready home. This next case involves complicity by a broker willing to launder crime money through a very clever scam. The case[8] shows how funds can be laundered by organized crime groups using the derivatives market.

Case Example 5.10 Money-Laundering via Derivatives Market (Australia)

In this method, the broker must be willing to allocate genuinely losing trades to the account in which criminal proceeds are deposited. Instead of relying on misleading or false documentation, the broker uses the genuine loss-making documentation to be allocated to the detriment of the dirty money account holder.

continued

---

[8] This typology was developed by the Financial Action Task Force (FATF), to assist members of industries at risk of being used for money laundering/terrorism financing (ML/TF) purposes to recognize ML/TF activities and techniques. This FATF typology was originally used within AUSTRAC's 'Securities and Derivatives' presentation delivered to members of the Australian financial markets sector in June 2008.

Influential People Connections

As an example, a broker uses two accounts, one called 'A' into which the client regularly deposits money which needs laundering, and one called 'B' which is intended to receive the laundered funds. The broker enters the trading market and 'goes long' (purchases) 100 derivative contracts of a commodity, trading at an offer price of $85.02, with a 'tick' size of $25. At the same time he 'goes short' (sells) 100 contracts of the same commodity at the bid price of $85.00. At that moment, he has two legitimate contracts which have been cleared through the floor of the exchange.

Later in the trading day, the contract price has altered to $84.72 bid and $84.74 offered. The broker returns to the market, closing both open positions at the prevailing prices. Now, the broker, in his own books assigns the original purchase at $85.02 and the subsequent sale at $84.72 to account A. The percentage difference between the two prices is 30 points or ticks (the difference between $84.72 and $85.02). To calculate the loss on this contract, the tick size which is $25 is multiplied by the number of contracts, 100, multiplied by the price movement, 30. Thus: $25 × 100 × 30 = $75,000 (loss).

The other trades are allocated to the B account, which following the same calculation theory of tick size multiplied by the number of contracts multiplied by the price movement results in a profit as follows: $25 × 100 × 26 = $65,000 (profit).

The account containing the money to be laundered has just paid out $75,000 for the privilege of receiving a profit of $65,000 on the other side. In other words, the launderer has paid $10,000 for the privilege of successfully laundering $75,000. Such a sum is well within the amount of premium which professional launderers are prepared to pay for the privilege of cleaning up such money.

As a transaction, it is perfectly lawful from the point of view of the broker. He has not taken the risk of creating false documentation, which could conceivably be discovered, and everything has been done in full sight of the market.

The final case example for 'influential people connections' attests to the risky business of crime money management (CMM) for those professional people who get involved with organized criminals. The following case highlights the risk:

Case Example 5.11 Risky Business of CMM (Netherlands)

On Monday, 31 October 2005, 36-year-old Dutch lawyer Evert Hingst was murdered in front of his house in Amsterdam. Among Hingst's clients were many noted and alleged criminals, including John Mieremet, who was once shot in front of Hingst's office. After this assault, Mieremet claimed that Hingst had tried to set him up. Mieremet was murdered three days after the liquidation of Hingst, on 2 November, in Thailand.

continued

> Hingst, a fiscal specialist, had been accused of assisting criminals to launder their money abroad. He was imprisoned for several weeks after police discovered three firearms and a large sum of cash during a raid of his office in 2005. A suspect for money-laundering, membership of a criminal organization, and possession of firearms, Hingst gave up his profession as a lawyer in July 2005. He had previously been arrested on charges of forgery of documents in 2004 (Nelen and Lankhorst, 2008: 127).

In sum, it is evident from the case examples presented that making and maintaining 'connections' is vital for a crime business that wants to grow and consolidate such growth. Ideally, such 'connectedness' will involve three domains—the criminal underworld, the legitimate business world, and various influential people in both the upper and under worlds.

'Fuzzy' Mapping of *Consolidating* Crime Business

This final section of the chapter presents a set of fuzzy, hypothetical scenario maps, similar to those presented for the previous phases of 'establishing' and 'expanding' a crime business. These maps show how criminals can entrepreneurially manage their illegal business activities at the 'consolidating' phase of a crime business using the business factors of *criminal, legitimate* and *influential people connections*.

Hypothetical scenarios

The following matrix in Figure 5.3 below offers a fuzzy mapping of three hypothetical scenarios at this consolidation phase for a criminal business.

With regard to the first scenario, for *Crime Group (A)* it relies, like the other criminal groups, on using past, current, or making new criminal connections to consolidate its illegal business. It is also evident it makes use of legitimate business connections, to a lesser extent, probably as a money-laundering scheme. Furthermore, Crime Group (A) has only limited connections with influential people. It prefers to rely on its trusted criminal networks for its business ventures. However, if it decides to go into a new niche market it will need to involve influentially-placed persons to assist them in the new marketplace. For instance, the derivatives market case where a share broker was needed to be part of a criminal conspiracy to launder crime money is a case in point.

In the second scenario, *Crime Group (B)*, whilst also relying heavily on its criminal networks to do business, has a higher need for making connections with legitimate business people. In other words, it needs legal structures to consolidate its crime business further, as shown in Figure 5.3. Also, they make more use of influential people. The case about the infiltration of Tongs (benevolent

'Fuzzy' Mapping of *Consolidating* Crime Business

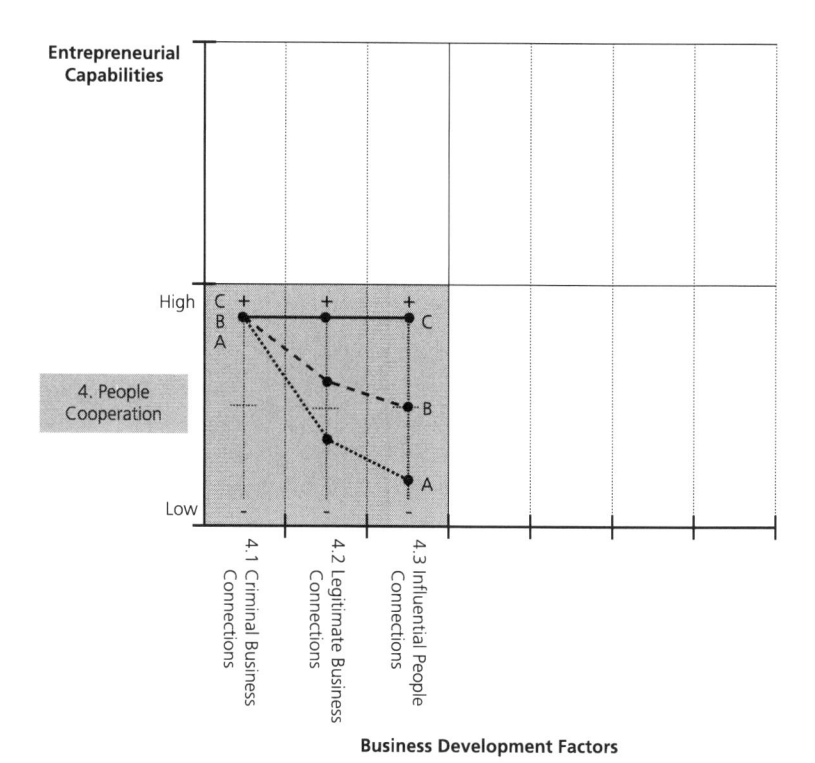

Figure 5.3 Fuzzy scenarios of entrepreneurial capability at 'consolidation' phase

business associations) by Triads is illustrative of this type of crime group mapping. Apart from utilizing legitimate business structures, this case example also highlights the added advantage for triad crime groups of building on influential connections within the Chinese community, for not only do Tongs contain influential Chinese businessmen but they are also highly regarded institutions within the Chinese culture.

For the third scenario, it is evident that *Crime Group (C)* follows the same trajectory as the other crime groups but at a much higher level across all three business factors. The Russian *vory v zakone* with their stranglehold on the Russian economy, politicians, businessmen, and society demonstrate such 'high achieving' criminal entrepreneurs, as represented by Crime Group (C) in Figure 5.3. Similarly, the Dai Huen Jai or BCB in the Chinese community can also be regarded as a high-achieving criminal syndicate.

To conclude, all three crime groups use their 'criminal connections' to the fullest extent, as would be expected. It is this social microcosm (Lampe, 2007) of the criminal underworld in which they learnt their trade. Growing up in street corner gangs and prisons are the places where a criminal lifestyle and career develops for most members of crime groups. Hence, it is only natural that they

Chapter 5: Consolidating the Crime Business

will rely on their criminal networks to establish, expand, and consolidate their illegal business enterprise. Furthermore, the qualitative variations in the hypothetical scenarios chart the way different crime groups can consolidate their illegal business operations. This variation reflects the extent to which different crime groups use their entrepreneurial capability for making and maintaining cooperation with a range of people in the under and upper worlds of society.

Summary

This chapter examined the third business phase of *consolidating* a crime business. The entrepreneurial capability of *people cooperation* is primarily related to this third phase of business consolidation through a combination of business factors. These factors are: 'criminal business connections' that operate as criminal cooperatives and social networks formed through gangs, prisons, and culture; 'legitimate business connections' including both professional people and business structures; and 'influential people connections' like politicians, government ministers, high-profile business people, and so forth. How each of these three business factors can be used entrepreneurially to consolidate an illegal business was illustrated through a variety of case examples.

Finally, the chapter presented three hypothetical scenarios illustrated as 'fuzzy' maps. These maps charted the various pathways different crime groups can take in how they choose to consolidate their illegal business operations.

6

Positioning the Crime Business

Introduction

In this chapter the final phase of *positioning a* crime business is considered. Firstly, the entrepreneurial capability of 'profit maximization' associated with developing a criminal business is examined. Secondly, business factors related to 'profit maximization' are discussed and illustrated through case examples of how they operate in criminal markets, both locally and globally. Thirdly, the 'fuzzy' mapping analytical tool is again used, as in the previous three chapters, to map out by 'hypothetical' case scenarios the contours of different crime groups at this positioning phase of their business enterprise.

Criminal Business Modelling: Positioning Phase

This phase of positioning a crime business requires, as noted in our operating framework in Figure 2.1, a strategic focus on 'sustaining' a criminal enterprise over time. An entrepreneurial strategy will focus on current market conditions and adopt a future-oriented view of how to sustain a business in the longer term. The following Figure 6.1 lists the key business factors associated with developing this fourth phase of 'positioning' a crime business.

As shown, the business development factors related to this 'profit maximization' capability are *'local' market share*, *'global' market share*, and *competitive advantages*. Figure 6.2, below, contains the matrix that results from the cross-matching of this 'profit maximization' entrepreneurial capability with its related business development factors.

Chapter 6: Positioning the Crime Business

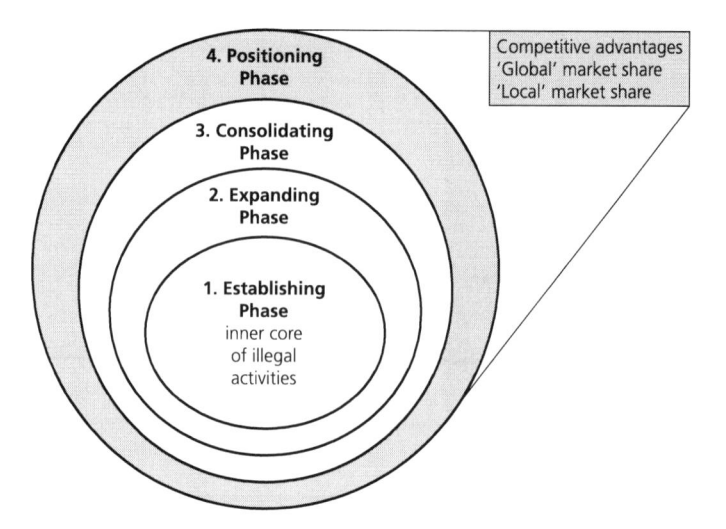

Figure 6.1 Crime business model: Phase 4—'positioning' business factors

As can be seen, the business factors associated with the 'profit maximization' capability are represented at the top right-hand side of the matrix. The other two entrepreneurial capabilities below profit maximization are *'people cooperation'* and *'decision-making under uncertainty'*.

Figure 6.2 Entrepreneurial capability by business factors at 'positioning' phase

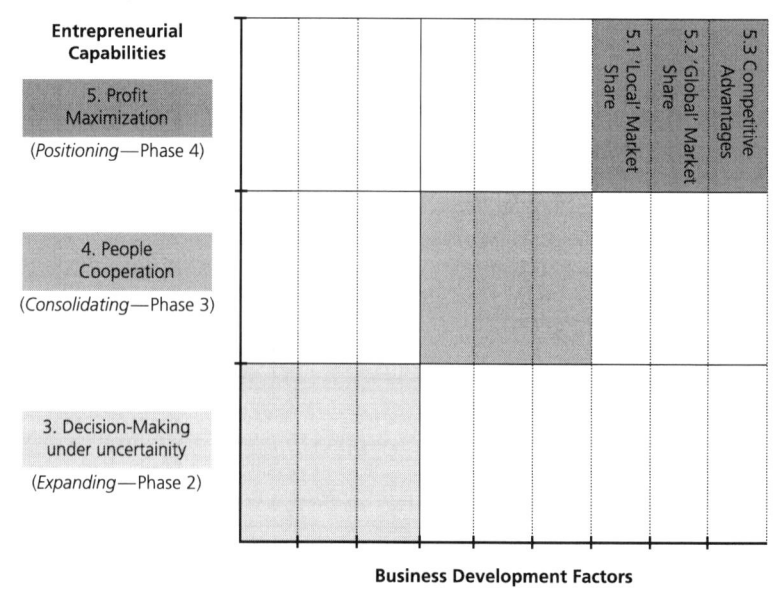

Entrepreneurial Capability: Profit Maximization

This capability of profit maximization involves a level of strategic entrepreneurialism, which has both short-term and long-term foci, to ensure the crime business is well positioned to capitalize on emerging business opportunities.

The aggressive pursuit of profit is a key driving force in criminal businesses, but it is not the only motivational factor involved. What motivates criminal entrepreneurs is a complex mix of several elements. For instance, the criminological literature identifies at least four motivational drivers (Thomas and Mancino, 2007; Audretsch and Keilbach, 2007; Markovski and Hall, 2007) which feed into the desire to engage in criminal entrepreneurialism. These motivations are: *allegiance* to a family crime business (destiny motivation); need to escape *poverty* (necessity motivation); a more *opportunistic* outlook in seeking out new business ventures (opportunity motivation); and finally entrepreneurs with a sense of *innovation* and creativity (innovative motivation). Moreover, whilst Duyne (2000) acknowledges that a 'crime-entrepreneur engages in a systematic planning of crimes for profit (p 371)' he also raises the interesting issue that if they are only in for profit then why do 'many crime-entrepreneurs (*who*)[1] should have quitted their industry after having amassed a handsome "retirement fund"' (p 372) stay on long after their use-by date? Duyne (*ibid*) posits that, 'Most crime-entrepreneurs continue beyond such a point, perhaps more addicted to a lifestyle than to the money they actually make'. He offers the following anecdotal evidence for this proposition:

> Part of their (*criminal*)[2] lifestyle is determined by their social environment, which consists mainly of like-minded risk seekers. Their incentives do not stem from a disciplined, beforehand calculation of the risks versus the rewards, but from the rough *expectancy* of huge rewards while (over)estimating their skills in beating the system and their competitors. This attitude was often expressed in the off-the-record interviews with detectives: 'I do not care for the big money anymore, I like the excitement of outsmarting you guys', remarked a hash wholesaler. Another boasted that he was the only one the law could never get at (up until now he has proved correct) (Duyne, 2000: 372).

Duyne's psychologically-oriented theory is an interesting addition to the other socio-cultural elements that drive and sustain a criminal entrepreneur's motivation over time.

However, such explanations are individualistic at their core and need to be understood in the context of a criminal 'microcosm' (Lampe, 2007), or as Duyne (2000) refers to it an 'addiction to a lifestyle'. For example, the cultural antecedents of Asian crime groups contain quite different and distinct understandings.

---

[1] Word in *italics* is by the current authors.   [2] Word in *italics* is by the current authors.

As Robinson (2000: 306) notes in relation to the Dai Huen Jai or Big Circle Boys (BCB) crime group:

> The Dai Huen Jai are about making money. They market heroin and do massive credit card frauds, and everything is done with a corporate strategy. They don't think of themselves as organized criminals, they think of themselves as organized businessmen.

Whatever the motivational mix may be for crime entrepreneurs, the overriding drive certainly at the beginning of their illegal entrepreneurialism is to maximize profit.

Market share has the potential to increase profits. By increasing market share a criminal entrepreneur changes the balance in the power structure of competitive markets. Increased market share reduces the financial impact from business rivals, customers, and new entrants in the marketplace as well as giving a criminal entrepreneur more bargaining power with suppliers. Opportunities to increase one's market share in the 'local' crime market or as a 'global' player arise from time to time. Market conditions are always in a state of flux. This is especially the case in a hostile and high-risk environment like the criminal underworld. As new business opportunities present themselves, alert criminal entrepreneurs will manoeuvre their crime business to exploit these opportunities for maximum profit. Therefore, such business manoeuvring involves looking at what competitive advantages exist, or can be created, to ensure one's crime business is strategically positioned for profit maximization.

Chapter 2 presented two fundamental business ideas with potential to increase market share, namely 'competitive market forces' and the 'supply-demand' equation. In relation to competitive market forces, entrepreneurially-oriented crime businesses face different types of constraints generally, to a greater extent, than legitimate businesses. For instance, criminal entrepreneurs have extra time pressure to make profits quickly since they are operating in a highly risky and dangerously volatile competitive environment. They can be arrested, closed down, or killed at any point in time—something legitimate entrepreneurs do not generally face. The worst that can happen to a legitimate entrepreneur is going bankrupt. Furthermore, smart criminal entrepreneurs can exploit market imperfections through seizing opportunities and thereby creating new economic value. However, imperfections create volatility in markets and hence environmental shocks (see Figure 2.6) for the unwary legitimate as well as the criminal entrepreneur. Territorial disputes can easily and quickly turn into gangland wars or hostile takeovers.

With regard to the 'supply-demand' equation, it is the interplay between suppliers and customers that creates the market dynamics whereby an increase in product price leads to rising supply and falling demand. Alternatively, when a decrease in product price occurs this leads to rising demand and falling supply. Such market dynamics reflect the 'elasticity' in the market. That is, the elasticity of demand and supply happens when price changes occur. Also, the 'price elasticity' in both demand and supply will vary from market to market. For instance, as shown on the graph (Figure 2.5 in Chapter 2), in a heavily-dependent drug market, where consumers are completely dependent on their daily dose, 'demand elasticity' may be very low.

In sum, the business factors—*'local' market share*, *'global' market share*, and *competitive advantages*—are the means by which criminal entrepreneurs attempt to position their crime businesses for increased profit-making. Case examples are presented below to illustrate the dynamics of competitive market forces and supply-demand elasticity as criminal entrepreneurs try to increase their business share in 'local' and 'global' markets.

'Local' Market Share

The 'local' crime market is the usual context within which most criminal entrepreneurs will seek to increase their market share. The first case example of increasing local market share involves Russian-style 'joint' ventures. Russia has not been marching towards democracy since the dismantling of the Soviet Union began in 1991 but rather as Serio (2008: 234) puts it '... closer to perfecting the notion of a criminal state'. Commercial opportunism in post-Soviet Russia for organized crime appears limitless. Doing business in Russia requires some sort of 'partnership' arrangement, usually in the form of a joint venture. While it is common in the world of organized crime to carry out joint ventures between crimes groups for specific illegal operations, in Russia such criminality also extends into legitimate business ventures. An illuminating example of the 'local' Russian way of turning a legitimate business 'joint venture' into an illegitimate 'one way' venture is provided by Serio (2008: 250):

Case Example 6.1 'One way' Russian-Style Joint Ventures (Russia)

The Russian joint venture factory of General Motors and Russian carmaker Avtovaz ground to a halt after the new management team forced on Avtovaz by the state halted component supplies. The Russian arms export agency, Rosoboronexport, reportedly close to the Russian president, seized control. The Russians claimed that the GM joint venture was profitable but that Avtovaz lost money on it and that the joint venture only made money because Avtovaz sold components at a loss.

Analysts speculated that one of the possibilities was that the Russian side was trying to raise prices so high as to make it unprofitable and then the Russian side would take over. This was a pattern long repeated across time. 'It's the typical Russian story. They let the American partners in and then start squeezing them out.' (*The Moscow Times*, 13 September 1994).

Chapter 6: Positioning the Crime Business

Serio (2008: 250) is quick to point out that many other forces were at work in the 1990s in the business environment that had more to do with the Russian way of doing things than with the traditional 'mafia.' However, it is equally true that criminal organizations are also part and parcel of the fabric of commercial life in Russia and were actively involved in many similar business shakedowns in the 1990s.

The next case example demonstrates how, in a relatively short time, a local street gang of 'new kids' on the block can grow its reputation for violence into a viable criminal business. In so doing, they dramatically increased their market share.

Case Example 6.2 'New Kids' on Block: the Case of MS-13 (Salvadorans)

MS-13 stands for 'Mara Salvatrucha', the name for a notorious organization that began in the 1980s as a relatively small gang on the streets of Los Angeles. Nicaso and Lamothe (2005: 211) quote a Newsweek article published in 2005, that described MS-13 as '... the newest "most dangerous gang in America"'. Nicaso and Lamothe (2005: 211) provide the following background of MS-13:

> Its original members were Salvadorans who had fled civil strife; among them were members of the El Salvadorian street gang La Mara and paramilitary groups. In America they and their children found themselves taunted by and preyed upon by local gangs in the L.A. ghetto. To protect themselves they banded together in a mara, or crew, and as the initial cell grew it attracted many Salvadorians as well as youths from other Central American countries. And like a lot of gangs that form themselves for self-defense, MS-13 soon recognized their own power and evolved into a local criminal organization that practiced extortion, drug trafficking, and violent robberies.

The rapid growth of MS-13's criminal empire is a classic tale of underestimating a crime group's potential by law enforcement. Not only was MS-13's potential overlooked but also, through fateful circumstances, law enforcement agencies were looking the other way.

> The growth of MS-13 was the result of several factors. Initially the group wasn't taken as seriously as the Crips or the Bloods (*notorious American street gangs*),[3] and while it was essentially ignored it was able to form a hard nucleus of leaders. After 9/11 resources were cut back, and in the FBI's Washington field office, gang investigators were reduced by 50 percent as agents were reassigned to terrorist-related activities. Now, however, MS-13 has become active in a range of activities, including murders, kidnappings, extortion, gang rapes, and drug and migrant smuggling (Nicaso and Lamothe, 2005: 212).

---

[3] Words in *italics* by current authors.

'Global' Market Share

Criminal markets are now more than ever before 'transnational' in nature. This is due in large measure to the way the legitimate economy has been 'globalized'. Globalization creates interlinking not only of the economic or financial sector, but across several spheres—social, environmental, political, and so forth. (See Figures 2.6 and 2.7 in Chapter 2). As Shelley is reported as commenting, 'Transnational organized crime will proliferate in the next century because crime groups are among the major beneficiaries of globalization' (Robinson, 2000: 316). The following case examples underscore the global interconnectivity of criminal entrepreneurialism.

On an international level, Nicaso and Lamothe (2005: 186) state that it is '... very difficult to overestimate the activities of Albanian organized crime'. These authors provide the following case example of 'The Corporation' and its global outreach.

Case Example 6.3 'The Corporation': Albanian Organized Crime (United States)

In the US, a series of stories began appearing in 2004 detailing how a group of Albanians—dubbed 'The Corporation' and directed by their alleged ringleader, Alex 'Alley Boy' Rudaj—orchestrated an attack on the American Cosa Nostra. According to American indictments filed in New York City, in 2001 the 37-year-old Rudaj led a crew of six of his henchmen on a raid on a social club where a powerful New York City LCN family operated a gambling racket using Greek front men. Armed with guns, Rudaj's crew swarmed into the mob-controlled club and violently attacked the workers.

Afterwards The Corporation began muscling in on at least six Astoria-area gambling clubs; these were added to several other clubs Rudaj's crew operated, bringing the total number of clubs to 50 and yielding $5.75 million in profits. They also attacked several associates of both the Lucchese and Colombo crime families (Nicaso and Lamothe, 2005: 184).

The global reach of organized crime works like a virus. Ironically, an organized crime virus can be spread 'globally' by law enforcement actions. MS-13, presented previously, started life as a violent paramilitary El Salvadorian street gang. It has since transformed itself into an international criminal organization through the efforts of law enforcement actions. As Nicaso and Lamothe (2005: 211) report:

Case Example 6.4 Spreading the Organized Crime Virus (Global)

A crackdown by US authorities led to the deportation of several members; the deportees banded together, however, and outposts of the gang popped up

continued

> throughout Central America. This effectively gave what was a local street gang reach across international borders. Investigators have uncovered a direct US-El Salvador route for the shipment of stolen high-end cars. And it was MS-13—known for the beheadings of their victims—that was behind a bus bombing in Honduras that killed 28 people.

As this case clearly demonstrates law enforcement actions, like all actions, have unintended and sometimes unforeseen consequences.

The next case example involves Africa and in particular, Nigeria. East Africa has been described as a 'black hole' where there is 'absolutely nothing you can't do' (Nicaso and Lamothe (2005: 240). The Nigerians are regarded as the most notorious of the African organized crime groups.

Case Example 6.5 'Black Hole' of Nigerian Crime Groups (Africa)

Generally, Nigerian crime groups have some degree of organization with a leader at the top and lieutenants below but, unlike the traditional hierarchical structure of the Italian mafia for example, Nigerian groups are cell-like syndicates, often breaking apart and reforming in other criminal initiatives with interchangeable members. Such small criminal groupings are along tribal lines or family ties, although most such crime groups have connections to government agencies since corruption is entrenched at all levels of Nigerian society, politics, the financial sector, and law enforcement. Money-laundering is rampant and Nigerian banks are used by crime groups from throughout Africa (Nicaso and Lamothe, 2005: 238).

Furthermore, the diaspora of Nigerian migrants in communities across the world provides an infrastructure for both international fraud and drug dealing rings, particularly heroin trafficking. According to Nicaso and Lamothe (2005: 237):

> The ease of getting drugs in and out of Nigeria—through porous borders and co-opted customs officials—has turned the country into an international hub for heroin trafficking. With the exception of marijuana and related products, Nigeria isn't a source country for narcotics, but criminal groups—including Asian syndicates, Italian organized crime, and Colombian cartels— operate throughout the country. Known as a drug-transit hub, the Murtala Mohamed International Airport (MMIA) in Lagos is under the control of crime figures and corrupted officials.

Clearly, Nigeria is a safe haven for crime groups as well as a transit hub into Europe for drugs and human trafficking, which makes it a global player of international reach into criminal markets. In this sense, Nigeria is a country where 'crime' is the 'industry' since it hosts a collection of criminal enterprises that conduct business in the same or similar kind of business area and/or markets.

Competitive Advantages

The final business factor for strategically 'positioning' a crime business for future sustainability is the notion of competitive advantage. This business factor separates out those criminal entrepreneurs who just survive and those that flourish. Several case examples are presented to show the diversity of the ways and means various crime groups use to gain a competitive advantage in crime markets. The 'strategic principle' behind these competitive advantages is elucidated as a reference point to understand how crime groups 'position' their illegal businesses.

The first competitive advantage strategy is clearly apparent in the way in which Albanian organized crime groups operate. For instance, Nicaso and Lamothe (2005) assert in the following case box:

Case Example 6.6 Strategy 1: Operate a 'Decentralized Command Structure'

The successes of the Albanian 'mafia'—particularly on the global stage—can also be attributed to the command structure of the groups that make up the wide federation. A Leadership Council oversees, but doesn't necessarily dictate, both local and international operations. The council is made up of elders who are the leaders of the *fis*, the family networks that govern individual groups. Some *fis* operations are controlled according to territory, particularly in the Baltic region, while others are built around *fis* members and their opportunities and specialties, such as a source and route for the transit of firearms, or alternatively, all activities in a specific region of influence. Many Albanian politicians and former military and espionage agents are believed to be members of individual groups, but *gjak*, or blood relatives, form the hard kernel of each cell. Family attachments, such as through marriage, make up a close but less trusted outer circle (Nicaso and Lamothe, 2005: 188).

This type of competitive advantage is of most value for major criminal organizations. For more cell-like syndicates and small networks a decentralized command structure is neither as great nor even a necessity.

Another competitive advantage strategy evident within the Albanian organized crime model is the use of 'specialists', mainly for finances and coordination. With regard to Crime Money Management (discussed in Chapter 3) Albanian crime groups appoint a financial officer '... whose job is to invest and launder the group's profits as well as to identify and exploit methods of repatriating funds overseas, particularly in groups with strong ties to their Albanian mother-*fis*' (Nicaso and Lamothe, 2005: 188). At the same time, a coordinator acts as a networker and fixer.

Case Example 6.7 Strategy 2: Create Specialists' Roles

The coordinator is a trusted blood relative who travels the world carrying messages, passing formation, and assisting Albanians who want to emigrate to either America or Canada. Often the coordinator has a public role, usually as a member of a cultural or social-awareness group. When a member of the group gets into legal difficulty with the law, it's the coordinator who navigates the judicial system, finding lawyers, arranging payment of fees and, when possible, corrupting or bribing police or judges (Nicaso and Lamothe, 2005: 188).

With regard to international fraud schemes, the small-scale operating principle of Nigerian organized crime groups is in stark contrast to other criminal groups that prefer to maximize profits with big-hit type scams. The next case example illustrates the Nigerian way.

Case Example 6.8 Strategy 3: Utilize 'Little and Often' Principle

Nigerian scams work on the principle of doing 'little' but 'often'. For instance, they are notoriously famous for the 'Nigerian Letter Scam' fraud. This scam involves mass mailing of letters to individuals and companies around the world with requests for money or other forms of assistance that will enable them to get their hands on the money of gullible victims who fall prey to such pleas for help.

The economy of scale of this 'little letter scam' lies in the 'often' mass mailings on a global scale to thousands of potential victims. Nicaso and Lamothe (2005: 239) make an interesting point on the operation of the 'Nigerian Letter Scam' fraud:

> These letters were often poorly written. But when the Nigerian fraudsters used word processing technology and even spell-check programs to improve their quality, the success rate dropped sharply and they went back to badly written, typed pleas for help.
>
> Observers believe that victims were initially drawn into the scam because they thought they were dealing with uneducated and naive Nigerians; once it appeared that they might be dealing with something other than dupes in a backward country, they became more cautious.

Moreover, as a further note, Nicaso and Lamothe (*op cit*) point out that even responding to such letters is a dangerous thing to do:

> Cautious respondents who sent a query letter but no banking information found their letterheads copied and used to get American or European travel

visas or to commit frauds against other companies. Victims who seemed exceedingly greedy were invited to meetings in Nigeria, where they were terrorized and held hostage while more information was extracted. Once more money had been taken from the victims' personal and country bank accounts, the victims were either released or murdered.

The next competitive advantage strategy is based on what Klerks (2003: 97) describes as the new 'networking paradigm'. This network paradigm is currently the dominant perspective from which to understand the operation of organized crime. As noted in Chapter 5, being connected to the right criminal, legitimate business, and influential people networks is of primary importance for criminal entrepreneurs to prosper and survive. Furthermore, as mentioned in Chapter 3, Grennan and Britz (2006) point out that criminal entrepreneurs are more likely to grow out of a life of crime where exposure to a criminal sub-culture (familial, ethnic, or simply gangs) provides the context for developing entrepreneurial vision and talent.

Case Example 6.9 Strategy 4: Recycle 'Crime Networks' and Utilize 'Porous Borders'

This new 'network' understanding of contemporary organized crime highlights the fluid nature of these loosely-joined entrepreneurial networks or 'criminal co-operatives' (Klerks, 2003: 101) which are highly flexible and adaptive criminal groups. These groups are smaller, independent, and largely autonomous entrepreneurial networks (Mackenzie, 2002; PJCACC, 2007) and are often willing to work with other criminal groups, regardless of loyalties and ethnic identity.

Such fluidity of transaction and association give networked criminal cooperatives a significant competitive advantage. This is not only over more rigidly structured crime groups but also, as 'moving targets', they make it very difficult for policing and law enforcement to get a fix on them for any length of time. By the time the police do become aware of a criminal operation the perpetrators of the illegal activity are generally long gone but also may have disbanded their alliance for that job and moved on to other joint ventures with new criminal partners and often in several different countries.

This is particularly evident in Europe where the porous borders of the EU allow for organized criminal groups to use several countries as 'criminal hubs' (OCTA, 2007).

Failed states and civil wars provide unique competitive advantages for organized crime. The business opportunities are basically twofold—firstly, it allows crime groups to 'support' the cause; and secondly to offer 'stability' of leadership in a destabilized situation. There are two particular strategies that organized crime employs to great effect.

Chapter 6: Positioning the Crime Business

Strategy 1—the first type of opportunistic exploitation, *'supporting the cause through crime'*, when civil strife and state unrest occur is something of a speciality for organized crime groups. They can play on both sides of the fence and come out a winner, no matter who ultimately wins the war in the country under siege. The following case box illustrates this strategy.

Case Example 6.10 Strategy 5: Exploit 'Failed States' and Civil Wars

Supporting the cause through crime

The complete breakdown of civil authority in Albania in 1997 led to widespread anarchy in which military arsenals were raided and thousands of automatic weapons were liberated. Anyone who wanted to arm themselves suddenly had the benefit of a full marketplace with competitive prices. Having accumulated firepower, some criminal organizations set themselves up as paramilitary units. Then, in 1998 and 1999, the war in Kosovo broke out, and again the traffickers were able to capitalize on chaos by organizing smuggling operations to support the cause (Nicaso and Lamothe, 2005: 187).

Stability of crime leadership

During the communist years the Fifteen Families—'fifteen fis'—had controlled organized criminal activity in Albania, primarily through smuggling and corruption. But with the collapse of the communist government and the military, the Fifteen Families were in essence the only groups that didn't descend into anarchy and chaos. This paradox echoes that of Sicily after World War II; when the Americans looked for leaders of strength who could govern there, they had only the Mafiosi to choose from (Nicaso and Lamothe, 2005: 187).

This double-sided dealing with less than reputable and even criminal groups in war-torn regions is especially evident in the political sector, for example, the pact the American CIA made with the Northern Alliance, made up mainly of Kurdish fighters, as well as Osama Bin Laden and his followers to take up arms against the Russian occupation of Afghanistan. Now the tide has changed after 9/11 and it is the Americans' turn to do battle in Afghanistan against the Taliban and Osama Bin Laden's terrorist organization and criminal groups who supply weapons and other resources against the USA.

Strategy 2—the second type of opportunistic exploitation, *'stability of crime leadership'*, as is evident in the case example above, has an ironic twist when democratic governments look to criminal organizations to provide 'stability'. Clearly, history has a way of repeating itself—and that is 'good business' for organized crime.

The next competitive advantage strategy was touched on in Chapter 2 when discussing the effect of 'successful' law enforcement activity in terms of market 'elasticity'. For instance, when a policing drugs bust takes place that is sufficient in size and scope to temporarily cut or significantly disrupt market supply then a higher market price will result. The 'perceived' extra profits to be made in this crime market will then encourage new or other competitive criminal groups to enter this market.

> ### Case Example 6.11 Strategy 6: Capitalize on Police Crackdowns
>
> What is considered 'successful' from a policing perspective is a very moot point, since such law enforcement successes can often have the unintended consequence of paving or smoothing out the way for another criminal group to fill the market vacuum.
>
> The earlier case example presented under the business factor of increasing a crime group's global market share about 'The Corporation', an Albanian organized crime group that systematically took over the Mafia's business interests in New York when sustained police crackdowns had the effect of weakening the Mafia's illegal operations, is again a case in point about what does 'success' mean.

Few criminal organizations can completely dominate a market and have a monopoly situation. However, when criminal groups join forces with others in a network or syndicated partnership arrangement then they achieve strength in a competitive market (Pérez, 2007). This type of market domination competitive advantage can be used to engage in price-fixing, among other things. The case example in Chapter 5 about the Hells Angels in Canada going into partnership with their drug market rival, the Italian Mafia, to avoid a turf war also had the added competitive advantage of '... fixing the price of cocaine at $50,000 a kilogram' (New Zealand Police Association, 2006a: 67).

> ### Case Example 6.12 Strategy 7: Make Strategic Alliances
>
> Strategic partnerships and alliances are a useful way to gain a competitive advantage over other business rivals as well as position one's business in the market to achieve sustainability in the longer term. Chinese Triads are particularly good at utilizing such competitively advantageous criminal alliances and 'loose cartels' (Chu, 2000: 135): 'Hong Kong triads are neither a centrally structured nor an unorganised entity, but loose cartels consisting of numerous autonomous gangs which adopt a similar organisational structure and rituals to bind their members together.'

The next competitive advantage is central to all crime groups as infiltration by law enforcement is a constant threat. However, some crime groups are better at ensuring impenetrability than others. Albanian criminal groups are specialists at this and hence achieve more of a competitive advantage in this regard than other crime groups.

Chapter 6: Positioning the Crime Business

> **Case Example 6.13 Strategy 8: Ensure Impenetrability**
>
> According to Nicaso and Lamothe (2005: 190) blood loyalty of the Albanian criminal groups makes them virtually impenetrable. 'This is the key', a Canadian law-enforcement officer said.
>
> > If a guy rats here, his entire family back in Albania is blamed. When we get a traditional organized crime informant in Vancouver, we can generally take him and his wife and kids into protective custody, into the [witness protection] program. With Baltics, there's no way we can even begin to identify relatives, never mind get a corrupt foreign government to protect mothers and fathers and children. Right away the entire clan goes 'in the blood' and there are bodies falling for generations to come, long after anyone even remembers why it all started.

For some crime groups, like the Mafia, attracting media attention, while not so good at one level, at another level is a useful business tool as it helps to reinforce their brand of 'reputational violence' (Gambetta, 1993). If your crime business, as in the case of the Italian Mafia, and to an extent Asian Triads, is 'protection services' then being seen as a 'credible protector' is good advertising. With regard to Triads, Chu (2000: 38) provides an interesting example of how one enterprising criminal used such 'branding' to his advantage:

> Since Triads have established their reputation for violence, some people are able to use this 'trademark' to make profits. For instance, in 1973 a total of fifty-seven people in well-paid occupations were telephoned by a man who demanded money from them in the name of a triad society. All paid except one, and as a result of this report to the police an arrest was made. The person concerned had made a very large sum of money but was in fact not a member of a triad society at all (*SCMP* 30 June 1975).

However, while there are some competitive advantages to having a 'high' media profile, crime groups in general, and Triads in particular, nowadays tend to want to keep a low profile. There are more business advantages to not being in the headlines every other day.

> **Case Example 6.14 Strategy 9: Keep a 'Low-Profile'**
>
> If a crime group gets too much media attention then the public demand tougher police and law enforcement actions. That is bad for illegal businesses. Albanian crime groups are a case in point, as Nicaso and Lamothe, (2005: 190) report. 'The Albanians don't have the media drawing power of a mafia hit or a Triad heroin-smuggling ring. People don't know about the Albanians. And the Albanians like it that way.'

In sum, it is evident from the case examples presented in this section that there are a wide and varied range of strategies that crime groups can use to 'position' their illegal business. The extent to which they choose some of these business factors over others, and in what combination, will to a large extent be determined by their entrepreneurial capacity and drive to maximize profit.

'Fuzzy' Mapping of *Positioning* Crime Business

This final section presents the fuzzy mapping of a number of hypothetical scenarios. These maps chart out how criminal entrepreneurs seek to increase their *'local' and/or 'global' market share* as well as exploit *competitive advantages* to position their crime business strategically to maximize profits.

Hypothetical scenarios

The following matrix in Figure 6.3 below offers a fuzzy mapping of three hypothetical scenarios at this positioning phase for a criminal business.

With regard to the first scenario, for *Crime Group (A)* it is clear this particular crime group seeks to exploit its 'local' market share to the maximum in terms of

Figure 6.3 Fuzzy scenarios of entrepreneurial capability at 'positioning' phase

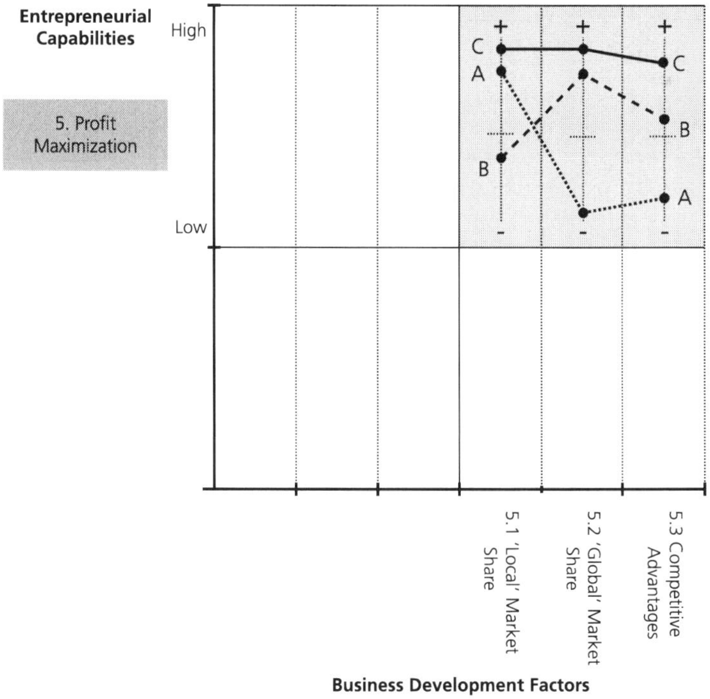

profit-making. It is also clear by its fuzzy scaling, that Crime Group (A) is content mainly to stay 'local' and not to become a big global crime market player. There can be several reasons for this reluctance to move beyond its regional boundaries. For instance, it may feel it is better to deal in its own back yard than to risk getting involved in global markets it knows little about. Such caution provides a sense of security and protection for it against global crime players. It also reduces the risk of attracting international law enforcement attention. Furthermore, it knows its local scene well and, like Russian crime groups, has well placed government officials, police, and politicians on its payroll to ensure its market share increases. If it went 'global' it would have to build new networks for production, distribution, and so forth. For Crime Group (A) the cost and risk is just not worth the effort.

Moreover, the competitive advantages it has in its local context allow it to specialize in particular scams and business shakedowns which provide plenty of opportunities to make money. For example, in Russia they have perfected the 'joint venture' scam with unsuspecting foreign investors as Serio's (2008: 251) account of a gullible American dentist makes clear.

> The 2006 experience of an American dentist who abandoned his dental practice in Moscow after being threatened by thugs is a typical example of what has occurred for the past twenty years and for at least five hundred years before that. When his clinic began to show a healthy profit, his Russian partner, true to Lenin's characterization, took a shortcut and started to squeeze him out. Typical of stories like this, the Russian partner had set up the accounts and controlled the paperwork, making the takeover a relatively easy undertaking. The dentist concluded, 'If you go into partnership with somebody and the company is losing money, it's your company. If you make money, it's theirs and they find a way to get it from you'.

In the second scenario, *Crime Group (B)* is doing relatively well in the 'local' crime market. Its illegal business is making good profits but the lure of getting into the 'global' criminal markets is the big attraction for this crime group. It also sees itself as having some competitive advantages over its rivals. It has a trusted cell-like structure based on tribal and blood ties that ensures impenetrability and prevents infiltration by law enforcement. Another competitive advantage is its expertise as a specialist scam group. Such a profile is similar to Nigerian crime groups where, from the safety of their home base in Nigeria, they can connect with all the major international organized crime groups. These criminal connections allow them to forge fluid networks to perpetrate a range of syndicated illegal business activities with other like-minded criminal entrepreneurs.

In relation to the third scenario, it is evident that *Crime Group (C)* is playing all the business factor 'keys' on the crime 'piano'. There is a continuous line between 'local' and 'global' crime markets because it has the organizational infrastructure and linkages with both criminal and legitimate business connections to move effortlessly between these market levels. Such economies of scale and scope give it the ultimate competitive advantage, that of immense power.

Such a scenario for Crime Group (C) is representative of Chinese Triads. They have access to a global infrastructure of 'Chinatowns' and 'Tong-like business associations' in every major city in the world.

To conclude, these hypothetical scenarios clearly illustrate the various business factor combinations possible that different profit-oriented entrepreneurial crime groups can use to position their illegal business operations strategically to survive in the long term. As each scenario demonstrates such groups vary in their ability to harness their entrepreneurial capability to maximize profits.

Summary

This chapter examined the fourth business phase of *positioning* a crime business. The entrepreneurial capability of *profit maximization* is primarily related to this fourth phase of business positioning through a combination of business factors. These factors are: attempting to increase one's 'local' market share; tactics to increase one's 'global' market share; and strategizing about using or developing 'competitive advantages'. How each of these three business factors can be used entrepreneurially to position an illegal business was illustrated through a variety of case examples. Finally, the chapter presented three hypothetical scenarios illustrated as 'fuzzy' maps. These maps showed various pathways different crime groups can take to position their illegal business operations strategically for future sustainability.

PART THREE

Policing Crime Businesses

This final section of the book contains three chapters (7, 8, and 9). Each chapter focuses, in different ways, on the vexing problem of how best to combat and police 'organized crime' and its variant forms. Chapter 7 introduces the concept of 'Knowledge-Managed Policing' (KMP) as an innovative perspective from which to view organized criminal entrepreneurialism. KMP involves balancing the mix of people knowledge and systems technology to optimize a police organization's performance. A case study of knowledge failure using a 'knowledge cube' tool illustrates the practical application of KMP.

Chapter 8 is operationally-focused. It presents an easy-to-use knowledge management tool termed a 'Crime Business Analysis Matrix' (CBAM). This tool provides the level of specificity required by policing to target criminal groups effectively. A case study illustrates the use of the CBAM system.

Chapter 9 looks to the future of policing. It examines the current UK 'joined-up multi-agency' approach. It includes a range of intervention strategies to police illegal business activities. The chapter proposes a strategic knowledge framework of sector policing to determine optimal policing strategies. However, knowledge sharing and international cooperation are preconditions for effectiveness. The chapter concludes with some speculative thoughts on charting out the future direction of policing illegal business entrepreneurialism.

7

Knowledge-Managed Policing: Principles and Practices

Introduction

This chapter presents a new perspective on policing organized crime, that of Knowledge-Managed Policing (KMP). It explores the extent to which a policing organization can optimize its policing knowledge (people and systems) to meet the challenges of a fast-changing, entrepreneurially-oriented organized crime global landscape. The problem with finding workable solutions to the complexities of organized crime initially involves freeing oneself from the mental constraints of pre-conceived ideas and established thinking. Einstein aptly notes, 'It is the theory that decides what can be observed' (<www.thinkexist.com>, 2009). A KMP perspective offers police executives, practitioners, policy makers, and government agencies a different vantage point for dealing with global organized crime. KMP is centred on the premise that people who are knowledgeable have the ability to integrate and frame information within the context of their experience, expertise, and judgment. The potency of this mix of people and knowledge is examined through the innovative notion of a 'Knowledge Cube' (KC). The cube integrates the dimensions of police knowledge categories, levels, and depth. The chapter concludes with a case study of suspected terrorism that demonstrates the practical application of this 'Knowledge Cube' tool. This KC tool can be used to plot the key knowledge points involved in any serious and complex investigation.

Application of 'Knowledge' in Policing

Knowledge originates in the human brain. Knowledge results from the combination of experience, context, interpretation, reflection, intuition, and creativity by human beings. Hence, 'knowledge', itself, cannot be stored in a computer.

Only some form of representation of knowledge can be stored in a computer as data or information like text, or a diagram, a picture, audio and video files, or some other representational system. Knowledge, therefore, is generally defined as the most valuable form of content in a continuum[1] starting at data, encompassing information, and ending at knowledge (Gottschalk, 2005). Two of the current authors[2] have written extensively about this hierarchy of knowledge as it applies to policing and law enforcement. Dean and Gottschalk (2007) include police 'intelligence' as a specific form of content in this 'knowledge ladder' continuum from data, information to intelligence, then knowledge. Sometimes wisdom is included beyond knowledge on the continuum as the ultimate end goal (Davenport and Prusak, 1998; Spiegler, 2000).

Typically, data is classified, summarised, transferred, or corrected in order to add value, and become information within a certain context. This conversion is relatively mechanical and has long been facilitated by storage, processing, and communication technologies. These technologies add place, time, and form utility to the data. Drucker (1995) notes information is 'data endowed with relevance and purpose'. Thus, information serves to inform or reduce uncertainty within a problem domain. When information is united with a context, it has utility that has relevance and purpose within that context (Grover and Davenport, 2001). The same can be said about 'intelligence' in that it is a form of data to which some relevance has been attached through an attempt to offer an 'organized' analysis of the information received by a crime analyst and/or intelligence officer within the context of its collection. Thus, 'intelligence' is placed between information and knowledge on the continuum as ideally intelligence represents, as Brodeur and Dupont (2006: 9) argue, a form of 'validated information'. In the current research literature (Poston and Speier, 2005; Ryu, Kim, Chaudhury, and Rao, 2005; Sambamurthy and Subramani, 2005; Tanriverdi, 2005; Wasko and Faraj, 2005) six characteristics of knowledge have been identified that distinguish it from information: knowledge is a human act; knowledge is the residue of thinking; knowledge is created in the present moment; knowledge belongs to communities; knowledge circulates through communities in many ways; and new knowledge is created at the boundaries of old.

Hence, for policing purposes, knowledge has the highest value, the most human contribution, the greatest relevance to decisions and actions, and the greatest dependence on a specific situation or context. It is also the most difficult of content types to manage, because it originates and is applied in the minds of human beings. People who are knowledgeable not only have information, but also have the ability to integrate and frame the information within the context

---

[1] This continuum is often referred to in the literature as a 'Knowledge Pyramid' or a 'data-information-knowledge-wisdom (DIKW) hierarchy (Rowley, 2007). Such a DIKW hierarchy, while part of the canon of information science and management, is nonetheless a contested notion by some academics (see Fricke, 2009).

[2] For a fuller treatment on what knowledge entails in policing the reader is referred to Dean, G. and Gottschalk, P. (2007). *Knowledge Management in Policing and Law Enforcement: Foundations, Structure, Applications*. London: Oxford University Press.

of their experience, expertise, and judgment. In doing so, they can create new information that expands the state of possibilities, and in turn allows for further interaction with experience, expertise, and judgment.

Therefore, in an organizational context, all new knowledge stems from people. Although knowledge cannot originate outside the heads of individuals, it can be argued that knowledge can be *represented* in and often embedded in organizational processes, routines, and networks, and sometimes in document repositories. However, knowledge is seldom complete outside of an individual. Moreover, institutionalized knowledge often inhibits competition in a dynamic context, unless the adaptability of people and processes (higher order learning) is built into the institutional mechanisms themselves.

Thus, when we speak of 'Knowledge Management', and in particular our concept of 'Knowledge-Managed Policing', it is in this dual or parallel-track sense of 'people' and 'systems', as indicated in Figure 7.1 below.

In essence, Knowledge-Managed Policing (KMP) is about getting the balance right between police officer knowledge and technological systems. The benefit of striving towards getting and maintaining a balance in the KM equation represented in Figure 7.1 is profound. It cannot be overstated how fundamentally important it is for police organizations to 'know what they have' in terms of policing knowledge (people and systems) to a level of audited detail. The possession of a whole-of-organization knowledge audit not only provides an invaluable organizational resource for training and educating staff but also allows the organization to 'harvest' and 'create' new knowledge (Dean and Gottschalk, 2007: 233) to apply to the emerging challenges facing policing. Law enforcement is involved

Figure 7.1 Two sides of knowledge-managed policing

Knowledge-Managed Policing:
is about the knowledge people possess in their heads and the various technological systems that can be used to explicate such tacit, experientially-learnt knowledge.

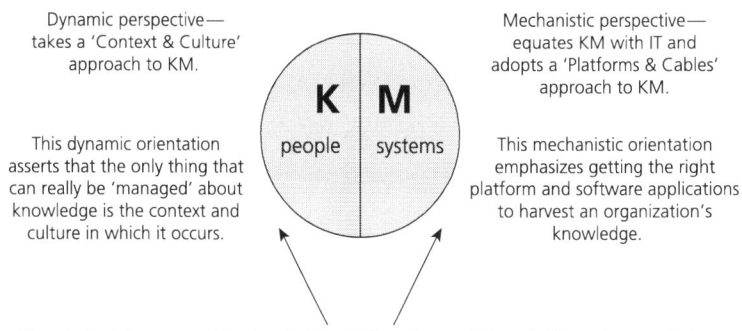

Dynamic perspective— takes a 'Context & Culture' approach to KM.

This dynamic orientation asserts that the only thing that can really be 'managed' about knowledge is the context and culture in which it occurs.

K | M
people | systems

Mechanistic perspective— equates KM with IT and adopts a 'Platforms & Cables' approach to KM.

This mechanistic orientation emphasizes getting the right platform and software applications to harvest an organization's knowledge.

Knowledge Management involves both a *philosophy*, consisting of different conceptual orientations or approaches, and a *practice* or technological base that revolve around a set of distinct yet complementary processes to do with *knowledge creation, capture, storage, retrieval, transfer, sharing, application,* and *integration*.

in a knowledge war with organized crime and terrorism. KMP is not an option for police organizations and governments; it is a necessity.

Knowledge Categories in Policing

'Policing knowledge' is a combination of the quality of the training, education, and experience that police carry around in their heads. Police knowledge can be categorized in various ways—for instance, in terms of types of actions or behaviours, or procedures and rules and so forth. From our perspective, police, at a minimum, require knowledge in the following categories: *legal, operational, administrative, technical, investigative, intelligence,* and *analytical.* Such knowledge categories equip police officers to carry out the diverse range of tasks and activities inherent in the job of policing.

These knowledge categories are numbered below in order of logical utility and not in terms of sequential actions. For instance:

1. Police officers will need *legal knowledge* to know what they can 'lawfully' do in a situation
2. They then need *operational knowledge* of the SOPs (Standard Operating Procedures) for the type of incident/crime involved
3. Following this, they need *administrative knowledge* of the organizational rules and regulations for tasks
4. This will also entail some *technical knowledge* about IT systems to enter data (records management) and what databases to use/search and so forth
5. Depending on the nature of the incident/crime some degree of *investigative knowledge* may also be required
6. Some *intelligence knowledge* input may also be required
7. Finally, some *analytical knowledge* like problem-solving skills may be necessary

The sequence and, therefore, use of a particular knowledge category will vary in actual practice owing to a variety of factors. These different types (categories) of knowledge can be thought of as 'cyclically interrelated' rather than as a set of step-wise actions to follow. Much of this type of categorical knowledge can be made explicit and written down as police doctrine and found in policy documentation (training manuals on law and duties, standing orders, operating procedures, and so forth). However, much also remains tacit—locked in the heads of experienced police and at different levels of expertise.

Knowledge Levels of Police

The knowledge categories listed above are subject to different levels of knowledge acquisition and sophistication by individual police officers. That is, police can be trained to achieve a basic level of core competency in each knowledge category. Furthermore, police can be trained as specialists to a more advanced level of competency in particular knowledge areas. Hence, there are levels of training and education that go into creating a 'knowledgeable' police officer.

To be useful, policing knowledge involves 'grafting' to quality training and education on-the-job learning and experience. This makes the value-added difference to the profession of policing. In this regard we make a fundamental distinction between 'professionalizing' and 'professionalism'. By this we mean that many occupations seek to 'professionalize' their service but not all such occupations would necessarily be regarded as 'professions'. We are aware the very terms 'professional' and 'professionalism' are highly contentious and hotly disputed with regard to who and what they apply to, by scholars, academics, practitioners, and the general public (Kulick, 2006; Flexner, 2001; Freidson, 2001; Krause, 1996; Pugh, 1989; Wilensky, 1964).

Notwithstanding such a minefield of divergent opinions on what being a 'professional' entails and means, for our purposes, we use the terms 'professionalized knowledge' and 'professionalism knowledge' in the following manner:

- When a police officer gains knowledge through experience and on-the-job learning to such an extent that it becomes *internalized* then that officer has 'professionalized' their working knowledge
- Such 'professionalized knowledge' becomes *'professionalism'* when that police officer develops and uses *higher-order critical thinking and analysis skills* and engages in *research-based practice* combined with *ethical integrity*

To make this distinction clear the following matrix diagram in Figure 7.2 is presented. As can be seen on the next page (Figure 7.2), cross referencing police knowledge categories with knowledge levels results in a matrix of the 'knowledge needs' for policing. The identification of such knowledge needs provides an invaluable guide to conduct an organization-wide audit of the knowledge strengths as well as the knowledge gaps. Such an audit enables better management of the policing knowledge resources within the organization in terms of the 'people knowledge' side of the KM equation (Figure 7.1). In our previous work on knowledge management in policing and law enforcement, Dean and Gottschalk (2007: 124) developed a mapping tool for the technological 'systems knowledge' side of this KM equation. This analytical mapping tool, when used in conjunction with the Knowledge Needs matrix above, allows a police organization to obtain a holistic snapshot of its current KM resources. This enhances policing capabilities and allows the organization to forward plan its strategic development.

Knowledge Depth to Police

With regard to the 'Knowledge Needs' matrix on Figure 7.2, there is a third dimension to be considered, that is the depth of such policing knowledge. The following Figure 7.3 illustrates this third dimension.

Chapter 7: Knowledge-Managed Policing: Principles and Practices

Knowledge Categories

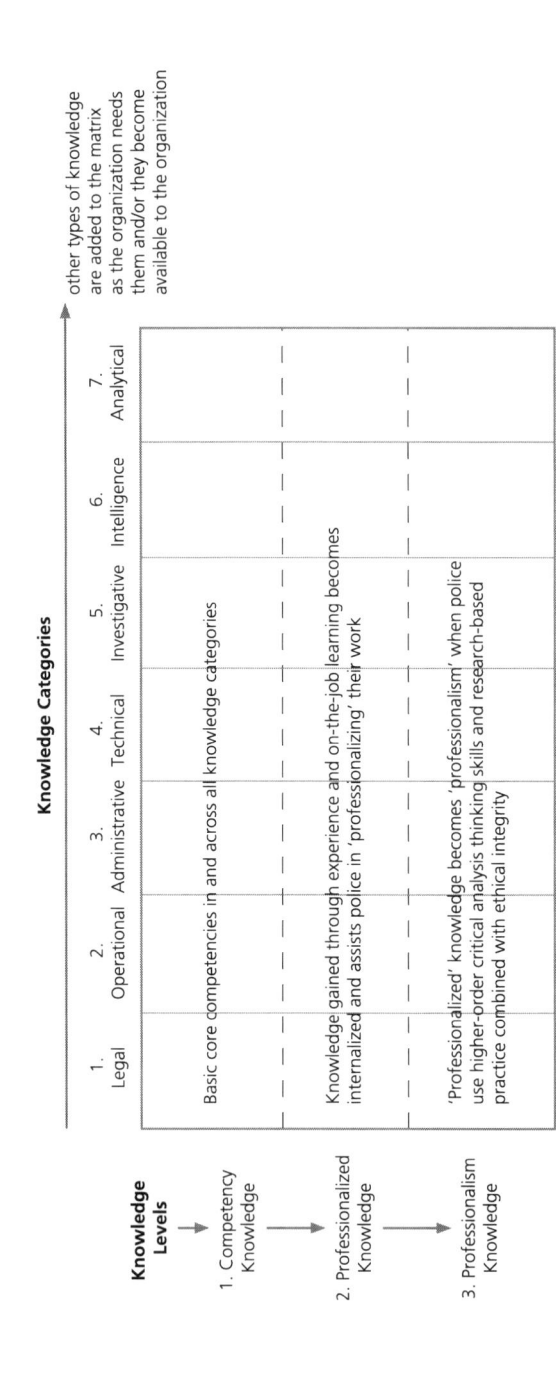

	1. Legal	2. Operational	3. Administrative	4. Technical	5. Investigative	6. Intelligence	7. Analytical	other types of knowledge are added to the matrix as the organization needs them and/or they become available to the organization
Knowledge Levels								
1. Competency Knowledge	Basic core competencies in and across all knowledge categories							
2. Professionalized Knowledge	Knowledge gained through experience and on-the-job learning becomes internalized and assists police in 'professionalizing' their work							
3. Professionalism Knowledge	'Professionalized' knowledge becomes 'professionalism' when police use higher-order critical analysis thinking skills and research-based practice combined with ethical integrity							

Figure 7.2 Matrix of knowledge categories and levels within policing

128

Knowledge Depth to Police

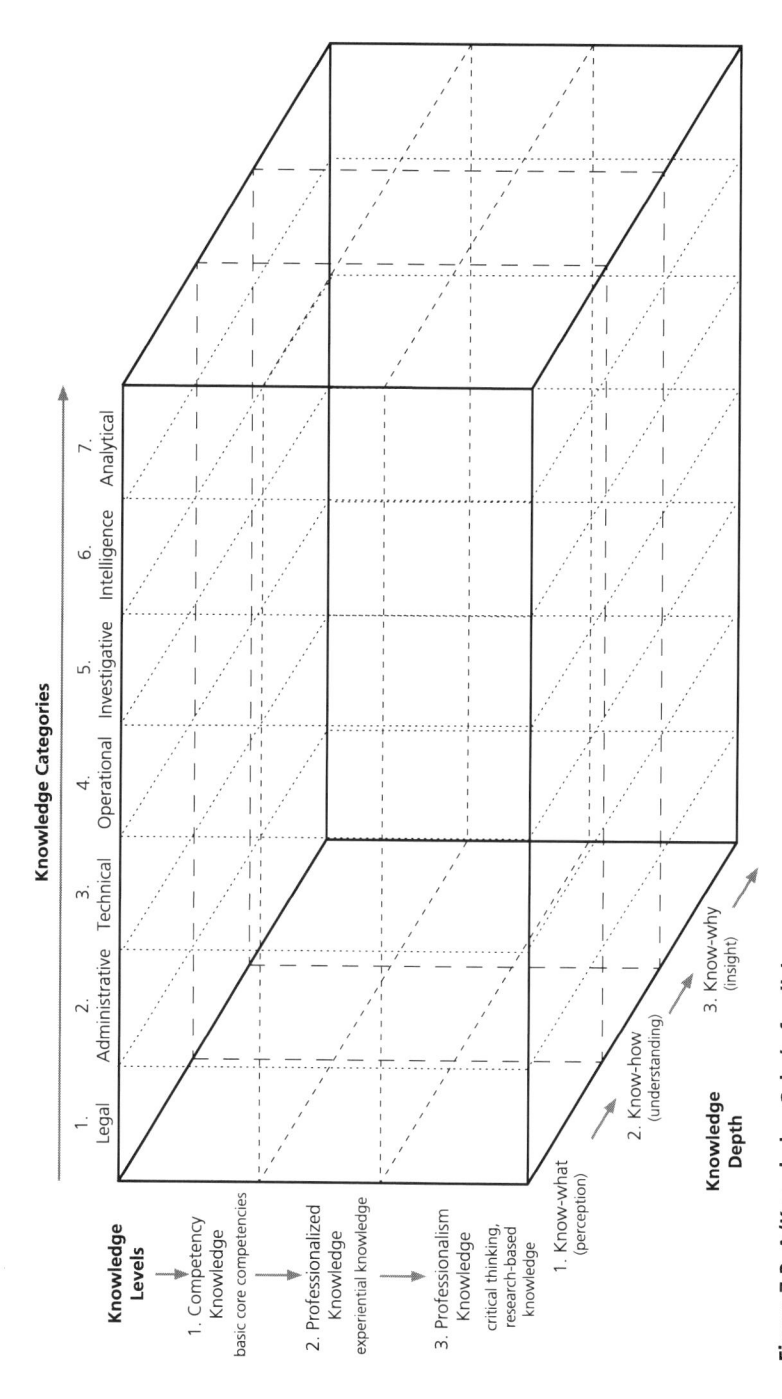

Figure 7.3 A 'Knowledge Cube' of policing

As can be seen, when depth of knowledge is added to the previous Knowledge Needs matrix, it turns into a three-dimensional 'Knowledge Cube'. It is apparent from Figure 7.3 that there is a progression to this depth of knowledge dimension, from simple *perception* to more *understanding* through to deeper *insights* about situations police officers deal with, either reactively or proactively. That is:

- *Perception Knowledge*—is 'know-what' knowledge, about what is happening and what is going on. A police officer perceives that something is going on, which might need his or her attention. The officer's knowledge is limited to perception of something happening. At this stage, the officer neither understands how the phenomenon is happening nor why it is happening
- *Understanding Knowledge*—is 'know-how' knowledge, about how to deal with the unfolding phenomenon. Such understanding is usually based on experience of similar situations over time. A police officer's knowledge is not limited to just a perception of something happening but also includes an understanding of how the phenomenon is happening
- *Insight Knowledge*—is 'know-why' knowledge, and is representative of a deeper form of understanding into a phenomenon. A police officer's knowledge extends beyond just the 'what' and the 'how' of the phenomenon's occurrence to seeking an understanding of why the phenomenon is occurring. Developing hypotheses about cause-and-effect relationships and empirically validating causality are important characteristics of 'know-why' knowledge

Police Knowledge Framework: Knowledge Cubes

In practice, the progression of a police officer's knowledge is more of a zigzagging path than a smooth transition from one knowledge level to another. For some police, all they need or want to know to do their job is a clear *perception* of 'knowing-what' is happening and going on in a situation, incident, and/or operation. However, with time and experience, police practitioners often want more of an *understanding* of situational dynamics and, therefore, 'knowing-how' to respond better to the emerging situation. In some officers this desire for understanding pushes them to learn or attain more in-depth knowledge about a particular phenomenon. Such officers will often seek to upgrade their skills and knowledge base through more advanced training and/or getting other educational qualifications. Armed with an expanded knowledge base, these officers may move onto developing tentative and deeper *insights* into 'knowing-why' the situation is happening and how it might change or develop for better or worse.

'Know-why' knowledge is the deepest form of understanding and insight into not only *what* is happening and *how* it is happening but also *why* it is happening. Such progressive deepening, in theory, should correlate with a police officer's movement down the various knowledge levels. For instance, as a police officer gets trained and educated in basic core 'competency knowledge' areas (across the knowledge categories 1 to 7) one would expect a gradual deepening of such 'know-what' (*perception* knowledge). In a similar fashion, as the internalization process of learning on-the-job takes place 'professionalized knowledge' develops. Thus, it would be expected that a police officer gradually develops more 'know-how' (*understanding* knowledge). Such understandings are based on their experiential learning in and with similar situations, jobs, and contexts. This is a particular human ability to transfer knowledge learned in one situation to solve problems in another situation.

The third knowledge level of 'professionalism knowledge' is generally achieved through a combination of higher education and a wealth of diverse and sustained experiences. Therefore, a police officer performing at this level would place more emphasis on 'knowing-why' a situation has developed the way it has and what can be done about it, as well as the likely scenarios which could result. Such insightful reflection and deeper understandings are evident in police officers striving to develop their abilities and capacities to their fullest extent.

The following Figure 7.4 contains a 'theoretical' Knowledge Cube example of the assumed correlation between the dimensions of a police officer's 'knowledge level' and 'knowledge depth' as they progress over time in experience, training, and education.

As shown, the plotting on the Knowledge Cube in Figure 7.4 is representative of the zigzagging path of knowledge acquisition. In the above example of the 'investigative knowledge' category, it is apparent that police practitioners progress from a competency-based form of knowledge in this category to deeper forms of knowledge about investigating crime. The precise path is as follows:

At *point A* there is a correlational link between an investigator's 'competent knowledge' and their use of 'know-what' knowledge at *point B*. As the investigator gains in competency *point B* changes into a new level of 'know-what' knowledge at *point C* (represented in Figure 7.4 by a deeper grey toning of point B to C within the domain of 'professionalized knowledge'). This movement from *point B* to *point C* is part and parcel of internalizing the learning-on-the-job. Over time the investigator accumulates experience and perhaps additional training, hence we would expect to see their investigative knowledge progressively deepen at *point C* and begin to move towards 'know-how' knowledge at *point D*. Not all investigators, or police officers for that matter, are necessarily interested in developing their knowledge base much deeper than this point (D). They have acquired a depth of knowledge at point D of a certain 'professionalized' level that serves them well enough in 'knowing-how' to do their job effectively and efficiently.

Therefore, the next movement in the knowledge acquisition process is from *point D* ('know-how' knowledge) to *point E* ('know-why' knowledge). Knowledge acquisition at this level requires a sustained investment by not only the investigator or police officer concerned, but also by the police organization in supporting the broadening and deepening of the investigator/police officer's knowledge base. This will usually entail a combination of advanced training and perhaps higher education.

Finally, the use of this 'Knowledge Cube' tool is not restricted to mapping out the developmental pathway of police officers' progressive deepening of their

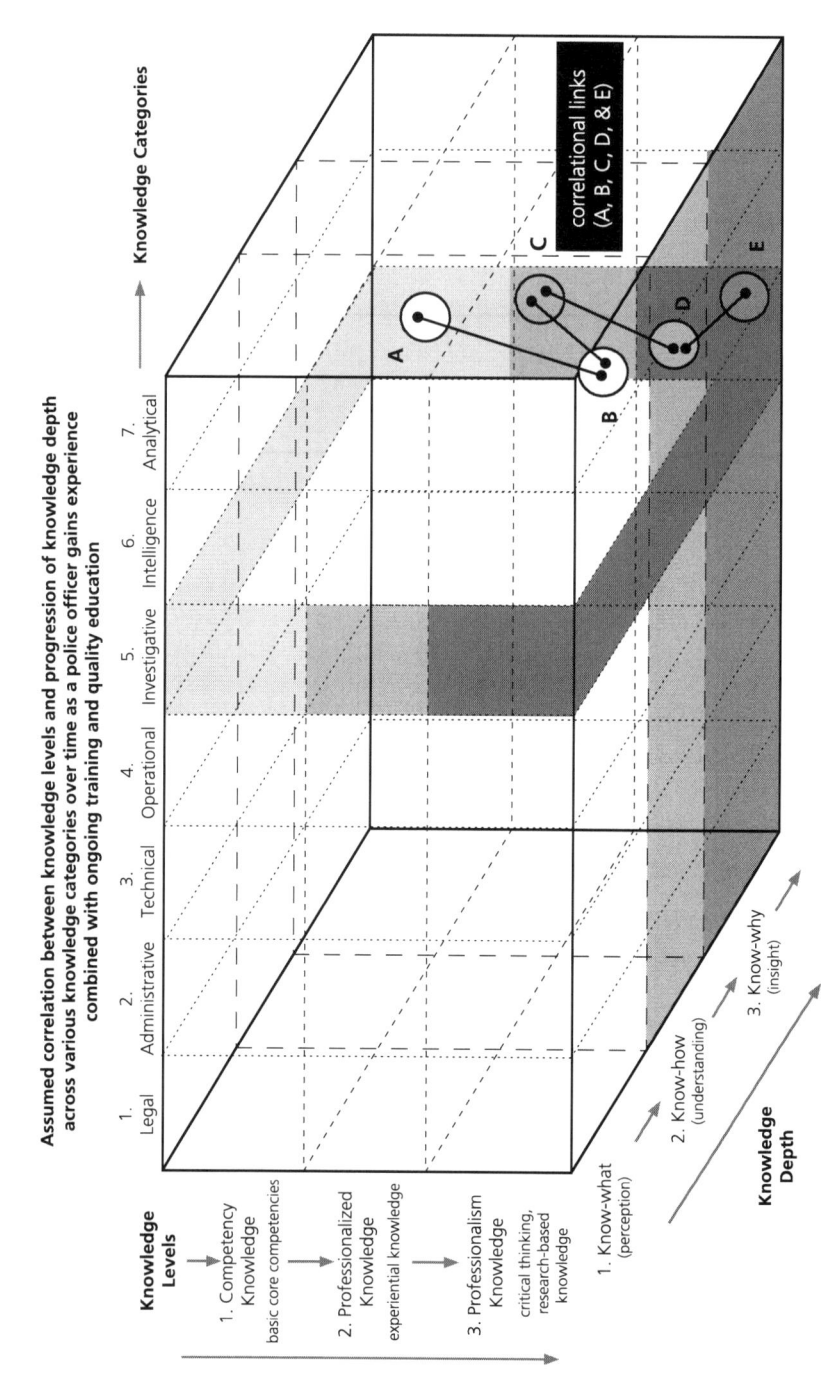

Chapter 7: Knowledge-Managed Policing: Principles and Practices

Figure 7.4 Plotting knowledge points on 'Knowledge Cube'

132

knowledge base. It has other practical relevance. This is the focus of the next section.

Case Study: Knowledge Failure of Suspected Terrorist

The case in question involves the arrest by the Australian Federal Police (AFP) of a Dr. Mohamed Haneef on charges of suspected terrorist[3] involvement in the UK in connection with incidents on 29 and 30 June 2007. Dr. Haneef, a medical doctor had been working in Australia as a temporary resident at the Gold Coast Hospital since September 2006, when he was arrested at Brisbane International Airport on 2 July 2007 at 11.05pm just before he was due to board a plane to return to India to support his wife who was in the final months of pregnancy. This case was the subject of a Judicial Inquiry into what turned out in the end to be a case of wrongful charging of Dr. Haneef. The AFP investigation into the Haneef case continues to receive extensive media criticism and as the Clarke Inquiry (2008: ix) has pointed out:

> It is understandable, given the media interest in the investigation from the start, the lengthy detention, the charging, and the spectacular and speedy collapse of the prosecution.

Hence, the case shows, amongst other things, what in our view was a clear case of knowledge failure at numerous levels of the investigation. Moreover, the focus of the subsequent Clarke Inquiry (2008) into the case was not about laying blame on the individual officers[4] involved in the Haneef affair but rather on conducting a detailed analysis of the operations of the Australian departments and agencies involved in the Haneef casel. In the words of the Clarke Inquiry (2008: vii):

> At the outset it must be said that this Inquiry was concerned with the operations of the relevant Australian departments and agencies during July 2007. It was not an investigation into whether Dr Haneef was guilty or innocent. He is, however, entitled to a presumption of innocence. Quite some time after the Inquiry began the AFP announced that he was no longer a person of interest. I do not find that surprising: I could find no evidence that he was associated with or had foreknowledge of the terrorist events or of the possible involvement of his second cousins Dr Sabeel Ahmed and Mr Kafeel Ahmed in terrorist activities.

---

[3] This case of suspected terrorism is, strictly speaking, not directly related to organized crime. However, it is nonetheless instructive for the purposes of demonstrating the utility of plotting an investigation on the 'knowledge cube' mapping tool. Furthermore, the link between organized crime and terrorism is substantial for both criminal domains derive mutual benefit from such an association, albeit for quite different motivations and aims. In this regard, Findlay (2007: 49) notes that '.... contemporary global terrorism exhibits and relies on the international enterprise networks essential for other forms of trans-national organised crime, such as drug trafficking, people-smuggling, and identity fraud'.

[4] Note: 'It is my opinion that the body of police officers involved, while never before having had to confront a crisis of the nature involved in this case, worked long hours in a thorough and dedicated way..... I interviewed a number of these officers, including some who have been singled out for criticism in the media, and I found them, almost without exception, dedicated, competent and impressive.' (Clarke Inquiry, 2008: x)

Background to the Haneef Affair

Two terrorism incidents occurred in the UK in late June 2007 that set in motion a series of events that enveloped Dr. Haneef and went on to ensnare various policing, law enforcement, and national security agencies in Australia in an unfolding crisis of dramatic significance in relation to how terrorism investigations are conducted. These UK-based incidents were:

- 29 June 2007—A vehicle containing an improvised explosive device was found in central London at about 1.40 a.m. UK local time. The Metropolitan Police Service subsequently found a second vehicle that contained an explosive device configured in a similar fashion and that had been parked about 400 metres from the first vehicle
- 30 June 2007—A vehicle (Jeep Cherokee) was driven into the front doors of Terminal One at Glasgow International Airport in UK. It burst into flames. One of its occupants, Dr. Bilal Abdulla, was arrested at the scene; the other occupant, Mr Kafeel Ahmed, suffered severe burns and was taken to hospital, where he later died

Chronology of key events in Haneef case

The table below provides a chronological sequence of the main events in the Haneef affair that are of interest to the examination of this case in relation to Knowledge-Managed Policing (KMP) and the analytical use of the 'Knowledge Cube' as presented in the previous section.

Table 7.1 Sequence of events in Haneef case[5]

Sequence	Events/(dates)	Actions
A	2 July 2007 (early morning) *MPS initial intelligence*	Counter Terrorism Command of the Metropolitan Police Service (MPS-CTC) in London contacted Australian Federal Police (AFP) Headquarters in Canberra, Australia and informed the APF that they wanted to contact Dr. Haneef urgently as he was considered to have a possible connection with the terrorist incidents in London and Glasgow. The nature of the possible connection was very unclear at this early stage of the UK incidents but the MPS-CTC thought a mobile phone subscribed in Dr. Haneef's name was of significance in the UK investigation into the London and Glasgow incidents.

---

[5] The persons involved in this case are referred to by an initial letter only. This is to restrict the identity of such persons to any further undue stress that reporting on this case may incur upon them. However, given that this personal information already exists in the public domain anyone who has followed this case in detail will be aware of the persons referred to in any eventuality.

Case Study: Knowledge Failure of Suspected Terrorist

Sequence	Events/(dates)	Actions
	2 July 2007 (later in morning) *MPS briefing in Canberra*	In-person briefing by MPS-CTC officer P on secondment to AFP in Canberra to Commander J—Manager of domestic Counter Terrorism based in AFP HQ in Canberra. The contents of this briefing reported to the Clarke Inquiry (2008: 46) is as follows: '"Officer P" said the phone had been used during the planning of and preparations for the incidents and that one of the people arrested in the UK, Dr. Sabeel Ahmed, had told police Dr. Haneef had left the phone at his (Sabeel's) home. "Commander J" said "officer P" told him the MPS-CTC considered Dr. Haneef to be their "number one most wanted person" in connection with the UK incidents and potentially a member of the group involved in the attacks. It was clear to Jabbour that locating Dr. Haneef was a high priority for the MPS-CTC at that time'.
B	2 July 2007 (afternoon) *Surveillance on Haneef*	Commander J instructed the Brisbane officer of APF to locate Dr. Haneef and put him under 24-hour surveillance. Dr. Haneef's premises located on Gold Coast and placed under surveillance. He was seen boarding a minibus bound for Brisbane International Airport.
	2 July 2007 (evening)	Local AFP officers keep Commander J in Canberra informed of developments and specifically sought his advice about what action to take when it became evident that Dr. Haneef was about to leave Australia.
C	2 July 2007 (late evening) *Decision to arrest*	Commander J considered there were 'reasonable grounds' to arrest Dr. Haneef based on information received from UK. A file note recorded at the time by one of the arresting officers stated: 'UK intelligence service has been working on this group for quite some time. The group has been using a mobile phone SIM card in Haneef's name. One of the Glasgow airport bombers has told Metropolitan Police that he has been in e-mail contact with Haneef within the last week. There has been money sent to Liverpool which has been linked to group.' (Clarke Inquiry, 2008: 49)
D	2 July 2007 (11.05 pm) *Haneef's arrest*	Dr. Haneef arrested at Brisbane International Airport. In this regard the Clarke Inquiry (2008: 52) noted that Dr. Haneef's actions in booking and attempting to board an international flight were such as to 'force the hand' of the AFP. Were it not for those actions, the AFP would probably have placed Dr. Haneef under surveillance and continued its investigation into his association with the people detained in the United Kingdom and his possible involvement in the terrorist incidents in London and Glasgow. *(Continued)*

Chapter 7: Knowledge-Managed Policing: Principles and Practices

Table 7.1 (*Continued*)

Sequence	Events/(dates)	Actions
E	3 July 2007 *Haneef interviews*	The local AFP arresting and investigating officers in Brisbane and the local Queensland police officers assisting with the investigation who had interviewed Dr. Haneef on all occasions did not accept that there was enough to charge and they were not prepared to charge Dr. Haneef formally (Clarke Inquiry, 2008: 49).
F	3–5 July 2007 *'Operation Rain'*	APF in conjunction with QPS (Queensland Police Service) started the formal investigation process called 'Operation Rain'. According to the Clarke Inquiry (2008: vii): After Dr. Haneef had been arrested the AFP and then the government—which had no intelligence supporting the existence in Australia of a terrorist cell involving Dr. Haneef—became concerned that there might be a terrorist attack imminent in Australia, as well as with the need to investigate whether Dr. Haneef was in some way involved in the UK incidents.
G	*Advice to charge Haneef from CDPP*	Commander J sought legal advice from an officer CP from the CDPP (Commonwealth Director of Public Prosecutions) who said the AFP had enough evidence to charge (Clarke Inquiry, 2008: xi). With regard to this advice, the Clarke Inquiry (*ibid*) noted: The advice given by 'CP' was obviously wrong and should never have been given. Apart from anything else, there was no evidence that in July 2006 there existed a terrorist organisation involving Sabeel Ahmed or Kafeel Ahmed. Even if there had been, there was no evidence that Dr. Haneef knew he was giving his SIM card to a terrorist organisation or knew facts that would have demonstrated that he was reckless in giving his SIM card to Sabeel. In short, the material was completely deficient in the most important respect. With respect to this CDPP officer's advice in fairness to officer CP it must be pointed out that CDPP officer: ... did not meet with the investigating team until ten days after Haneef had been arrested. At that meeting, 'CP' was informed that Haneef's SIM card had been found on Kafeel Ahmed at Glasgow airport – an inaccuracy which was corrected the following day by the AFP in the briefing paper for 'CP', but was never specifically drawn to his attention.... The AFP also incorrectly told DPP that Haneef and his cousins had shared

Case Study: Knowledge Failure of Suspected Terrorist

Sequence	Events/(dates)	Actions
		a house – expressly denied by Haneef in his interview – and suggested there was evidence of Sabeel Ahmed holding 'radical views.' (Lynch, 2009: 2)
H	Contrary advice from ASIO	ASIO conducted its own concurrent investigation of the Haneef allegations of terrorist involvement at the time and according to the Clarke Inquiry (2008: x):
		ASIO *did* have the same information and, being Australia's primary intelligence organisation in relation to domestic matters, had furnished intelligence to the AFP.
		Furthermore, the ASIO investigation came to the conclusion and documented it in writing at the time as stated in the Clarke Inquiry (*ibid*) where it surfaced that the:
		Acting Secretary of the Department of Immigration and Citizenship, Mr Bob Correll, had in his possession a document in which ASIO had said there was no evidence that Dr. Haneef had foreknowledge of or participated in the UK terrorist incidents.
		Moreover, as pointed out in the Clarke Inquiry (2008: x) the AFP material provided to the then Minister for Immigration and Citizenship, the Hon. Kevin Andrews MP, '. . . . contained information that was somewhat equivocal and, at its highest, was in complete conflict with the assertions of ASIO'.
I	12–13 July 2007 Initial UK intelligence supplied to AFP corrected	According to the Clarke Inquiry (2008: 92): The initial information provided to the AFP by the Metropolitan Police Service was that Dr. Haneef had left his mobile phone, and the SIM card, with Dr. Sabeel Ahmed. However, it was eventually corrected by the Metropolitan Police Service on 12 and 13 July. On 12 July the MPS informed the AFP that both the phone handset and the SIM card had been in the possession of Sabeel Ahmed when he was arrested—that is, the SIM card had not been in Kafeel's possession at the time of the incident in Glasgow. On 13 July the information was further corrected by the MPS, which revealed that Dr. Haneef had given to Sabeel a SIM card only and not his mobile phone handset, which he had brought with him to Australia. Also, the intelligence about Haneef being in 'email contact' and 'sending money' to a terrorist group was later corrected by MPS as wrong. *(Continued)*

Chapter 7: Knowledge-Managed Policing: Principles and Practices

Table 7.1 (Continued)

Sequence	Events/(dates)	Actions
J	14 July 2007 Decision to charge	Commander J, in spite of conflicting advice from ASIO and his subordinate investigating officers as well as the correction by the MPS that the original intelligence it had supplied to the AFP was factually wrong about the location of Haneef's SIM card and handset (which was the most crucial 'evidence' the AFP had against Haneef), still took the final decision to charge Haneef with supporting terrorism. The Clarke Inquiry (2008: xi) is most telling on this decision: My view is that, although I respect Commander 'J's' belief that he was obliged to follow the CDPP advice, Commander 'J' had formed a strong opinion that Dr. Haneef was implicated and so was more receptive to 'CDPP officer's' advice. It is my view that 'J' had become suspicious about Dr. Haneef and had lost objectivity. He was unable to see that the evidence he regarded as highly incriminating in fact amounted to very little. Had he not become so close to the case, there is a strong possibility he would have taken more notice of his investigating police officers, who had interviewed Dr. Haneef for many hours and reached the conclusion that his was a plausible story.
K	27 July 2007 CDPP drops charges	The charges against Dr. Haneef were dropped and he was released from immigration detention into residential detention. His passport was not returned (*Herald Sun*, 2009). ..... what started as a small investigation blew out, coming to involve an investigation of nearly 50 people from Perth to North Queensland and occupying the attention of many officers, from the AFP, the Queensland Police Service, other members of the Australian Intelligence Community (in particular, ASIO and the Defence Signals Directorate) and the Australian Customs Service. Clarke Inquiry (2008: xi) The AFP have estimated that the cost of the Haneef investigation and subsequent events at AUS $8.2 million as of 26 May 2008 (*Herald Sun*, 2009).

Case Study: Knowledge Failure of Suspected Terrorist

The following Figure 7.5 contains a plotting of this chronology of events onto the 3-D grid surface of a 'Knowledge Cube' as shown below.

As is evident from Figure 7.5, the various 'knowledge points' that occurred in the AFP-led investigation of Dr. Haneef reveal a pattern of knowledge competency at certain points and knowledge failure at others. For instance, it is clear that from *point A* when the initial intelligence from the MPS-CTC was received by the AFP that a competent level of knowledge (*points B, C, D*) was applied to the case that extended into a professionalized running of the investigation (*point E*) up to *point F*. This is notwithstanding the legally 'grey' decision to arrest Haneef (*point C*) in the first place. As the Clarke Inquiry (2008: vii) made clear, Haneef's imminent departure 'forced the hand' to some extent of the AFP to arrest him before the presumed intelligence supplied by the UK could be properly validated. However, at *point C* a more worrying phenomenon emerged than just the legal aspect as Justice Clarke notes:

> Notwithstanding Dr. Haneef's action in endeavouring to fly to Bangalore, India, on 2 July was capable of creating—and did create—a perception that he was fleeing the country and was probably involved in the terrorist events. In my opinion this perception coloured the entire investigation (Clarke Inquiry, 2008: vii).

This perceptual reading of Haneef's actions as those of a guilty person on the basis of as yet unsubstantiated intelligence is one of the most crucial and critical knowledge errors to avoid in the early stages of any investigation. As can be seen on Figure 7.5 *point C* is located in the legal category of knowledge at a core competency level but also it intersects with the 'know-what' knowledge depth based on initial perceptions before a fuller understanding can be obtained.

At *point G* it is evident, as noted by the Clarke Inquiry, that the CDPP was given a *black and white* picture of Haneef by the AFP which, to a large extent, determined the legal advice offered by the CDPP officer to charge Haneef. Again, note that *point G* is located at a 'perceptual' depth of knowledge only for the CDPP officer. Furthermore, it can be surmised that the CDPP officer would also have been influenced in his perception that this *black and white* picture was being presented by a reputable and therefore reliable source, Commander J from the AFP.

Finally, it is clear on the chronology table that *point H* contradicted knowledge *point G* and furthermore *point I* added even more weight against the final decision to charge Haneef, which eventually occurred at *point J* again by Commander J of the AFP. This decision at *point J* can be understood in individual terms as a loss of objectivity and an error in judgment on the part of Commander J, as noted in the Clarke Inquiry (2008: xi):

> It is my view that (Commander J) had become suspicious about Dr Haneef and had lost objectivity. He was unable to see that the evidence he regarded as highly incriminating in fact amounted to very little. Had he not become so close to the case, there is a strong possibility he would have taken more notice of his investigating police officers, who had interviewed Dr Haneef for many hours and reached the conclusion that his was a plausible story.

However, laying individual blame is not the objective of this Knowledge Cube exercise but rather understanding how and why such a knowledge failure at an individual level

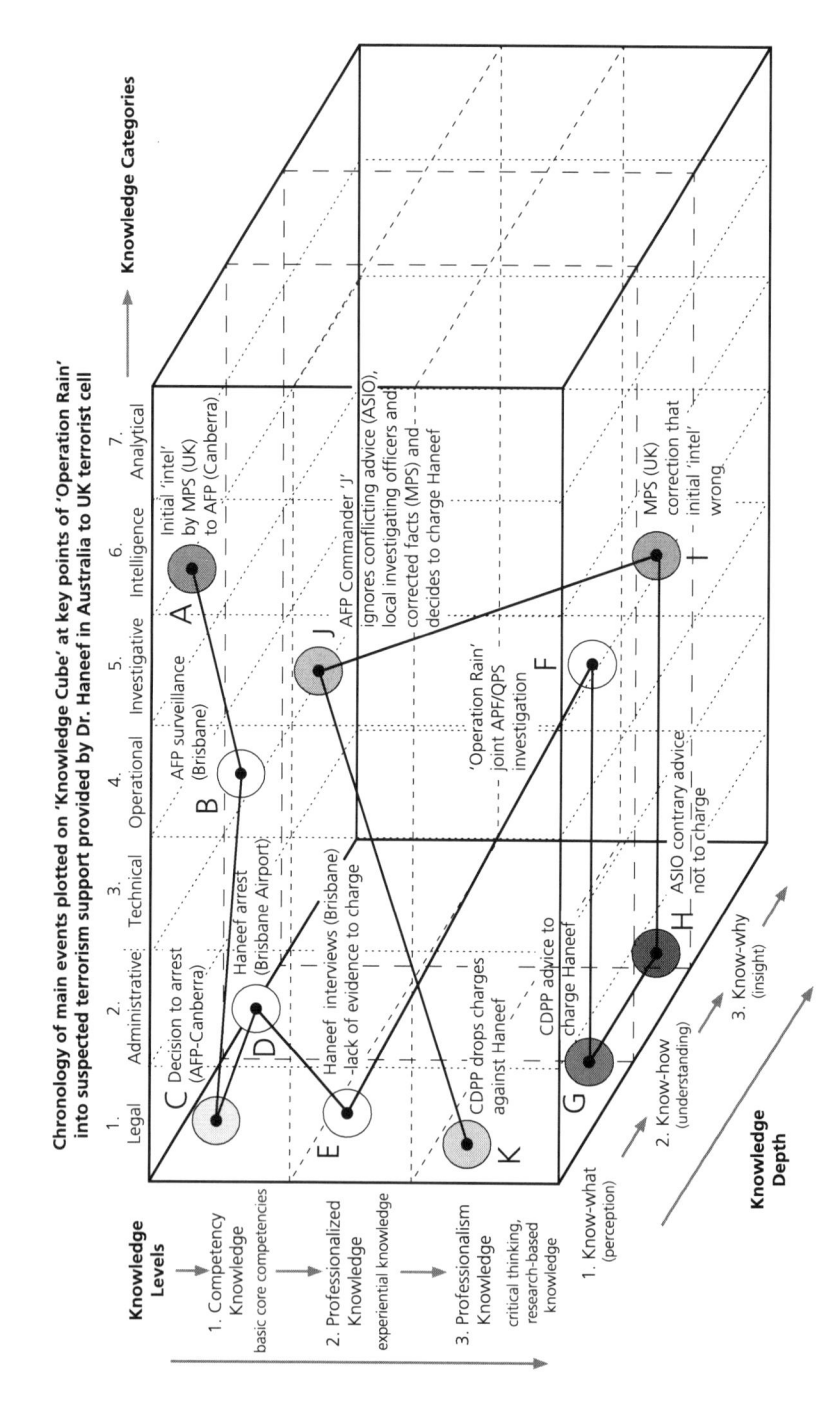

Chapter 7: Knowledge-Managed Policing: Principles and Practices

Figure 7.5 Knowledge Cube of failed terrorism investigation

140

can occur. Clearly it can be assumed that a police officer like Commander J should have a level of *experiential, professionalized knowledge* in investigations in order to be put in charge of an operation like this in the first place. Thus, why the knowledge failure at this level? Part of the answer lies in the lack of depth applied to this experiential knowledge of Commander J. As can be seen on the 'Knowledge Cube' Commander J's decisions were based only on the 'know-what' knowledge of perceptions. Such perceptual knowledge did not develop to deeper understandings or insights.

When the CDPP applied a level of *professionalism knowledge* to its original advice to charge Dr. Haneef at *point K* then it realized there was insufficient evidence to sustain such a charge. Moreover, what 'evidence' that was offered by the AFP was based on inaccurate, misleading intelligence and in some instances factually wrong information.

Perhaps, the most evident aspect of knowledge failure is at the *investigative team* level in the lack of 'reflective' knowledge applied to the case. As Clarke (2008: xi) notes:

> . . . . I record my surprise that not one of the people involved in the police investigation and the charging whom the Inquiry interviewed stood back at any time prior to the decision to charge and reflected on what Dr Haneef was known to have done. That was to give a SIM card registered in his name—a card that could have been bought for a small sum of money, even with a false name in the United Kingdom—to his cousin, who had asked for it, about 12 months before the terrorist attack. If the police officers had reflected on those basic facts they would have realised that in such circumstances the evidence demonstrating criminal intent or recklessness would have had to be very strong indeed if a conviction were to be secured. Only one person who provided a statement to the Inquiry seems to have expressed that view at the time: the CDPP specialist counsel who appeared in the bail application emphatically questioned the case. By then, of course, Dr Haneef had been charged.

Reflective knowledge of the type that Justice Clarke is talking about in the above quote is part and parcel of a university education for becoming a 'professional'. The ability to *analyse critically* and *reflect on* a given phenomenon or set of facts and to *explore in depth* the situation rather than just be content to know *what* (perceptions) is happening but not to seek to know *how* (understandings) and *why* (insights).

In sum, as the plotting of this 'Knowledge Cube' reveals and the Clarke Inquiry confirms, only a superficial level of competent legal and investigative knowledge was applied in this case and this was restricted to mainly procedural, operational, and administrative matters like the arrest and detention of Dr. Haneef. Furthermore, no-one at any point in the 'Operation Rain' investigation ever really reached an insightful depth of knowledge in the case. It is also clear that there were mistakes of detail, and an over-reliance on overseas intelligence and information that was never properly cross checked or validated. There were deficiencies in the system of judicial oversight (Clarke Inquiry, 2008: x) particularly with regard to the wrongful charging of Dr. Haneef, and finally a lack of professional refection by the key players which led to the ignoble outcome that eventuated. Perhaps the most telling insight to emerge from this 'Knowledge Cube' application is that this lack of *reflective knowledge* is a *systemic issue*. It is deeply embedded in the police culture and mentality of 'group think'. The ability to reflect organizationally on differential knowledge in a non-defensive, open-minded manner is not solely an issue at the level of individual officers.

Summary

In this chapter Knowledge-Managed Policing (KMP), which involves balancing the mix of people knowledge and systems technology to optimize a police organization's performance, was explored. The focus of the chapter was on the people side of policing knowledge.[6] To that extent, police knowledge is a combination of the quality of the training, education, and experience police practitioners carry around in their heads. At a minimum, police officers require a broad base of different types or categories of knowledge (*legal, operational, administrative, technical, investigative, intelligence,* and *analytical*) to equip them for the job. Police officers attain such knowledge to various levels from basic *competency,* to on-the-job *professionalized* knowledge, and finally to a level of *professionalism* knowledge. Professionalism involves higher-order thinking and critical analysis combined with reflective thought and merges with ethical practice and integrity. Furthermore, such knowledge acquisition involves a progressive deepening of knowledge from simple *perception* to more *understanding* through to deeper *insights* about policing serious and complex situations and crimes. These three dimensions of policing knowledge—categories, levels, and depth—were conceptualized as a 'Knowledge Cube'.

Finally, the chapter presented a case study of knowledge failure in a suspected terrorism investigation using the 'Knowledge Cube' as a practical mapping tool. The case study clearly demonstrated how, by plotting the key knowledge points of an investigation, a 3-D zigzagging path can be arrived at that shows co-occurring relationships. These relationships illustrated the *types* of knowledge utilized in the investigation along with the various knowledge *levels* involved and the *depth* of knowledge progression reached, or failed to be reached, in the case study. The most striking aspects to emerge from the application of the 'Knowledge Cube' tool to this knowledge failure case study were: firstly, the extent to which the investigative team suffered from a lack of 'reflective' knowledge about the particulars of the case. This lack of refection raises serious concerns about the existence of an ingrained 'group think' mentality in policing at a much more systemic level than just individual officers. Secondly, the superficial depth of legal and investigative knowledge brought to bear on such a serious case. Combined, these two salient features, along with others, inadvertently contributed to an ignoble outcome of knowledge failure.

---

[6] The systems technology side of policing has been extensively dealt with by two of the current authors (Dean and Gottschalk) in a companion work published by Oxford University Press in 2007 entitled *Knowledge Management in Policing and Law Enforcement: Foundations, Structures, Applications.*

8

Policing Criminal Businesses

Introduction

This chapter applies our crime business modelling framework of 'business phases' to the policing of entrepreneurially-driven organized crime groups. Initially, the chapter considers the influence of culture and market spheres on how crime groups operate their criminal businesses. Different cultures shape and structure business models. A case study of human trafficking illustrates these cultural variations in crime business models. In relation to crime markets, it is the dynamic interconnectivity of market spheres which shapes illegal business activities. A case study of business, crime, and politics in Montenegro illustrates this interconnectivity. Next, the chapter presents an application tool termed a 'Crime Business Analysis Matrix' (CBAM). This tool is designed to achieve the level of specificity required by policing and law enforcement agencies to target criminal groups effectively along the local-global crime continuum. Finally, the chapter concludes with a case study which illustrates in detail the use of the CBAM tool on outlaw motorcycle gangs (OMCGs), with particular reference to the Bandidos group in Norway.

Policing in Context

Everything has a context. A context provides a reference point to make sense of a phenomenon. Having a context in which to locate a phenomenon makes specificity possible. Otherwise, all that can be said about any phenomenon will remain full of abstraction and vague generality.

Policing is no different; it must be context-specific to be meaningful. Therefore, our business phases model of *establishing, expanding, consolidating,* and *positioning* an illegal business exists in specific contexts which, in turn, are shaped by different cultural traditions and market dynamics. There are two key contexts—culture and markets—which provide the essential focal points of reference from which to view, appreciate, and understand in a knowledgeable manner the business operations of specific entrepreneurially-driven criminal groups.

In relation to the first context—the cultural dimension of organized crime—it is clear there are important variations in cultures in different countries across the globe. Significant socio-cultural and political differences impact on legitimate businesses. Thus, it is equally the case that the same cultural variations will also impact on how criminal businesses are structured and managed in different countries.

With regard to the second context—crime markets—it is the market that makes organized crime possible. The same market forces and factors that apply to legitimate business markets are also mirrored in crime markets. As previously discussed, illegal business markets operate, to a large extent, in terms of supply and demand and the dynamics of market elasticity based on economics of scale and scope.

At a practical level, where these two key contexts—criminal cultures and crime markets—intersect is in the organizational structure that various crime groups use to operate their criminal business.

Criminal Structures

The extant criminological literature has identified a change in the criminal landscape in relation to the types of organizational structures used by criminal enterprises. As Ridley (2008: 28) notes:

> The 'traditional monolithic hierarchical structures of organized crime themselves have changed, and smaller, equally ruthless organized crime groups have become apparent forming confederations of associations based upon ethnic and linguistic affinity, and engaging in common types of criminal enterprise.

Such a trend by criminal groups away from hierarchical to more associational structures of mutual business benefit has led policing agencies, especially in the United Kingdom, Australia, and Europe, to rethink the extent and breadth of organized crime, and how best to respond to it. This in turn has led to what Ridley terms a 'reevaluated model' of how criminal groups are structured and how they operate. For example, the creation of SOCA (Serious Organised Crime Agency) in the UK in 2006 by merging NCS (National Crime Squad) and the NCIS (National Criminal Intelligence Service) as well as other elements from the immigration, customs, and security services highlights how the perception of organized crime has dramatically changed (Gilmour, 2008). For as Harfield (2008: 68) notes with the introduction of SOCA, the emphasis on dealing with 'organized crime' has changed from detection, investigation, and prosecution to 'intelligence and disruption'. This is a tacit admission that the way conventional policing is organized, especially local police forces in the UK, appears to be unable to address effectively such new developments in 'organized crime' (Harfield, 2008).

A parallel rethink and reorganization of the agencies responsible for policing organized crime in Australia also underwent a similar metamorphosis to that in the UK with the merger of the National Crime Authority (NCA) with the Australian Bureau of Criminal Intelligence (ABCI) and the Office of Strategic Crime Assessments (OSCA) to form a new agency known as the Australian Crime Commission (ACC). The emphasis of the ACC is on the collection of high-grade intelligence and sharing such intelligence in multi-agency partnership arrangements whereby other agencies like the Australian Federal Police (AFP), state police services/forces, and the Australian Customs Service (ACS) carry out the investigative work based on ACC intelligence (Australian Crime Commission, 2007).

In the EU, Europol, in its latest OCTA (Organized Crime Threat Assessment) report (2007), documents the same trend found in the UK and Australia in terms of threat level to society. The Europol analysis has moved away from hierarchical models of criminal organization to more what it terms 'oriented clusters' of criminal enterprise. The OCTA (2007: 9) report defines the concept of 'oriented clusters' as a convergence of a number of criminal groups that can be differentially structured along either hierarchical or network models of organization themselves, but which strategically join together temporarily or on a more longer-term basis, to pursue common criminal objectives:

> Single criminal groups with common objectives no longer operate in isolation and this creates a powerful convergence of criminal intentions and resource. Strategic direction for their activities can be determined by policies decided by the leaders of the most dominant criminal group or by regular meetings of the most influential representatives of the individual groups. The presence of such 'oriented clusters' that are led by, at least, coordinated by a common centre of influence is assessed as a major threat. These clusters may combine the strengths of both hierarchies and networks so that very high levels of effectiveness, diversification and specialisation can be achieved.

Such findings do not deny the existence or powerful influence of more traditional hierarchical structures of organized crime. Such hierarchical structures are exemplified by the Sicilian Mafia (or *Cosa Nostra*) (Gambetta, 1993) and derivative forms like the Calabrian 'Ndrangheta' (Paoli, 2003) and the Neapolitan Camorra (Roberti, 2008) as well as Asian variants in relation to Chinese 'Triads' (Huisman, 2008) and the Japanese 'Yakuza' (Hill, 2003). What is of interest here is the emergence of new forms of criminal organization like 'oriented clusters', 'cell-like' criminal groups, and 'loose networks' of criminals (OCTA, 2007: 9-10) that run parallel with traditional criminal hierarchies. The essential point is that all such structural variations and models of criminal organization co-exist and inhabit the same criminal underworld. Hence, the diversity of structural variations must be taken into account in any cultural and market mapping of the 'organized crime' landscape.

Business Models: Cultural Variations

The notion of a 'business model' is a concept that is problematic because it is not culture-free. That is to say, how a business operates is very much dependent upon the cultural context in which it is embedded (Siegel and Nelen, 2008). In other words, businesses in criminal markets do not operate in a vacuum. Every global illegal business must carry out its criminal profit-making activities in specific localized contexts and cultures. These localized contexts mirror the trading patterns of particular regions with their own set of historically embedded traditions and customs.

Criminal businesses share the same contextual drivers as legitimate businesses in legal markets. Therefore, these cultural variants must be factored into their operations if they want to remain in business. The only difference is criminal businesses have available to them a range of illegal business practices, such as violence and corruption, which legitimate businesses do not use or, more precisely by definition, must not use to be considered legitimate.

Therefore, the 'business phases' of *establishing, expanding, consolidating*, and *positioning* in our crime business modelling framework are 'general and universal processes' with regard to the development of any business enterprise, criminal or legitimate. However, how businesses operate in terms of a 'business model' is 'particular and specific' to their cultural context. In other words, business models are shaped by factors that exist in the context of particular countries and their specific national, geographical, and socio-cultural traditions and heritage. Given the contextual variation present in a particular country's market economy there will also be variations in the business models used in that country which reflect regional differences. There can be no single generic business model that will cover all the myriad criminal business enterprises involved in worldwide illegal market activity. The following case study illustrates this variation in business models within the global crime market of human smuggling and trafficking.[1]

Case Study: The Business of Human Trafficking

There are a number of context-specific business models operating within the global crime market trade of trafficking in people. This is a crime market of huge profitability for criminal business enterprises. As Galeotti (2005: 3) notes:

> The second most lucrative criminal business, after narcotics, is the trade in people. It is estimated that between four and five million people are smuggled each year, most want a new life elsewhere, but up to a million trafficked against their will, usually to be forced into prostitution or slavery, a trade in misery earning organised crime an

---

[1] Zhang and Pineda (2008: 42) note that the terms human trafficking and human smuggling were used interchangeably for many years in the literature with little differentiation between the two concepts. However, now the term 'human trafficking' has been accepted by the UN Convention against Transnational Organized Crime to cover both trafficking and smuggling of people.

estimated $9.5 billion in profits annually. Furthermore, it feeds into and services other vices and criminal activities. Illegal migrants may be forced into slavery at their destination, made into prostitutes or used as drug 'mules'.

It is little wonder that so many crime groups of different ethnic and cultural backgrounds are involved in this global crime business. The Transnational Crime and Corruption Centre (TraCCC) has systematically documented (Shelley, 2003) the human smuggling and trafficking of women. It involves a wide and diverse spread of criminal groups from Russia, the Balkans, and Asia, especially Chinese criminal organizations, right through to African and American crime groups.

It is clear from the research by TraCCC that there are at least six different business models operating in the global trade in people (Shelley, 2003: 123). These six business models reflect the cultural context in which they are embedded. Each illegal business model mirrors the historical and geographical realities that drive the market forces present in that cultural context for a particular national and/or regional crime group. Accordingly, Shelley (2003: 123-129) has labelled each business model of human smuggling and trafficking with reference to the main cultural context of particular organized crime groupings. The six business models are as follows:

Model 1: Natural Resource Model: Post-Soviet Organized Crime
Model 2: Trade and Development Model: Chinese Traffickers
Model 3: Supermarket Model: Low Cost and High Volume US-Mexican Trade
Model 4: Violent Entrepreneur Model: Balkan Crime Groups
Model 5: Traditional Slavery with Modern Technology: Trafficking out of Nigeria and West Africa
Model 6: Rational Actor Model: Dutch Approach to Regulation

The first crime business model views people as a 'natural resource', like oil or gas, that can be traded in a market economy. Russian crime groups are considered specialists in this type of business model (*ibid*: 123). Since the collapse of the Soviet Union and the breakdown of the economies of many post-Soviet satellite communities, women in particular, became a readily available resource which Russian organized crime groups could exploit for financial gain. The business revolves solely around recruiting women via various scams and then selling them on either directly to other crime groups or through middlemen who deliver them to markets to 'serve clients' (*ibid*). The business focus is on short-term profit with little or no concern about maintaining supply. This is presumably in the belief that scores of women will continue to be readily available. The mindset is similar to the raping of the environment through aggressive exploitation of natural resources, such as the cutting down of acres of virgin forests to supply the insatiable demand for timber with no concern for the sustainability or welfare of the environment. This 'Natural Resources' model for a crime business with its short-term, exclusive focus on profits does not reflect an integrated approach to business development. Hence, organized crime groups that are less sophisticated in a business sense and who are not adverse to the use of extreme violence and the violation of human rights would be attracted to this business model. This crime business model offers short-term profitability with little set-up costs to the business and minimum infrastructure requirements.

The second business model reflects more a 'Trade and Development' orientation. In this T&D model the emphasis is on an integrated approach to people smuggling and trafficking. That is, the organization of the business is such that it controls the trafficking process at all stages from recruitment to debt bondage and placement in a brothel. Such an integrated business structure is capable of generating very lucrative profits as well as allowing for the development of the business in the longer term. Hence, it is of little surprise to find that this type of 'T&D' business model is favoured by Chinese and Thai organized crime groups, given the long trading history of China and the fabled Chinese entrepreneurial business acumen. With respect to the 'development' side of people smuggling and trafficking Shelley (*ibid*: 124) notes 'Much of the profit is repatriated and eventually leads to further entrepreneurship throughout Thailand and southern China'.

The third business model takes a 'supermarket' approach to people smuggling and trafficking. Shelley (*ibid*: 125) notes this is a 'low cost and high volume' model exemplified by the US-Mexican trade in human trafficking in that the business maximizes profits by moving large numbers of people at a relatively cheap rate per individual to smuggle them across the US border. Hence, this is a trade that is based on large-scale supply and constant existing demand. This type of large-scale smuggling operation factors in a number of business costs, such as the fact that a certain percentage of those smuggled will be caught by law enforcement authorities, as well as the need to pay off border officials to turn a blind eye. However, the huge profits involved in such large-scale trafficking makes such opportunity costs (capture and corruption) relatively negligible. Some idea of the size of the profitability of this 'Supermarket' crime business model can be gained when one considers that in the year 2000 alone '1.8 million individuals were arrested on the border' (*ibid*). In spite of this staggering number of arrests people smuggling and trafficking from Mexico across the US border shows no signs of abating in the foreseeable future. When huge money is to be made, crime flourishes.

The fourth business model operates as more of a 'violent entrepreneur model' of people smuggling and trafficking according to Shelley (*ibid*: 126) than the other models. Balkan crime groups are the main exponents of this type of business model. The underlying instability and civil conflict that regularly flares up in the Balkan region produces conditions of vulnerability for many women who then become ensnared in trafficking. Hence, this is primarily an 'opportunistic' business model. Criminal entrepreneurs can financially exploit such regional instability as supply and demand are ever present. For instance, the Balkan region provides the supply side for trafficked women and the brothels of Western Europe provide the constant demand side of the business equation. Very substantial amounts of money are generated from the highly profitable sex markets of Western Europe. In this context, Balkan trafficking groups act as middlemen for organized crime groups particularly from Eastern Europe who control much of the prostitution market for the rest of Europe. However, as Shelley (*ibid*: 126) points out Balkan crime groups are not simply content to play a middleman role but also use extreme violence to move into and take over existing markets in Western Europe and the UK from other crime groups. In fact, violence is regularly used in all stages of their trafficking operations not only against competitors and law enforcement personnel who get in the way of their business ventures but also against trafficked women and their family members in the source countries of the Balkan region (*ibid*). Given the huge profits to be gained from sex trafficking, it is unsurprising that Balkan crime groups will use excessive violence to get and maintain their market share. Certain aspects of the T&D model of human trafficking used by Asian crime groups, particularly the Chinese, can also be found in the 'violent entrepreneur' model. For example, Balkan crime groups use profits from the trafficking trade '. . . to finance other illicit activities at home and for investments in property and trade businesses domestically and abroad. The money is returned through wire transfers and cash carried by couriers to the home country' (*ibid*: 127). This type of re-investment strategy is typical of a more integrated approach to managing a crime business.

The fifth business model is based on a 'traditional slavery' approach to human smuggling and trafficking. However, it uses modern technological means to exploit the vulnerabilities of young girls and uneducated women. Shelley (*ibid*) identifies Nigeria and West Africa as the prime sites for this type of human exploitation. This model exemplifies, perhaps more than the other business models, the significance of the cultural context for understanding the operations of organized crime. As Shelley (*ibid*) notes, 'Using female recruiters who conclude contracts with girls and women by manipulating voodoo traditions, they are able to force compliance through psychological as well as physical pressure'. Nigerian organized crime groups have melded modern transport links and sophisticated technologies with such tribal customs in order to exploit uneducated women. As a result, African trafficking has risen tremendously in Europe since the late 1990s. A worrying aspect according to Shelley (*ibid*) of this rapid rise of Nigerian organized trafficking is that such groups have diversified into other illegal activities and are now regarded as '. . . . multi-faceted crime groups, in which the trade of women is only one part of their criminal activities'.

The sixth business model which is termed a 'Rational Actor' model is directly associated with the Dutch approach to organized crime groups involved in human smuggling and trafficking. As Shelley (*ibid*) explains:

> The model, as employed in the Netherlands, presumes that the brothel owner is a rational businessman and seeks to maximize his profits. In response, a licensing system is established whereby the local government sets the conditions by which brothels operate. Regular controls by multidisciplinary teams are held to check the compliance with these criteria.

Therefore, this model is not so much a business model for an organized crime group but rather an administrative response model of law enforcement in that, to deal 'effectively' with sex trafficking, law enforcement has essentially 'decriminalized' it. This administrative approach to human trafficking is similar to what the Dutch have also done with the illegal drug trade. Such an administrative approach works so long as a crime group can see it is in their financial interests to 'cooperate' with the law enforcers (police, public officials, city councils) and still make a tidy profit. Hence, it becomes a 'rational' business decision by a crime group to accept a regulatory framework if this means they are left alone by the authorities to run their 'decriminalized' business. The fly in the ointment here, of course, is that such a regulatory approach by the authorities can only work in a context where prostitution is decriminalized. It is a legal regulation model whereby the state takes over the role of regulating the sex industry market. The assumption for this regulation model is that this will reduce some of the worst aspects of the criminal element in the market, such as violence and violation of human rights towards trafficked women. Hence, under such a legal regulation or administrative approach to organized crime, the law enforcement role changes from one of investigation to inspection. For countries that continue to criminalize the sex industry such a regulatory approach to human trafficking would be of limited value.

Market Spheres: Dynamic Interconnectivity

There are 'global spheres of influence' (see Chapter 2) in market economies with a dynamic interconnectivity to reshape how markets operate. Markets are driven by a range of push-pull factors which cause various market spheres to 'balloon' out in importance, relative to other spheres, at particular times and in particular global contexts. The point is such dynamic reconfiguring and reshaping of global spheres of criminal market activity, as they balloon in and out under the pressure of various push-pull factors, present opportunities for entrepreneurial criminal initiatives and also for law enforcement intervention. In other words, the dynamic interconnectivity of criminal market spheres can act as a two-edged sword, in that real-time dynamics operating in various spheres can both expand criminal business entrepreneurialism as well as slash crime businesses through properly targeted law enforcement activity.

Global crime always involves multi-layered market spheres (*economic, social, technological, political*, and *environmental*) which are played out in localized contexts. Therefore, the key to policing organized crime effectively is to use market dynamics as an intervention strategy. The knowledge task is picking *which* global market spheres to target for *what* crime groups, *when* and *where* and *under what 'local' market circumstances*. Such strategic targeting produces a disruptive influence 'ripple effect'. Most police/law enforcement intervention occurs at a local level; therefore, logic dictates there must be localized multi-agency and multi-disciplinary involvement to deal with the global business reach of organized crime. Police must involve themselves in strategic partnerships. This is a subject of crucial importance taken up in the next chapter. Our purpose in this chapter is to locate together our 'business phases' framework with the drivers and push-pull factors inherent in crime market spheres. The aim of this co-location is to achieve the level of specificity required by policing/law enforcement executives, managers, practitioners, and other government agencies to target criminal groups effectively along the local-global crime continuum. The following Figure 8.1 is suggestive of the interrelationship possibilities between crime business phases and criminal market spheres.

As can be seen in Figure 8.1 there is a list of several of the main push-pull factors. These factors exert influence in and through the five key spheres (*economic,*

Market Spheres: Dynamic Interconnectivity

Key Business Phases and Global Spheres of Criminal Market Activity

Criminal Market Activity

Economic Sphere — Opportunity costs of Business
- 'Invisible hand' of the market

Social Sphere — Supply/Demand
- Increasing social polarization
- Continuing social & economic inequalities

Technological Sphere — Business Efficiencies
- Developments in market globalization
- Development of digital technologies
- Sophistication of criminal activities

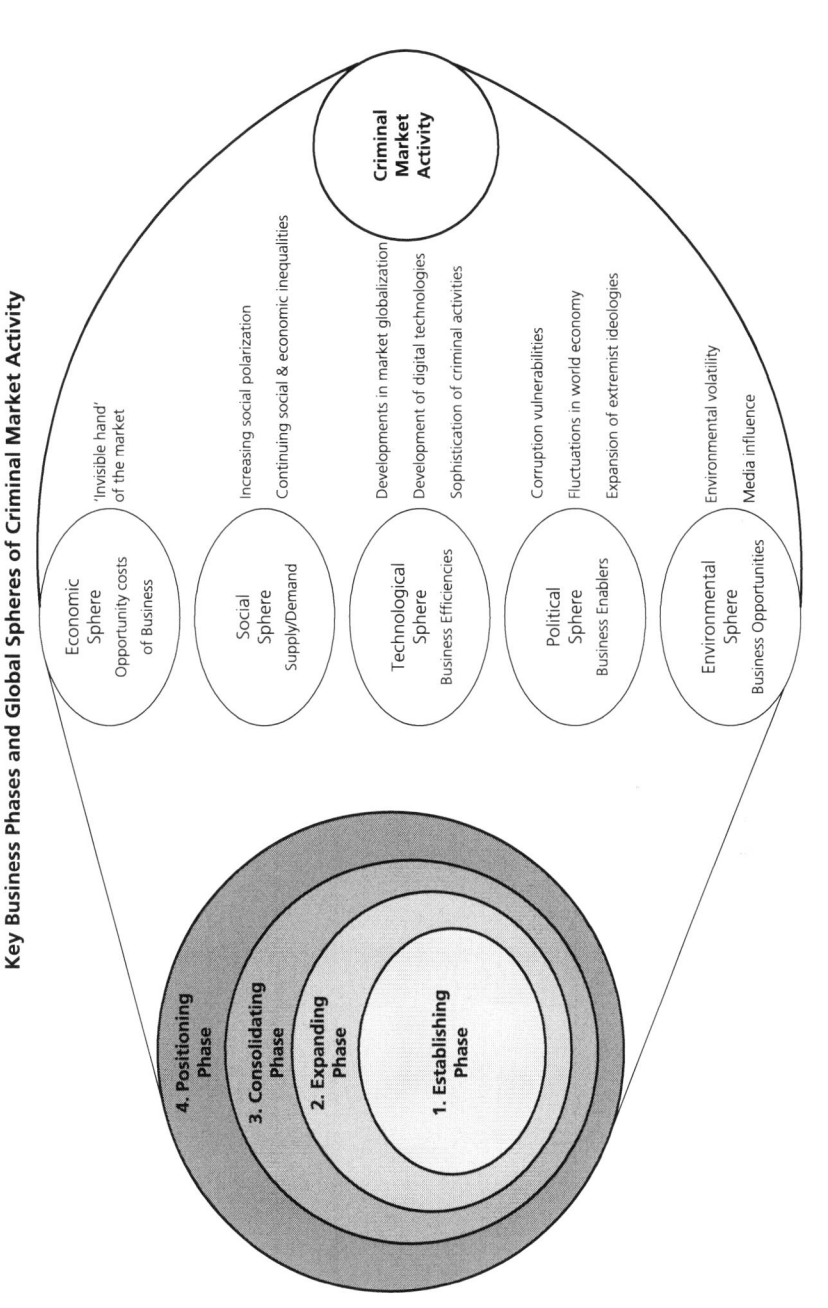

Political Sphere — Business Enablers
- Corruption vulnerabilities
- Fluctuations in world economy
- Expansion of extremist ideologies

Environmental Sphere — Business Opportunities
- Environmental volatility
- Media influence

4. Positioning Phase
3. Consolidating Phase
2. Expanding Phase
1. Establishing Phase

Figure 8.1 Interrelationship of crime business phases to criminal market spheres

Chapter 8: Policing Criminal Businesses

social, technological, political, and *environmental*) identified in the organized crime literature. The above diagram is relatively self-explanatory. Moreover, each of its component parts—business phases and criminal market spheres—have been discussed at length in Chapter 2. The following case study about criminal market activity in Montenegro and the ballooning out of the political sphere as a result of certain push-pull factors is a further illustrative example of the interrelatedness of criminal entrepreneurialism and market spheres.

Case Study: Business, Crime, and Politics in Montenegro

Milo Đukanović, Montenegro's Prime Minster, was one of NATO's most important allies in the Kosovo-war. Đukanović emerged on the political scene in 1990. Đukanović served three consecutive terms as Prime Minister from 1991 to 1998 (1991–1993, 1993–1996, and 1996–1998); he was then President of Montenegro from 1998 to 2002 and Prime Minister again from 2003 to 2006. Although Đukanović chose to step down in late 2006, he returned to office as Prime Minister in February 2008. His coalition won the 2009 early election with an absolute majority, securing him a sixth term in office (<http://en.wikipedia.org/wiki/Milo_Dukanovic>, 2009). Đukanović was instrumental in Montenegro's increasing separation from Serbia, culminating in the victory at the 2006 independence referendum. He has become a national symbol of independence (Guardian, 2003).

In 1999 US President Bill Clinton invited Đukanović to Hotel Elephant in Ljubljana, Slovenia, to show appreciation for his courage and loyalty to the NATO alliance. It was widely reported at the time that during these friendly conversations, Clinton found it necessary to also discuss Đukanović's affiliation with cigarettes (Guardian, 2003). In the 1990s, illegal cigarette smuggling was seen as a way of helping the republic survive the effects of war and sanctions levelled against the regime of the former Yugoslav President, Slobodan Milosevic, and Đukanović, who was a close ally of Milosevic during this period. However, when Đukanović sided with NATO against Milosevic he gained a certain degree of 'political insurance'. At that time Đukanović was probably seen as too important a player for the NATO alliance to pursue the illegal cigarette smuggling allegation. In Montenegro under Đukanović the illegal cigarette smuggling market was expanding.

In July 2003, the Italian prosecutor's office in Naples named Đukanović as a linchpin in the illicit tobacco trade which used Montenegro as a transit point for smuggling millions of cigarettes across the Adriatic Sea into Italy and into the hands of the Italian mafia for distribution across the EU (Guardian, 2003). Đukanović is formally under investigation in Italy for alleged involvement in cigarette smuggling. According to reports by the Italian Customs Police and Financial Police, *Guardia di Finanza*, the Prime Minister's former associates were also being investigated. The information from the official reports was first published by the Italian newspaper *La Repubblica*. The accusation was contained in a report based on a year-long investigation which included transcripts of bugged telephone conversations between Đukanović and Italian mafia. Furthermore, Italian media and western diplomats in the Balkans reportedly said: 'It can be seen that Milo Djukanovic was in charge of monitoring the activities of the organisation led by Paolo

Savino.' Mr Savino is a senior figure in the Camora, the Naples-based mafia. Another news agency, the French, AFP, said the investigation was opened after a key witness involved in the smuggling ring came forward and provided information on Đukanović and his associates. In an interview, the Prime Minister stated that he did not know why an investigation has been launched against him and said he was 'ready to do everything to establish the truth' over allegations that he has been involved in cigarette smuggling. La Repubblica said investigators had been told Đukanović would not be protected by diplomatic immunity as Montenegro did not have diplomatic representation abroad.

Cigarette smuggling is a serious problem for Italy, with $2 billion to 3 billion in potential tax revenue being lost every year, according to treasury officials. Montenegro is considered a key part of the tobacco smuggling route from the former Yugoslavia to Italy, with ships carrying contraband cargo across the Adriatic for distribution throughout Europe. Everyone who visited the Balkans after the outbreak of the war in the early 1990s could not avoid seeing street sellers of all ages offering cartons of Marlboro for no more than $8.00. In London, like most other EU countries with high taxes on cigarettes, the price at that time for a carton of cigarettes would have been considerably higher—at least ten times this amount.

The operation of this crime business works on wholesale dealers who buy the cigarettes directly from the producers on the global market. The goods are delivered to one of Europe's two free trade zones, Rotterdam in the Netherlands or Zug in Switzerland. From there the cigarettes are sent via a corrupt third country like Egypt or Lebanon to Montenegro. From Montenegro's ports the cigarettes are smuggled 'back' across the Adriatic Sea into Italy and into the hands of the Italian mafia for distribution across the EU. Companies, like the Montenegrin Tabak Transit, allegedly controlled by Đukanović, taxed the transit with $30.00 per carton. This taxation business made Đukanović annual profits of tens of millions US dollars and still the cigarettes could be sold to smoking EU-citizens for about half of the normal price.

It is clear from this case study that various push-pull factors operating in the global political sphere assisted in maintaining and developing a profitable crime business in the illegal tobacco trade. It is also evident that other global spheres of influence, such as social, economic, and environmental, were involved in the expansion of the illegal cigarette smuggling in Montenegro. These market spheres allow organized crime to flourish when unusual circumstances like war and other volatile environmental conditions exist. The cultural antecedents in Montenegro helped to shape and define the way this particular crime business model operated.

Operational Knowledge Framework: Crime Business Analysis Matrix

The four Chapters 3, 4, 5, and 6, which comprised Section 2 of this book, contain a series of hypothetical scenarios of various crime groups at each phase (*establishing-expanding-consolidating-positioning*) of criminal business

Chapter 8: Policing Criminal Businesses

development. These crime group scenarios were constructed using a 'fuzzy' mapping tool developed by the principal author (Dean). These fuzzy maps assist police in analysing the business profile and performance of crime groups as they develop over time through each phase of *establishment, expansion, consolidation*, and *positioning* of their illegal business activities. In this section, these four business phases are combined into one matrix configuration. This matrix diagram provides a holistic graphical analysis of a crime business across its entire business development lifecycle. The following Figure 8.2 contains this Criminal Business Analysis Matrix (CBAM) diagram.

As can be seen, down the left-hand side of the matrix are the five key entrepreneurial capabilities[2] for a particular crime group. Whilst, the bottom axis contains the business development factors associated with each capability at each phase of *establishing, expanding, consolidating*, and *positioning* of the crime business.

This CBAM tool works as an analytical and strategic planning application for policing organized crime groups. It does this by evaluating the relative strength (*fuzziness factor*) of each business factor associated with a particular entrepreneurial capability for the specific crime group targeted for police/law enforcement assessment. Naturally, police knowledge of how strong a specific business factor is for a particular crime group may not be very accurate in this initial evaluation. This could be due to insufficient information or poor intelligence about a particular group and their business factors. Given this knowledge gap, it is still a very worthwhile assessment exercise to make some initial 'guesstimates'. The point is that such knowledge should be continually updated as new intelligence comes to hand thereby increasing the accuracy level of the data.

A primary benefit of using this CBAM tool is that it trains police and other law enforcement practitioners *to think holistically in a business-like manner* about how organized entrepreneurial criminality works, as a profit-making business in a crime market. Policing practitioners and law enforcement executives get better at hypothesizing about criminal businesses by using this CBAM tool. Furthermore, by continually updating the accuracy levels of various business factors then potential possibilities for intervention become 'seen' on the CBAM diagram. Such visualization makes the task easier to plan multi-agency and multi-disciplinary operations strategically to disrupt and dismantle selected business factors for particular crime groups. The following case study illustrates the use of the CBAM application with 'Outlaw Motor Cycle Gangs' (OMCGs) and with particular reference to the Bandidos group in Norway.

---

[2] It should be noted at this point that it would be a rare 'individual' crime entrepreneur who possesses all of the five core entrepreneurial capabilities to a similar level of competency. Hence, what is assessed is the 'collective' strength of each entrepreneurial capability for the crime group as a whole—be they a group of business-oriented criminals working independently or as part of an alliance of criminal groups in a network, syndicate, or cartel arrangement.

Operational Knowledge Framework: Crime Business Analysis Matrix

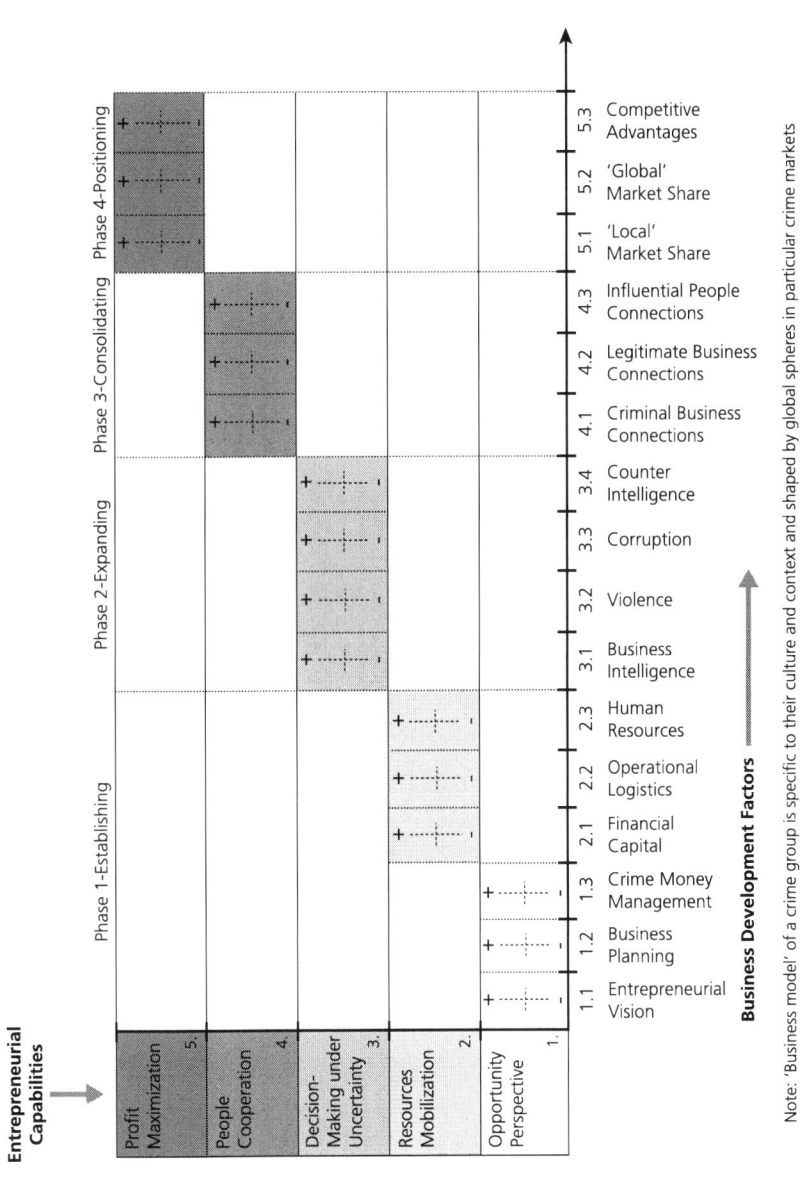

Figure 8.2 Criminal Business Analysis Matrix for policing organized crime groups

Note: 'Business model' of a crime group is specific to their culture and context and shaped by global spheres in particular crime markets

155

Case Study: Outlaw Motorcycle Gangs—Bandidos in Norway

This case study of OMCGs will firstly provide a brief overview of the crime business profile of this global organized crime group. This will be followed by a description of some of the more prominent types of OMCGs before presenting an example of the application of the CBAM as a knowledge tool for policing an OMCG, the Bandidos, in Norway.

Crime business profile

The origins of Outlaw Motorcycle Gangs (OMCGs) date back to post World War Two in the 1940s of the United States of America. The first Hells Angels Motorcycle Club was formed in 1948 with its original chapter in California (Abadinsky, 2007).

Interestingly these motorcycle clubs were formed as a social outlet for bored ex-military personnel who were trying to adjust back and fit into civilian life after the horrors of the Second World War (Richter, 2000). Hence, from the very beginning these clubs provided a social milieu for an alternative, military-style mateship and camaraderie.

Somewhere over the last half century this alternative motorcycle lifestyle became derailed into a general lawlessness and has now developed into a highly organized criminal enterprise. Interpol lists a trio of American OMCGs—the Hells Angels, Bandidos, and the Outlaws—as being the big international movers and shakers in the illicit drug trade. The Hells Angels are the largest OMCG with some 1,800-patched members and several thousand associates spread over 22 countries (New Zealand Police Association (2006c: 71).

Outlaw Motorcycle Gangs (OMCGs) are involved in the trafficking of multiple types of drugs, and specific drug activity tends to depend on the geographic region. That is, the distribution of drugs in a given geographic area reflects the preferences of the drug consumers in that area. For example, while marijuana and cocaine are the main drugs used in Canada and the USA, the demand for amphetamine is primarily in Scandinavia, Australia, and New Zealand. In fact, there is some evidence that methamphetamines are the new drug of choice, certainly in so far as New Zealand is concerned:

> ... a new and more potent form of 'ice' (methamphetamine hydrochloride), which comes in a crystal rock form and is specifically manufactured in China for the New Zealand 'pipe' market. The 'rock crystals' are sold individually or in five-rock bags. ... One South Island officer told *Police News*: 'Gangs aren't really interested in dealing cannabis any more, it's all about dealing meth these days because its easy to conceal and our staff have trouble locating it', he said (New Zealand Police Association (2005: 12–13).

Nevertheless, OMCGs as a club and OMCG members individually will generally deal in any drug that provides a source of income. After all, the aim is to make money no matter how.

The main business strategies used by OMCGs are violence and corruption. The OMCGs use violence as a tool in order to control their criminal networks and intimidate rivals (Richter, 2000). Intimidation as a business tactic does not stop at their competitors but also extends to law enforcement, the police, and court system. For instance, potential witnesses in gang trials are intimidated and tactics are used to disrupt or delay judicial proceedings. For example, in Canada:

> By 1998, the Hells Angels had become so powerful that they were intimidating prosecutors, police officers, journalists, jurors and judges. Some police officers refused to work on cases associated with the gang, fearing gang reprisals against them and their families (New Zealand Police Association (2006a: 66).

In terms of operational logistics for their crime business, the main OMCGs, for instance the Hells Angels and their rivals the Bandidos, tend to use smaller, less powerful gangs as their 'intermediaries' or distribution agents for illegal drugs. Such lower-level street gangs are known as 'puppet' gangs. For instance, in Canada:

> Hells Angels Nomads used 'puppet' gangs, such as the Rockers, the Evil Ones and the Para-Dice Riders, to do their intimidation, bombings and retribution. These 'puppet' gangs, as they were known, paid a 10% tithe (of their monthly earnings) to the Hells Angels. The Hells Angels would collect the money at monthly meetings called 'le messe' – (in French) 'the mass'. Gangs in Australia and New Zealand, operating in similar vein, are known to call their Sunday meetings 'church' (New Zealand Police Association (2006a: 66).

Clearly the business advantage of using 'puppet' gangs to carry out criminal acts on behalf of the big OMCGs is to insulate themselves from prosecution.

Estimates vary as to the extent of the profit derived by OMCGs with regard to their illegal business activities, especially the illicit drug market. Some indication of the multimillion dollar business empire of globally-connected OMCGs can be gauged through various reports. For instance, 'The FBI estimates that the annual income of the Hells Angels' worldwide operations is US $1 billion'. (New Zealand Police Association (2006a: 67). Moreover, the United Nations estimates the illicit drug market to be worth more than US $400 billion worldwide (Moran, 2002: 5).

Furthermore, the cost to the community of the illicit drug market has reached staggering proportions. For example:

> A conservative estimate prepared for former US President, Bill Clinton, during his time in office, said that the cost to America was approximately $400 billion a year. A similar study in Australia three years ago, said that the cost to Australian taxpayers of illicit drugs was estimated at $1.7 billion (New Zealand Police Association (2006a: 68).

Types of Outlaw Motorcycle Gangs

There are a multiplicity of locally-based motorcycle gangs associated with the big three OMCGs—the Hells Angels, the Bandidos, and the Outlaws. Depending on the country, various local brands or clubs have emerged. For instance, in Canada, OMCGs go under labels like the Rockers, the Evil Ones, Satan's Choice, and the Para-Dice Riders to name but a few (New Zealand Police Association (2006a). By contrast, in Australia, local variants are the Finks, the Vipers, as well as the main gangs, the Bandidos, Outlaws, and Hells Angels (CMC, 2000). In New Zealand, there are several local gangs most notably, the Mongrel Mob and Black Power, as well as an assortment of other gangs like the

Chapter 8: Policing Criminal Businesses

Epitaph Riders, the Outcasts, the Forty-Fives, the Southern Vikings, Satan's Slaves, Sinn Fein, The Lost Breed, the Road Knights, Highway 61, Head Hunters, and the Lone Legion gangs (New Zealand Police Association, 2006b).

Two of the most influential OMCGs are the Hells Angels and the Bandidos. For example, the Hells Angels are considered the primary producers and distributors of illegal drugs within the United States. They have been identified as involved with marijuana, methamphetamine, cocaine, hashish, heroin, LSD, PCP, and diverse pharmaceuticals.

On the other hand, the Bandidos are more expansive in their outlook and consequently use their worldwide network of chapters to distribute marijuana, cocaine, and amphetamine. Frequently, the retail distribution of drugs is normally handled by hang-arounds, prospects, and support clubs, with Bandidos members normally distributing at the wholesale level (National Alliance of Gang Investigators Association (NAGIA), 2005). This means that the OMCGs are seeking control over existing criminal networks and subordinates. Such control is maintained by intimidation and violence.

The Bandidos, also called the 'Bandido Nation', is a fast growing outlaw motorcycle club with 100 chapters in the United States, 90 chapters in Europe, and another 20 in Australia, 8 in Southeast Asia, and 1 in Latin-America (Bandidos, 2009). In total, 218 additional chapters are currently in the process of setting up new shops in Russia and other Eastern European countries (*ibid*). The Bandidos are organized by local chapters, with state and regional officers, as well as a national chapter made up of four regional vice presidents and a national president. The Bandidos also have a large number of 'support clubs'. These groups usually wear reverse colours (gold border with red background rather than the Bandidos' red-border-and-gold background). They also commonly wear a 'support patch' consisting of a round patch in Bandidos colours on the front upper left of the colors (vest), as worn by the member. Most of these clubs are regional (*ibid*).

Application of CBAM: Bandidos in Norway

A recent example of the Bandidos in Scandinavia can be found in the southernmost parts of Norway. In the city of Kristiansand the local police have, since 2004, received information on how the locally based Bandidos[3] chapter is gradually trying to take control over the amphetamine market in the region. The local Bandidos chapter in Norway became a full member in 2003. It did not take the newly formed local chapter long to begin to flex its muscles towards the local amphetamine dealers. They were given a clear message from members of the newly established club to either sell the amphetamines supplied by them or they would claim a 20 per cent tax from all they sold (Norwegian Police University College, 2008). The message was followed up by a wave of violence and threats towards a substantial number of drug dealers in the region. The police received detailed information on how this activity went on and also on how the activity was linked to the formal structures in the Bandidos organization. Hence, it is clear this Norwegian-based chapter of the Bandidos was in expansion mode for its illicit drug market crime business.

---

[3] It should not be assumed that all of members of this local Bandidos chapter are necessarily involved in criminal activities and the drug trade. Some members of OMCGs are simply in it for mateship and love of bike riding.

Case Study: Outlaw Motorcycle Gangs—Bandidos in Norway

The following Figure 8.3 represents an analytic mapping based on police reports, empirical research, and available open sources of this local Norwegian Bandidos crime group. This data allowed the Bandidos' expertise in applying their entrepreneurial capabilities to various business development factors to be assessed and hence to construct the CBAM below.

As can be seen, Figure 8.3 is divided[4] by thick dotted lines into the four business development phases of *establishing-expanding-consolidating-positioning* of a crime business as it develops over time.

In this example we have also marked out the expansion phase in a different tonal shade. We term this area a 'blue zone' because it is the point at which a crime group comes to the attention of the police to such an extent that the crime group gets noticed. As mentioned previously, the nature of illegal business activities by organized criminality is generally hidden from public view. It is this invisibility of crime groups that gives them a competitive advantage against policing, as such crime groups are often able to keep their activities below the police radar. However, when they use violence and intimidation then a 'blue zone' attention point registers with the police or other law enforcement agencies. For instance, this study will illustrate how such a 'blue-zone' was registered by the local police when the Bandidos started to interfere with the previously established balance in the criminal market in the Kristiansand region. These 'eruptions' of violence and threats of violence were picked up by the local police who analysed them correctly as important 'awareness indicators' of the ongoing rivalry between competing criminal groups for market share.

Hence, how a crime business develops depends, to a large extent, on the type of business choices made during these phases in the lifecycle of an illegal business enterprise. Such choices are based on and conditioned by several factors. Some of these factors are external to the business, like the operating context of a crime market environment as well as cultural influences and political considerations in the countries where crime groups have a base or in which they operate. Such externalities can be considered as macro-level factors that influence a crime business. Thus these external, macro-level factors permeate down into business choices made at a more internal or micro-level as depicted by the range of business factors on which a crime business develops, as shown on the horizontal axis of Figure 8.3. Furthermore, the key drivers behind the development of a criminal business enterprise are the entrepreneurial capabilities of a crime group at each phase in the development of the illegal business. Hence, each business phase of the Bandidos in Norway is examined in detail with regard to the type and nature of the business development model implied.

Establishing phase

Certain assumptions have to be made depending on at what phase of development a crime business is in when it comes to the attention of police for closer scrutiny. Hence,

---

[4] These dotted line separation points are conceptual rather than actual. That is to say, to aid analysis it is conceptually useful to draw a distinction at these points between how the various business development factors relate to each of the four key business phases in theory. In reality, it can be assumed that how these various business development factors operate is more interlinked and chaotic than shown on the CBAM.

Chapter 8: Policing Criminal Businesses

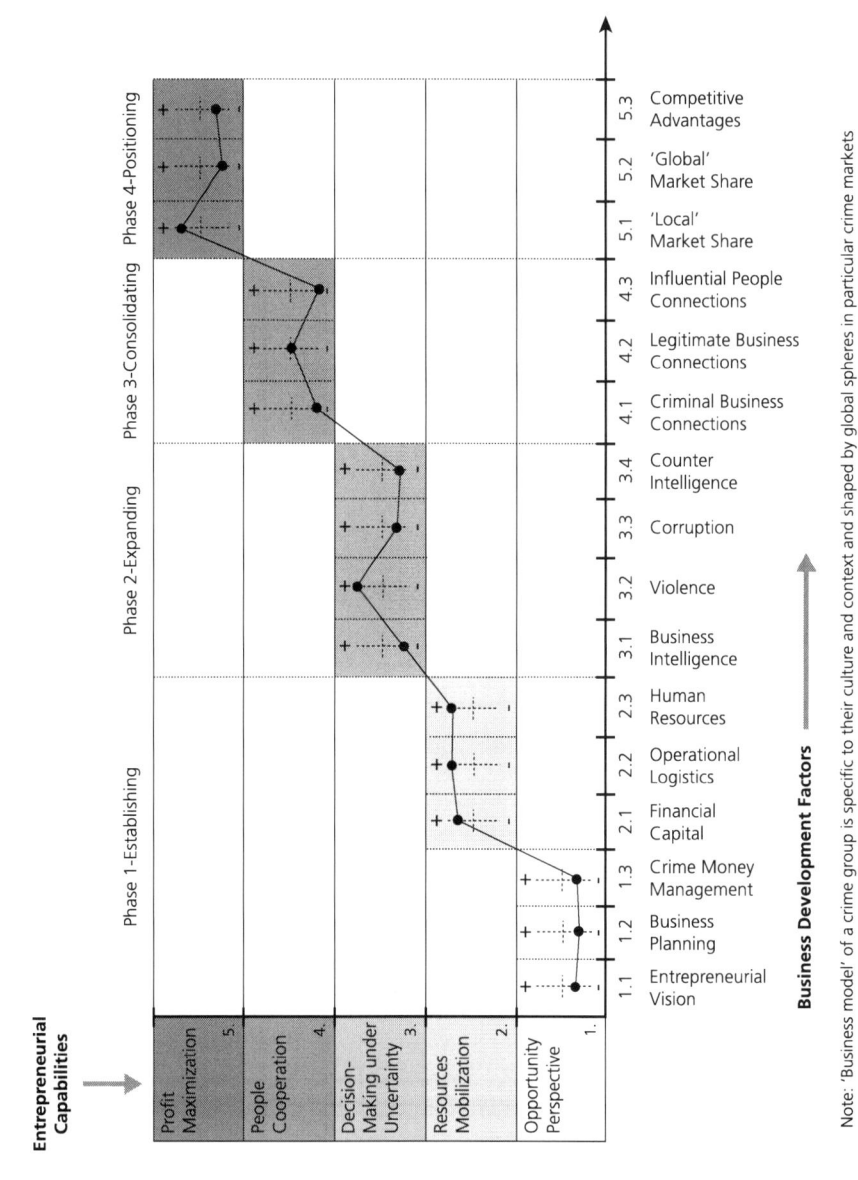

Figure 8.3 Application of CBAM tool to Bandidos crime business in Norway

Note: 'Business model' of a crime group is specific to their culture and context and shaped by global spheres in particular crime markets as with any business enterprise there are a set of pre-existing capacities and capabilities contained within any working group by virtue of its composition and access to resources. The same holds true in so far as the Bandidos crime group is concerned in this case study. At the time of coming to police attention, the Bandidos crime group had already established itself in the illegal drug trade and was now in 'expansion' mode. Hence the fuzzy scaling evident on Figure 8.3 for this first phase of *establishing* the crime business is based on the following assumptions.

Opportunity perspective—with regard to this initial entrepreneurial capability within the Norwegian branch of the Bandidos crime group it is assumed that a moderate low level of *entrepreneurial vision (1.1)* is involved in its desire to expand its illegal drug business. Such strong-arm tactics are a well-worn method in the criminal underworld for increasing one's market share by removing rivals. Hence, it is hardly a new or original entrepreneurial vision. The motivation for the Bandidos to consider muscling in on the operations of rival drug dealers would appear to be out of pure greed to increase their money-making capacity rather than any significant display of depth to their entrepreneurial vision.

Furthermore, it can be assumed that there must be at least a minimal level of *business planning (1.2)* involved in taking control over the amphetamine market in the Kristiansand region in the southern part of Norway from rival drug dealers. The level of planning is rated as low given that their entrepreneurial idea is simply to stage a hostile takeover where necessary from rival dealers. Hence, there is little need for a sophisticated business plan involving a complicated set of tasks and activities. Given such an uncomplicated business plan, it is also most likely that the Bandidos would not have devoted much more than a cursory look at doing anything different from the usual way this crime group *manages its crime money (1.3)*. That is, other than how much more profit it expected to 'bank' and 'clean' from its expansion takeover.

Resources mobilization—in relation to this second entrepreneurial capability, since the Bandidos have a pre-existing illegal drug enterprise which it can be assumed returns them reasonable profits then they would probably have sufficient *financial capital (2.1)* already available to them to run the planned takeover operation without having to look elsewhere for money. Hence, this business factor is rated as relatively high for working capital.

In terms of working out the *operational logistics (2.2)*, to make the planned takeover happen this is also rated as relatively high. The rationale here is that like most OMCGs the use of strong-arm tactics is something the Bandidos excel at and even specialize in to a large extent. The Bandidos in Norway would also benefit from such 'reputational violence' market branding strategy by OMCGs.

Moreover, given the simple business plan to take over by force if necessary the operations of rival drug dealers in the Kristiansand region of southern Norway it can be assumed that in relation to the *human resources (2.3)* needed then it would be Bandidos members themselves involved. Thus, this crime group would have the necessary staff internally to carry out in theory a successful takeover expansion of the illicit drug market trade. Hence, the high rating given in terms of having the capability already available to them for expansion.

Expansion phase

With regard to the 'expansion' phase proper an interesting pattern or fuzzy assessment is evident as can be seen on Figure 8.3 for each of the four business development factors used to evaluate this phase of business modelling.

Decision-making under uncertainty— this entrepreneurial capability is the key driver behind an expansion strategy for a criminal business enterprise. The business development factors available for crime business expansion are *business intelligence, violence, corruption,* and *counter-intelligence.*

In terms of *business intelligence (3.1)*, as can be seen on Figure 8.3 by the relatively low rating on fuzzy scale for this business factor, it appears that the use of *business intelligence* about their crime competitors does not appear to be any more sophisticated than establishing that their rivals are ripe for 'taking over'.

However, with regard to the use of *violence (3.2)* as a viable business option for expanding a crime business a very different picture emerges. It is clear that this local Bandidos crime group readily employs such a violence option as indicated by the high rating given on the fuzzy scale for this business factor. Hence, it would appear that this Bandidos group 'positively' values violence as a means of expansion of its illegal drug market as well to control its competitors through intimidation and fear. Of course, such a 'positively' high assessment does not imply there is anything 'positive' in terms of being optimistic or affirmative about violence from a societal perspective.

What is analytically interesting is this strong assessment of the level of violence this local Norwegian Bandidos group is prepared to use. For instance, as depicted on the CBAM in Figure 8.3 above, in terms of this third entrepreneurial capability, decision-making under uncertainty, this Bandidos group uses violence as the business strategy for 'expanding' its business enterprise as it would probably have used for 'establishing' it. That is, using the business option of *violence* is generally used by crime groups to 'establish' a foothold in a crime market and if this is done by an already existing criminal organization like the Bandidos, this continued use of violence is considered as part of an 'expansion' phase.

In fact, this local OMCG crime group continues to use violence as its preferred *modus operandi* to such an extent that it does indeed spill over into the conceptually different domain of 'expanding' its crime business. Hence, it can be reasonably assumed on the basis of its continuing use of violence that this local Bandidos group does not *see* or *recognize* or maybe even *ignores* the need to vary its business strategy when it comes to a different evolutionary point in developing its crime business.

This is a very salient finding as it implies a less sophisticated approach to business development by this local crime group. Hence, one would expect this local crime group to continue to use violence as the preferred option across all four key business phases. Furthermore, one can also surmise that the use of violence by this local Bandidos group will get more extreme if it runs into any opposition to its business plans to take over and/or expand its crime market in drug dealing. Such suppositions are borne out by subsequent events in terms of this local Norwegian Bandidos group chapter of this global OMCG. After the local Norwegian police in Kristiansand started an open investigation into the Bandidos and subsequently charged the local president and most of the members with almost 30 violent crimes during a seven-week period the use of violence towards victims and witnesses by the crime group dramatically escalated.

This escalation was entirely predictable by this group as the option to use violence appears to be the only business option this local chapter of the Bandidos relies on in all circumstances. Clearly, violence works for them. It was successful again at the level of intimidation of victims and witnesses. For although the local Kristiansand case against the Bandidos was relatively clear and straightforward evidentially, when it became time for court the case collapsed since many of the most important victims and witnesses refused to give evidence. Subsequently, the president was cleared and the members who were convicted did not receive anywhere near the level of punishment requested by the prosecution service. Thus, it seem like the Bandidos were successful in not only establishing but also expanding their drug business in southern Norway.

As for the use of *corruption (3.3)* as a business option at this 'expansion' phase, given that the Bandidos are 'muscling in' and 'taking over' a share of their competitors' slice of the illicit drug market it seems unlikely that the Bandidos would need or have little use for exercising corruption, as indicated by the low rating on the fuzzy scale. It appears from all accounts that violence is the business option of choice for the Bandidos in this part of Norway.

The final business factor for this expansion phase is the use of *counter-intelligence (3.4)*. The low rating for this business factor is very similar to that for the use of business intelligence. It would seem the Bandidos did little if any *counter-intelligence* towards the local police in Kristiansand because, not surprisingly, the police did pick up threats of violence in the 'blue-zone' of the CBAM and possibly they also analysed them as 'awareness indicators' of an expanding criminal business organization.

Consolidation phase

It is clear from the previous discussion of the expansion phase, that the Bandidos crime group, at the time of writing, is firmly located at this junction in its criminal business enterprise development. Therefore, the assessment of the business factors associated with this next consolidation phase is of necessity more speculative in nature. However, given the Bandidos group's distinct business trajectory that has become apparent in the previous business phases it is unlikely that such a trajectory will alter much under this consolidation phase, or indeed the next phase of positioning its crime business. In other words, the fuzzy patterning evident across the 'high' and 'low' business factors seen so far on Figure 8.3 is likely to continue across the remaining two phases of business development, unless some exceptional circumstance occurs in the foreseeable future to alter the business profile already set for the Bandidos. Thus, with regard to the third consolidation phase, the key entrepreneurial capability it involves is people cooperation.

People cooperation—this entrepreneurial capability contains three business factors that all revolve around 'making connections' with different types of people and at different levels for facilitating further criminal business development.

The first level of connectedness concerns making *criminal business connections (4.1)* through forming alliances and networks based on mutual assistance. It would appear that this Norwegian Bandidos group saw little point in working cooperatively with its rivals. It relied exclusively on violence to get what it wanted rather than wasting time building mutual trust and cooperative relationships. This is arguably its Achilles heel. Thus, as indicated in Figure 8.3, on the fuzzy scale this business factor is assessed as very low in terms of cooperating with criminal rivals.

By contrast, the next business development factor, that of using *legitimate business connections (4.2)* to further this local Bandidos group's expansion plans, attracts a slightly higher rating at the mid-point level on the fuzzy scale. The reason for this is that using legitimate business connections and structures is a favoured business strategy that Bandidos chapters in other countries engage in quite substantially (Nicholas, 2006; *The Australian*, 2007). Hence, a case can be made that the local Bandidos chapter in Norway would certainly be aware of this business option even if it has not as yet exploited it to its fullest potential. However, further police intelligence in Norway is needed to confirm the use and extent of this business strategy. Thus a mid-range rating is a reasonable assumption at this point in time.

The third and final business development factor that of making *influential people connections (4.3)* is given a low rating on the fuzzy scale for the local crime group as it seems unlikely that these Norwegian Bandidos would either need or want much in the way of influential leverage to pursue their strong-arm takeover plan of rival drug dealers in the local region of Kristiansand.

Positioning phase

This final phase is an interesting one to profile from a business development point of view for this local Norwegian Bandidos crime group, in that what works for a business at one level may not work at another level. As the business trajectory of the Bandidos clearly illustrates in Figure 8.3 they have successfully expanded their illegal drug business mainly through the use of violence. Their business development has been this almost exclusive 'one-factor' approach to establishing, expanding, and consolidating their crime business. Hence, one would not expect the Bandidos to be different in this final phase of *positioning* their crime business for future survivability.

Profit maximization—as can be seen on Figure 8.3 there are three business development factors ('local' market share; 'global' market share; and competitive advantages) associated with this final entrepreneurial capability at this crime business positioning phase.

The first business development factor involves ways to position a crime business so as to increase its *'local' market share (5.1)*. Clearly the Bandidos takeover of rival drug dealers in the local context of the Kristiansand region in southern Norway was highly successful as indicated on the fuzzy scale for this business factor.

However with regard to the second business development factor, that of *'global' market share (5.2)*, it is salient to recall the example noted earlier where the court case against the president of this local Bandidos chapter in Kristiansand on violence-related charges collapsed owing to important victims and witnesses refusing to give evidence after being subjected to fear and intimidation by members of the Bandidos.

Under further analysis, this example of 'success' by the local Bandidos crime group in beating the police charges through the use of extreme violence as their preferred and only business option in dealing with all opposition can be read another way.

From a global market share perspective, the use of unrestrained extreme violence can also be understood as having the potential to bring this 'local' chapter into conflict with its 'global' organization. That is, its strong preference for violence, both towards outsiders and insiders, can also be its undoing, not only internally, but also with regard to its global masters. For instance, uncontrolled violence can make it appear as a 'rogue' OMCG in so far as the global Bandidos network is concerned. For, not long after the failed court case in Kristiansand, a massive conflict broke loose in the local Bandidos chapter. In part, this conflict was seen as retribution towards some of the members who appeared to cooperate with the police investigation. These members were punished for having been 'too cooperative' in the ongoing police investigation at the expense of the president and other members. Settling 'scores' by violent behaviours is, of course, a traditional means of reasserting one's control in the criminal underworld. However, the conflict is still not settled and the newly established chapter is now officially 'frozen' (Norwegian Police University College, 2008).

One can only speculate about how much this unsightly eruption of external and internal displays of extreme violence by the local Norwegian chapter of the Bandidos was influential in its 'freezing' by the global 'Big Brother' OMCG organization of the Bandidos. For instance, in New Zealand in 2006 a violent gang clash broke out between the Hells Angels and a local gang, the Mongrel Mob, in Wanganui. The gang fight erupted to such an extent that police in the Armed Offenders Squad raided the respective headquarters of the rival chapters. The OMCG leadership was not pleased since the policy of most OMCGs is not to draw public attention, especially police notice, to themselves:

> The emphasis for today's gangs is on being as covert as a Diplomatic Protection Squad officer's vest. That's why the gang stoush in Wanganui between the Mongrel Mob and Hells Angels will not have gone down well with the leadership of the Hells Angels in particular, because it has again raised their profile at a time when they have been working hard to lower it (New Zealand Police Association (2006c: 71).

In fact, a cogent argument can be made that the over-use of violence by the Norwegian chapter of the Bandidos, apart from raising its profile to an unwanted level, actually works against it as well in terms of the business development of its criminal enterprise, not only 'locally' but more importantly from a business positioning of its crime business for 'global' market outreach. The basis for this argument can be seen in the 'under-use' of the other three business development factors at this 'expansion' phase of its crime business, namely in the low use of the factors of *business-intelligence (3.1)*, *corruption (3.3)*, and *counter- intelligence (3.4)* that are associated with this entrepreneurial capability of decision-making under uncertainty.

Hence, in terms of a rating for this second business development factor to do with increasing a crime group's 'global' market share it is evident that this local Bandidos chapter can only receive a low score of the fuzzy scale at this point in time. Clearly, the local Bandidos in Kristiansand have done themselves no favours 'globally' in the way they have behaved with unrestrained violence and intimidation as their only business option for all situations. Moreover, in the light of this pattern it would also appear to be the case that the local Bandidos are not that interested in expanding into the global illegal drug trade at any significant level anyway in the foreseeable future.

The third and final business development factor, that of *competitive advantages (5.3)*, as can be seen on Figure 8.3, is again rated as relatively low for similar reasons as the last business factor discussed about the local Bandidos disadvantaging themselves in relation to a global market presence. As noted on several occasions the sole reliance on the business option of violence, while giving a competitive advantage at the local level, is problematic in the long term as a strategy for both local and global positioning of a crime business.

To conclude, the overall picture that emerges from the application of this CBAM tool of the local Norwegian chapter of the Bandidos, as a part of a global OMCG, is one of a relatively unsophisticated crime group. This lack of sophistication is evident in a number of its entrepreneurial capabilities and limits this local crime group to any further expansion of its illicit drug business beyond a certain point in its chosen criminal market business. Essentially, its over-reliance on expressive violence was at the expense of other business factors that it could judiciously have used to grow its crime business without attracting all the troubles it did from the police and its 'big brother' global organization.

Finally, the utility of this CBAM application is twofold. Firstly, such a matrix design is capable of capturing the knowledge of a crime business in terms of specific business factors and their entrepreneurial significance with regard to a crime group's actual business capabilities. Secondly, the matrix provides a holistic profile about how such a crime group travels over time in relation to the development of its crime business. Combined, these two advantages give police and law enforcement organizations a highly competitive edge against organized crime groups.

Summary

This chapter applied the 'business phases' framework, presented in Chapter 2, to policing entrepreneurially-driven organized crime. The key influences of culture and market spheres on criminal business development were discussed in detail and supported with case studies.

Different cultures shape and structure business models. Such cultural variation in business models is evident in human smuggling and trafficking. Shelley (2003) identified six such business models of human trafficking. They were: the *natural resource* model of post-Soviet Russia; the *trade and development* model of Chinese traffickers; the *supermarket* model based on US-Mexican trade; the *violent entrepreneur* model of Balkan crime groups; the *traditional slavery using modern technology* model coming out of Nigeria and West Africa; and finally the *rational actor* model in the Netherlands that is more a Dutch policing approach based on a regulatory model.

In relation to crime markets, global crime relies on the use of multi-layered spheres of influence—*economic, social, technological, political*, and *environmental*—to gain and maintain a foothold in localized criminal contexts. The dynamic interconnectivity of these spheres was evident in the ballooning out of the political sphere in Montenegro as a result of certain push-pull factors in that cultural context. This in turn allowed organized criminal entrepreneurialism to spread like a virus into other countries.

Finally, this chapter presented the operational utility of combining the 'business phases' framework with the entrepreneurial capabilities and related business factors of crime groups. This resulted in an application tool, termed a Crime Business Analysis Matrix (CBAM). The CBAM tool takes into account the cultural and contextual factors, noted above, which impact upon how criminal business models work in various countries and across various crime market spheres.

CBAM operates as a knowledge management system by incorporating emergent forms of criminal organizational structures like 'criminal co-operatives' (Klerks, 2003), 'oriented clusters', 'cell-like' criminal groups, and 'loose networks' of criminals (OCTA, 2007). These emergent criminal structures co-exist alongside more traditional criminal hierarchies, yet all inhabit and feed off the same global criminal landscape.

Furthermore, the CBAM application as a knowledge management tool captures policing knowledge of a crime group's actual entrepreneurial capabilities in relation to specific business factors used to develop their crime business over time. This knowledge capture is represented in 'fuzzy maps', which reveal points of strength and vulnerability in the business profile of a crime group. The chapter concluded with a detailed case study of an Outlaw Motorcycle Gang—the Bandidos in Norway—using the CBAM application tool. The overall picture that emerged of the local Norwegian chapter of the Bandidos was one of a relatively unsophisticated crime group. Their lack of entrepreneurial sophistication limits this crime group's illicit drug business and exposes their vulnerabilities, to such an extent that it is unlikely their crime business will grow much beyond increasing their local market share.

9

Future Policing of 'Organized Crime'

Introduction

This final chapter brings together a number of thematic strands and their implications for policing organized crime. Initially, the chapter reviews the definitional difficulties associated with 'organized crime' and how it has morphed into a continuum of criminal forms. It then looks at the current UK experiment with using a whole-of-government, joined-up, multi-agency approach in dealing with 'organized crime' and its variant forms. Next, the chapter develops further the essential idea behind this book; which is, knowledge is a value-adding resource that provides policing with competitive advantages in the 'knowledge war' against entrepreneurially-driven criminal groups. In this regard, the chapter introduces a strategic knowledge framework based on sector policing. In this knowledge-driven strategy of sector policing the relative quantum of knowledge is the contingency factor that determines the optimal strategy police and law enforcement should adopt in the knowledge battlefield with organized crime. The later part of the chapter focuses on the array of intervention strategies (civil, criminal, and market-based) available to combat entrepreneurial crime. The problematic issue of 'knowledge sharing' between and across policing, law enforcement, and government agencies is discussed in terms of new developments with integrating *emergent* and *engineering* approaches to sharing knowledge. The final section deals with the key factors of *politics, law, culture,* and *capacity,* which can either enable or disable international cooperation in policing. The book concludes with some speculative thoughts on charting out the future direction of policing illegal business entrepreneurialism.

Morphing of 'Organized Crime'

Defining what 'organized crime' is has bedevilled politicians, police, academics, and governments for decades (Rawlinson, 2008; Lampe, 2008; Abadinsky, 2007; Leong, 2007; Grennan and Britz, 2006; Reichel, 2005; Lyman and Potter, 2004; Albanese, 2004). As the now retired Deputy Director General of the National Criminal Intelligence Service (NCIS) in the UK put it '"Organised crime" is distinguished as a term in common daily use, behind which lies at least four decades of failed attempts to arrive at a single satisfactory definition' (Gaspar, 2008: 18). No-one is any closer to agreement. In its absence police operate on less than adequate definitional versions for legal purposes. Legal framing of what is believed to constitute 'organized crime' highlights some key characteristics but inevitably misses others.

This definitional dilemma, in part, is due to the way 'organized crime' morphs into other forms of criminality that have different labels. For instance, some forms of commercial crime like insider trading, or fraud can be labelled as 'economic' crime; others use the label of 'white-collar' crime or 'enterprise' crime. Furthermore, if a fraud occurs outside the borders of a country or 'between countries' it can be labelled as an 'international crime' (Gaspar, 2008: 8). Moreover, to add another layer of confusion, if the fraudulent activities 'flow over national boundaries' it can also be properly regarded as a 'transnational crime' (*ibid*). Even if such finer points of delineation between 'international' and 'transnational' can meaningfully be made, such attempts are largely futile because these terms are used almost interchangeably in the literature. Alternatively, this 'international/transnational' fraud can rightly be considered as a 'global' crime. In the case of the infamous Nigerian scams such fraud is also labelled as 'organized' crime. In the UK it is likely to attract another label as being a 'serious crime' as well as being an 'organized' crime. Then there are 'environmental' crimes like illegal timber logging which is, alternatively, 'serious', 'transnational', 'global', and an 'organized' crime depending on who is doing the categorical framing and legal defining of this type of 'crime'.

Some academics deal with this definitional quandary over 'organized crime' by locating it under a more inclusive label like 'enterprise' crime. Siegel (2008: 280) defines the label 'enterprise' crime as 'crimes of the marketplace'. He includes 'organized crime' under *marketplace crimes* along with 'white-collar' crime and 'cyber' crime. Furthermore, Siegel (*ibid*) defines the common link between these three distinct categories of 'enterprise' crime (white-collar, cyber, and organized crime) as 'crimes of illicit entrepreneurship'. Moreover, Siegel (*ibid*) defines the distinguishing feature between 'white-collar' crime and 'organized' crime as turning on whether or not the people, institutions, and/or organizations involved in illegal activities for the 'acknowledged purpose of profit' did so through 'legitimate business transactions' (white-collar criminals) or through 'illegitimate business enterprise' (organized criminals). Since Siegel defines 'cyber' crime as involving people 'using the instruments of modern technology for criminal purposes' he presumably lumps *cyber crime* under the 'enterprise crime' label. It is hard to imagine how *white-collar* and *organized crime* could function without using the 'instruments of modern technology' for their 'criminal purposes' (*ibid*).

To base a definitional distinction of crime types (*white-collar* and *organized*) on a legitimate/illegitimate dichotomy of business activity is a hair-splitting exercise that confounds the definitional predicament even more. As Robinson (2000: 28) points out, organized criminal groups have no reason to rob a bank anymore, they can simply buy one. For instance, 'Russian "businessmen" are believed to have several thousand IBCs and banks registered in Niue'. In fact, the government of Niue now offers banking licences to anyone:

> For under $20,000, you can buy your very own Niue-authorized financial institution, which, as one brochure touts, 'provides access to the international credits market, as well as to the international mutual funds market and the securities market, [and] allows the bank to conduct FOREX transactions and, with minimal expense, to solve problems of liquidity.' At least three company-formation agents easily located on the World Wide Web offer such banks for sale and list branch offices in Moscow and St. Petersburg (Robinson, 2000: 28).

The usefulness of a distinction based on legitimate verses illegitimate business activity has long been superseded by white-collar and organized criminals. Moreover, as Smith (1974: 10) pointed out more than two decades ago the 'business' of 'organized crime' operates on 'the same fundamental assumptions that govern entrepreneurship in the legitimate marketplace: a necessity to maintain and extend one's share of the market'. Furthermore, the 'business' of crime is not a local issue anymore, it is global. Arnaud De Borchgrave from the Centre for Strategic International Studies notes: 'As legitimate business understood and adjusted to the complexities of the new global marketplace, so did international criminal organizations.' (Robinson, 2000: 13). For instance, according to Robinson (2000: 337) 'Drug trafficking now accounts for 2 percent of the world's economy'. The Serious Organised Crime Agency (SOCA) in the UK broadly estimates that the economic and social costs of serious organized crime, including the costs of policing it, is upwards of £20 billion a year (SOCA, 2006/7).

Hence, whatever the term 'organized crime' means 'definitionally', in a conceptual sense it is clear that it exists on a continuum of business criminality. Such a criminal business continuum will range from 'local' criminal entrepreneurs seeking to start up in a crime market to established entrepreneurially-oriented crime groups. Some criminal entrepreneurs will specialize in particular illicit goods and services. Others will diversify across various legal and illegal market sectors to position their illegal business activities strategically on a 'global' scale.

To fight the variety of morphing forms 'organized crime' transforms itself into along this local-global criminal continuum requires a fresh way of thinking.

New conceptualizations, inventive innovations, and bold experimentation are needed in policing to combat entrepreneurial criminality. Whatever innovations come forth, hard decisions and dedicated commitment to the long road ahead on the part of governments, politicians, and policing institutions worldwide is the only way forward in the battle with 'organized crime'. The next section looks at how the UK is experimenting with new ways to combat 'organized crime' and its variant forms.

Combating Organized Crime: UK Approach

For some time the UK Government has recognized that the way traditional police forces were organized in the UK made them largely unable to address effectively new developments in 'organized crime' (Harfield, 2008). Thus, the UK Government embarked on a grand experiment in taking a more whole-of-government, joined-up, multi-agency approach in dealing with the myriad forms of entrepreneurial criminality. The creation of the Serious Organised Crime Agency (SOCA) in 2006 exemplifies this joined-up, multi-agency perspective. According to the SOCA website it is:

> ... an Executive Non-Departmental Public Body sponsored by, but operationally independent from, the Home Office. SOCA is an intelligence-led agency with law enforcement powers and harm reduction responsibilities. Harm in this context is the damage caused to people and communities by serious organised crime (<http://www.soca.gov.uk/aboutUs/index.html>, 2009).

The following Figure 9.1 provides a snapshot of how SOCA is currently structured at the time of writing in terms of joined-up agencies.

There are five generic aims (<http://www.soca.gov.uk/aboutUs/aims.html>, 2009) that guide SOCA's activities. They are:

1. To build knowledge and understanding of serious organized crime, the harm it causes, and of the effectiveness of different responses
2. To increase the amount of criminal assets recovered and increase the proportion of cases in which the proceeds of crime are pursued
3. To increase the risk to serious organized criminals operating in the UK, through proven investigation capabilities and in new ways
4. To collaborate with partners in the UK and internationally to maximize efforts to reduce harm
5. To provide agreed levels of high quality support to SOCA's operational partners and, as appropriate, seek their support in return

These aims reflect a shift in emphasis away from the more traditional 'detection, investigation, and prosecution' of organized crime groups to an 'intelligence and disruption' focus, as noted by Harfield, (2008: 68). How well this whole-of-government approach succeeds in combating organized crime in the UK is too early to tell but there are encouraging signs (Leong, 2007).

Chapter 9: Future Policing of 'Organized Crime'

UK whole-of-government, joined-up, multi-agency Approach to Organized Crime

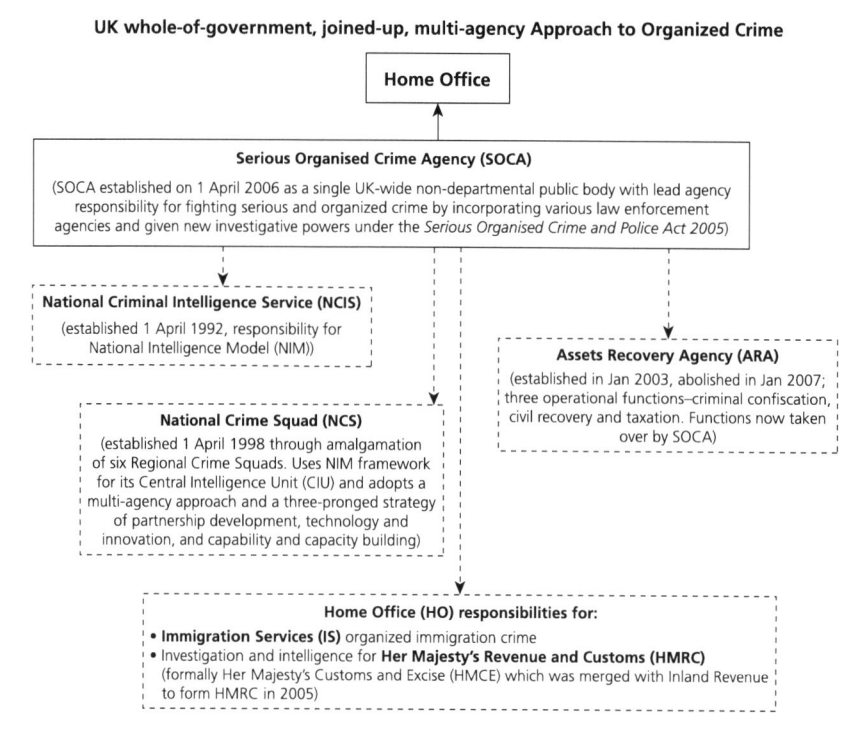

Home Office
↑
Serious Organised Crime Agency (SOCA)
(SOCA established on 1 April 2006 as a single UK-wide non-departmental public body with lead agency responsibility for fighting serious and organized crime by incorporating various law enforcement agencies and given new investigative powers under the *Serious Organised Crime and Police Act 2005*)

National Criminal Intelligence Service (NCIS)
(established 1 April 1992, responsibility for National Intelligence Model (NIM))

Assets Recovery Agency (ARA)
(established in Jan 2003, abolished in Jan 2007; three operational functions–criminal confiscation, civil recovery and taxation. Functions now taken over by SOCA)

National Crime Squad (NCS)
(established 1 April 1998 through amalgamation of six Regional Crime Squads. Uses NIM framework for its Central Intelligence Unit (CIU) and adopts a multi-agency approach and a three-pronged strategy of partnership development, technology and innovation, and capability and capacity building)

Home Office (HO) responsibilities for:
- **Immigration Services (IS)** organized immigration crime
- Investigation and intelligence for **Her Majesty's Revenue and Customs (HMRC)** (formally Her Majesty's Customs and Excise (HMCE) which was merged with Inland Revenue to form HMRC in 2005)

Figure 9.1 UK approach to combating organized crime

The key to SOCA's success or failure will lie in how well it can develop its strategic partnerships. Such partnerships are the cornerstone of this whole-of-government, joined-up approach. There are three pillars which are necessary for such partnership collaboration to work. These pillars are: alignment, boundaries, and commitment (Owen, Goldwasser, Choate, and Blitz, 2008). Alignment is about ensuring all partners are on-board with the new SOCA strategy for combating organized crime. This will involve both vertical and horizontal alignment for partner agencies. Boundaries are a 'big ticket' issue for strategic partnerships. Research shows that failure rates for strategic alliances hover around 50 per cent (David and Bamford, 2005). As Owen *et al.* (2008: 64) argue, the majority of strategic partnerships fail in the business realm 'because they are very hard to manage well'. Such partnerships are built on trust. Whilst the context of government agencies is different in several respects from a business environment, nonetheless the same principles of trust building, mutual respect, two-way sharing of information and knowledge, and so forth still apply and perhaps even more so in a whole-of-government approach. As for the third pillar, commitment, joined-up agencies must foster a collaborative climate which can only be enabled by good leadership, supported by performance incentives and long-term learning strategies, or else commitment will die and so will the partnership (Owen *et al.* 2008: 63).

In sum, it is clearly a more enlightened strategic position to take a coordinated and integrated multi-agency approach using multidisciplinary investigative teams rather than just relying on the police alone to deal with organized crime. This is especially the case in the light of this work's focus on criminal entrepreneurialism and the knowledge war this entails.

Knowledge War: Policing Criminal Entrepreneurialism

Knowledge is the main resource for an organization's competitive advantage. Police organizations are, first and foremost, 'knowledge' organizations. Policing involves the use of information and intelligence combined with 'interpretation, reflection, and context' to produce knowledge (Biloslavo, 2005). Police officers are knowledge workers who use their brains as a 'Knowledge Cube' to make sense of information and intelligence. This is especially so with regard to police investigations which are characterized as knowledge-intensive and time-critical police work (Chen *et al.*, 2002; Hughes and Jackson, 2004).

Criminal organizations are also, to an increasing extent, 'knowledge organizations' that develop over time as business entities as shown in this work. This is clearly so when a crime group is entrepreneurially-driven to success in its illicit business activities. Knowledge is a resource that provides a competitive advantage to such criminal entrepreneurialism. Moreover, Bennet and Bennet (2005a) define knowledge organizations as complex adaptive systems composed of a large number of self-organizing components. These self-organizing components seek to maximize their own goals but operate according to rules in the context of relationships with other components. In an intelligent, complex, adaptive system the agents are people. The systems (organizations) are frequently composed of hierarchical levels of self-organizing agents (or knowledge workers), which can take the form of teams, divisions, or other structures that have common bonds. Thus, while the components (knowledge workers) are self-organizing, they are not independent from the system they comprise (the professional organization).

There are other recognizable features that distinguish knowledge organizations from more bureaucratic organizations. For example, a knowledge organization's focus is on flexibility and customer response rather than a bureaucracy's focus on organizational stability and the accuracy and repetitiveness of internal processes. In the knowledge organization, current practices emphasize using the ideas and capabilities of employees to improve decision-making and organizational effectiveness. In contrast, bureaucracies utilize autocratic decision-making by senior leadership with unquestioned execution by the workforce (Bennet and Bennet, 2005b).

Moreover, in knowledge organizations, transformational and charismatic leadership is an influential mode of leadership that is associated with high levels of individual and organizational performance. Leadership effectiveness is critically contingent on, and often defined in terms of, leaders' ability to motivate followers toward collective goals or a collective mission or vision (Kark and Dijk, 2007). Entrepreneurial criminals also display a type of motivational leadership in that they command a level of respect in how they run their crime business, although, it should be noted that the basis of such respectful leadership in a criminal organization is often due to fear and intimidation rather than natural charisma. The point being made though is that leadership effectiveness is a contributing factor for organizational performance in criminal organizations as well as police organizations.

Police organizations and criminal organizations have to rely substantially on their stock of knowledge as a resource. Such resource knowledge adds capacity to their performance capabilities and also positions them to build on competitive advantages. To that extent, policing and criminal entrepreneurs are engaged in a knowledge war. In other words, if policing has more knowledge then crime groups, then organized crime can be fought in a more efficient and effective way and the balance is tipped in favour of the police winning the war. Alternatively, if police have less knowledge compared to organized criminals, then organized crime will gain the upper hand to expand, consolidate, and successfully position their crime businesses. Therefore, it is not the absolute amount of knowledge that policing has that is important but rather it is the relative quantum of knowledge that will to a large extent determine how winnable this knowledge war is for policing against organized crime. This is the subject of the next section.

Strategic Knowledge Framework: 'Policing Sector' Positioning

This strategic knowledge framework is based on the premise that the quantum of knowledge, in terms of people and systems assets, that a particular police organization possesses determines the optimal policing strategy to adopt towards organized crime.

Therefore, policing organized crime requires a contingent strategy that takes into account the relative position of a police organization's knowledge quantum in relation to that of entrepreneurially-oriented criminal groups. Hence, when the relative 'knowledge quantum' of police versus criminal groups is cross-tabulated in terms of low to high ratios of knowledge then the resulting matrix produces four distinct sectors as shown in Figure 9.2 below. As can be seen, we have defined these policing sectors as random policing, disadvantaged policing, targeted policing, and competitive policing.

Whilst this sector matrix is largely self-explanatory, each sector and its implications for policing entrepreneurially-driven criminal groups will be briefly discussed in turn.

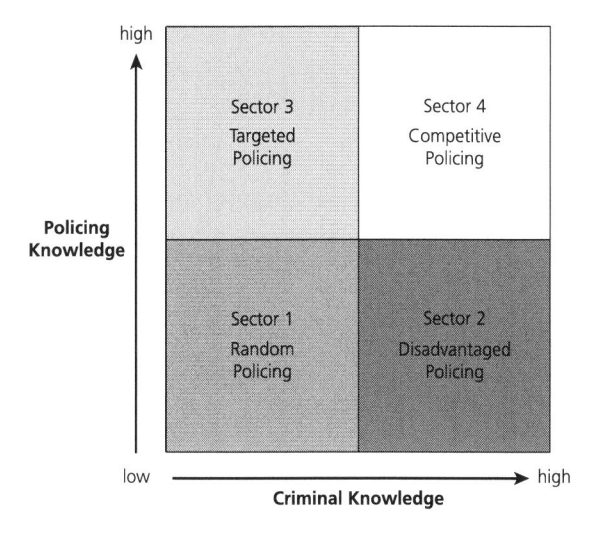

Figure 9.2 Strategic knowledge framework for sector policing of organized crime

Sector 1: Random Policing

In this first sector, both police and criminals suffer from lack of knowledge. Thus, it becomes random who succeeds and who fails. Both criminal entrepreneurs and investigating police officers only have basic knowledge of how a crime business operates. Most of this crime business knowledge is based on the personal experiences of both the criminals and the police. To some extent we can hypothesize that such basic knowledge is limited to *know-what* (perceptual/procedural knowledge), where both sides know what is going on, but they do not know how it is going on, and they do not know why it is going on. In other words, the criminal entrepreneurs are not very sophisticated. They are typically opportunity-based without understanding how to improve business performance. Similarly, police officers observe what is going on, but they do not understand how, and they certainly do not understand why. Also, police actions are only understood in terms of what is done in policing, as they do not know how their actions work and why some of their actions work while other actions do not work. This situation causes randomness on both sides. Because they have so little task-specific knowledge, randomness occurs both among criminal entrepreneurs and police officers in their crime and law enforcement respectively. Randomness is lack of order, purpose, cause, and predictability. Thus, for sector 1, we suggest that the optimal policing and law enforcement strategy has the following characteristics:

- *Time frame*: Some weeks up to some months
- *Goal*: Catch-of-the-day approach (eg seizing drugs, locking up prostitutes, arrest illegal immigrants, and so forth)

- *Forecast*: Chaotic, turbulent, and dynamic criminal environment
- *Change*: Results in quantitative terms
- *Action*: Short-term gain rather than long-term prevention
- *Resources*: Division of labour based on need-to-know management
- *Analysis*: Identifying the most likely time and place for next criminal activity
- *Decision*: Hierarchical organizational structure (bureaucratic model)

Sector 2: Disadvantaged Policing

In this second sector, criminals are ahead of police. For example, criminal business enterprises may have knowledge of money-laundering procedures and methods and knowledge of information and communication technology that are completely unfamiliar to law enforcement agencies. Hence, for sector 2, we suggest that the optimal policing and law enforcement strategy has the following characteristics:

- *Time frame*: Some days up to some weeks
- *Goal*: Catch-of-the-day approach
- *Forecast*: Chaotic, turbulent, and dynamic criminal environment
- *Change*: Results in quantitative terms
- *Action*: Short-term gain rather than long-term prevention
- *Resources*: Division of labour based on need-to-know management
- *Analysis*: Information-led identifying and solving crimes based on random policing opportunity
- *Decision*: Hierarchical organizational structure

Sector 3: Targeted Policing

In this third sector, police can be in charge of the situation and can prevent crime and solve crime, because they are ahead of criminals in terms of relative knowledge quantum. Police have a better understanding of the organized crime phenomena in terms of security, psychology, technology, and other factors influencing organized crime. Therefore, for sector 3, we suggest that the optimal policing and law enforcement strategy has the following characteristics:

- *Time frame*: Some months up to some years
- *Goal*: Closedown of criminal enterprises and preventing establishment of new criminal activity
- *Forecast*: Predictable environment
- *Change*: Results in society qualitative terms
- *Action*: Focus on criminal organization rather than criminals
- *Resources*: Knowledge management for knowledge sharing and knowledge development
- *Analysis*: Business analysis of criminal enterprises
- *Decision*: Knowledge organization structure

Sector 4: Competitive Policing

In this fourth and final sector, both criminals and police officers work in knowledge organizations characterized by innovative knowledge. Criminal knowledge organizations are able to adapt quickly to new market conditions, law enforcement strategies, customs control procedures, and other factors influencing business performance. Similarly, police knowledge organizations understand criminal business enterprises in terms of their structures, markets, roles, and relationships. Hence, for sector 4, we suggest that the optimal policing and law enforcement strategy has the following characteristics:

- *Time frame*: From weeks to years
- *Goal*: Limit criminal industries in terms of size in the legal economy
- *Forecast*: Stable environment
- *Change*: Results in quantitative terms
- *Action*: Short-term gain combined with long-term borders for crime
- *Resources*: Knowledge workers
- *Analysis*: Identifying criminal businesses and their performance
- *Decision*: Vertical knowledge-based decision-making

The suggested policing strategy of adopting a contingent approach to organized crime, as outlined above, with regard to the four policing sectors implies that police organizations have to invest in knowledge resources. That is, police have to invest in people knowledge and systems knowledge, in order to position the organization successfully in policing the sectors (that is, sectors 3 and 4 on Figure 9.2) that will count in this knowledge war with criminal entrepreneurialism. In other words, given that police organizations have limited budgets with which to fight organized crime they have to prioritise and position themselves strategically to police those sectors of entrepreneurial criminality where they can get the best bang for their bucks. In this regard, the UK experiment in a whole-of-government, joined-up, multi-agency approach in dealing with the myriad forms of entrepreneurial criminality as exemplified by SOCA is the only rational way forward. Such a holistic, joined-up approach allows police organizations and other law enforcement and community agencies to plan, develop, and put in operation a wide and diverse range of intervention strategies to disrupt and dismantle organized crime. What these intervention options are is the focus of the next section.

Intervention Strategies against Illegal Business Activities

This knowledge-driven strategy of sector policing combined with a whole-of-government, joined-up, multi-agency and multi-disciplinary investigative approach can target, in a very focused and precise manner, an array of intervention strategies (Leong, 2007). These strategies can be tailored to disrupt as well as dismantle organized crime groups and their networks through a range of civil and criminal legislative remedies as SOCA attempts to do. Moreover, there are also a number of market-based remedies available to destabilize and highlight the invisibility of organized criminal entrepreneurialism. The following Figure 9.3 outlines such intervention strategies.

As can be seen, there are five top-level intervention strategies arranged in an ascending hierarchy from 'civil' to 'criminal' legislative remedies. These strategies range from administrative, regulatory, revenue, asset recovery, and finally prosecutorial in nature. Each intervention strategy involves a regime level or system of rules which can be applied to particular illegal business activities as shown. Examples of each regime level can be seen on the left-hand side of the figure along with the extent to which each type of intervention strategy has the potential to disrupt and dismantle organized criminal entrepreneurialism.

On the top right hand side of Figure 9.3 are some suggested intervention strategies that are essentially market-based remedies. Rather than wait for the *invisible hand of the market*, with all due respect to Adam Smith (Dictionary of Economics, 2002), to intervene in an illegal business enterprise, police and government agencies can do a lot of destabilizing with regard to the delicate supply and demand balance of market behaviour. The precise details of how such market-based strategies work is a matter that is betted discussed in the context of police-oriented training courses rather than in this work.

Finally, in the bottom right-hand corner of Figure 9.3, there is a dotted line box that contains an 'investigation equation'. The significance of this box is to underscore the point that for a good number of these remedies some type of investigation will have to be done and it is of crucial importance that such an investigation is conceived of in terms of the dynamics of time, cost, and quality. In other words, investigating organized criminality is often a lengthy, time-consuming, costly, and complex undertaking that requires quality investigators in order to succeed. In this regard, the UK approach of investing heavily in a whole-of-government approach recognizes that the fight against organized crime is not short term. Vast sums of money have to be committed to it and the best and brightest of multidisciplinary practitioners are needed on the job. The next section looks at how multidisciplinary teams working at the coalface will need to share their knowledge. Knowledge sharing is a key ingredient that gives the competitive edge to the knowledge-driven strategic positioning approach advocated in this book for policing criminal entrepreneurialism.

Knowledge Sharing: Local and Global Policing Partnerships

As we have noted several times in this work, knowledge resides within individuals. More specifically, it is the employees (police and civilians) of a police organization who create, recognize, archive, access, and apply knowledge in carrying out the tasks of policing (Liu and Chen, 2005). Consequently, the movement

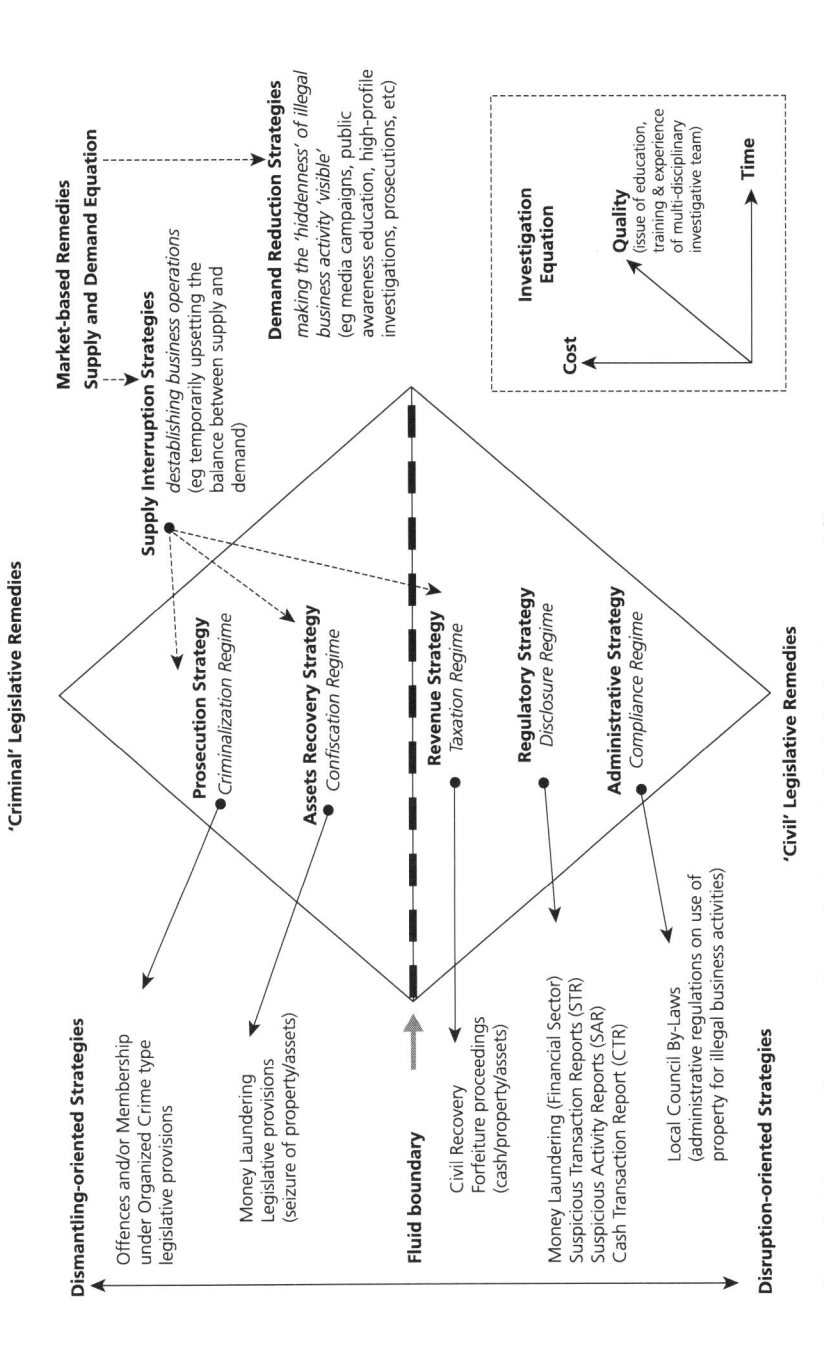

Figure 9.3 Intervention strategies against organized criminal entrepreneurialism

of knowledge across individual and organizational boundaries is dependent on employees' knowledge-sharing behaviours (Liebowitz, 2004). In this regard, Bock *et al.* (2005) reiterate an all too familiar finding; in that, extensive knowledge sharing within organizations still appears to be the exception rather than the rule. Moreover, police organizations are perhaps even more an 'exception' in their desire to share knowledge, given that the nature of their knowledge often requires tight security controls on it. As Gaspar (2008: 26) notes, this is one of the tension spaces of contemporary policing:

> For law enforcement officers there are new skills to learn. It will be necessary to make appropriate judgments about when to share information and when to restrict it. This requires an understanding of the tension that is inherent in the purpose of security controls and data protection and the benefits of information sharing.

Apart from this security of information/knowledge concern in policing, the most crucial problematic aspect of knowledge sharing is that it simply cannot be forced. Sharing knowledge comes about in a social context where individuals are motivated to share with each other their ideas and experiences. In this regard, Van den Hooff and Huysman (2009: 1) use the term an 'emergent approach' towards knowledge sharing. They argue that 'knowledge sharing is not dependent on management intervention but on the social capital of a group of people'. Moreover, the implication for management of this emergent quality to knowledge sharing is:

> .... the awareness that knowledge cannot be directed from the outside has pushed the role of the manager to the periphery of KM (*knowledge management*).[1] Consequently, though knowledge sharing is crucial to an organization, it is inherently emergent in nature. (Van den Hooff and Huysman (2009: 1))

This emergent approach to knowledge sharing is in alignment with the 'Context and Culture' philosophical orientation noted previously in the work in relation to Knowledge-Managed Policing (KMP) in Chapter 7 and in Figure 7.1.

However, there is an alternative approach to knowledge sharing, which Van den Hooff and Huysman (2009) define as the 'engineering approach'. This approach assumes that knowledge sharing can be managed. The key assumption here is that management, while it cannot directly command knowledge sharing, can nonetheless play an indirect role through creating a stimulating environment where people can share their knowledge.

Again, the overlap with the 'Context and Culture' orientation to KM as discussed previously is also evidenced in this engineering approach whereby the more IT-focused 'Platform & Cables' approach to Knowledge-Managed Policing (Chapter 7, Figure 7.1) can play a support role to the organizational context and culture rather than being the dominant orientation. Figure 9.4 below expands

---

[1] Words in italics are those of the current authors.

Knowledge Sharing Models:
Integrating Emergent & Engineering Approaches*

Emergent approach to constructing knowledge

assumes knowledge is embedded in and its meaning shaped by the social interactions of the context in which it is practiced. 'social capital' underpins this emergent view of knowledge

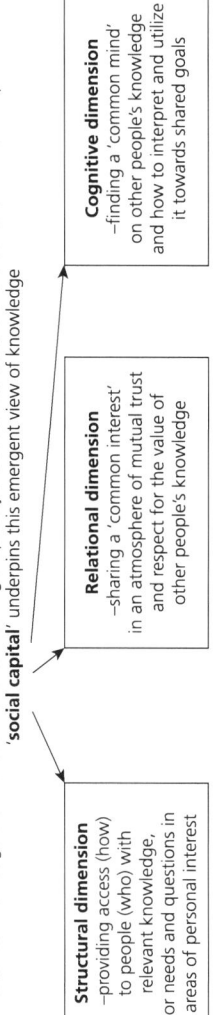

Structural dimension
—providing access (how) to people (who) with relevant knowledge, or needs and questions in areas of personal interest

Relational dimension
—sharing a 'common interest' in an atmosphere of mutual trust and respect for the value of other people's knowledge

Cognitive dimension
—finding a 'common mind' on other people's knowledge and how to interpret and utilize it towards shared goals

Engineering approach to managing knowledge

assumes knowledge cannot be directly controlled by management but can only be indirectly influenced by providing the context (stimulating and trusting) and means (processes and incentives) to make and manage the knowledge of individuals 'collective' as a valued organizational resource. 'organizational capital' underpins this engineering view of knowledge

Structural infrastructure
—extent to which an organization's structure facilitates knowledge sharing

Cultural infrastructure
—establishing a knowledge-friendly culture through a positive orientation towards knowledge and creativity

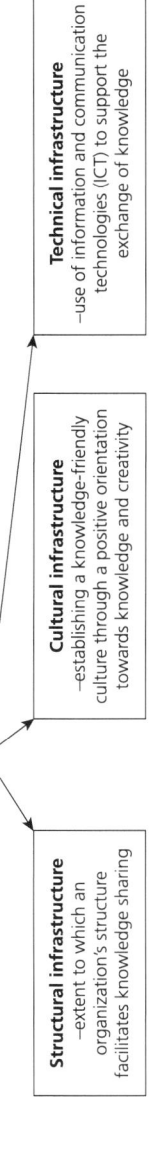

Technical infrastructure
—use of information and communication technologies (ICT) to support the exchange of knowledge

Figure 9.4 Integrating emergent and engineering models of knowledge sharing

*Source: material extracted from Van den Hooff, B., and Huysman, M. (2009). Managing knowledge sharing: Emergent and engineering approaches. *Information & Management*, 46, (1), pp. 1–8.

more on how these two approaches can act in an integrated way as compatible models for knowledge sharing.

As can be seen, the notions of 'social capital' and 'organizational capital' and their associated dimensions are prominent concepts within this knowledge sharing framework. Moreover, Van den Hooff and Huysman (2009:7) draw out the following observations from the findings of their research into these two approaches:

> As for practical implications, our results indicated that management could indirectly promote knowledge sharing through the creation of an environment that fostered social capital by:
> - creating an organizational structure that showed who was responsible for which knowledge activities and that had little formal barriers to interaction between different parts of the organization;
> - establishing a knowledge-friendly culture with openness, innovativeness, a willingness to share, etc.
> - establishing and maintaining an IT infrastructure that efficiently and effectively helped organizational members to learn what is relevant knowledge, where it is located, and how to contact those possessing or needing it.

In so far as Knowledge-Managed Policing of organized crime is concerned, there is value-adding benefit to the argument that by aligning the *social* and *organizational capital* inherent in the *emergent* and *engineering* approaches to knowledge sharing in the manner suggested by the Van den Hooff and Huysman (2009) research, it may become possible to overcome, to a significant extent, many of the difficulties associated with sharing knowledge in and between people in an organizational context. The next section builds on this issue of knowledge sharing with particular reference to the need for international cooperation in policing.

International Cooperation in Policing

The issue of international cooperation between police and law enforcement agencies is no longer something that only concerns police managers and executives. It is also highly relevant to 'local' police officers on the beat. In this regard, Gaspar (2008:8) asserts that 'Bowling argues that there is no part of policing that does not have an international dimension'. According to Gaspar (2008: 20):

> The nature of the globalization of the markets has increased the risk of international crimes. . . . . This has broadened the nature of organized crime and places the investigator in the position of needing international co-operation in the generation of information, the design and execution of proactive operations and prosecutions.

Moreover, we argue that this need for international police cooperation is not restricted to just the big policing issues of terrorism, and serious and/or organized crime. However, given the focus of our work on policing illegal business entrepreneurialism the absolute central importance of international cooperation in policing cannot be overestimated. Gaspar (2008: 24) underscores this point when he refers to a study by Shaw of transnational organized crime groups which '...found that just under 50 per cent of such groups were categorized as spreading their business across five or more countries'.

Brown (2008: 29) identifies four main factors that influence the policing and law enforcement environment in relation to international cooperation: 'These "enablers" are—Politics, Law, Culture and Capacity.' For example, in so far as the political dimension of policing and law enforcement cooperation is concerned, Brown (2008: 27) considers it as a macro-level enabling factor where '....political agreement and consensus has to be sought as a precondition for action'. In other words, international cooperation cannot exist without political will as a prerequisite condition, whereas the enabling effect of the law can be considered as more of a micro factor because it is wholly dependent on the political will of the legislature. According to Brown (2008: 32):

> When engaging at the international level, there are two chief factors to consider in this respect: the negotiating of international agreements and their national implementation. Framing international laws that can accommodate the different types of legal jurisdiction and practice is no easy task.

Furthermore, whilst 'politics' and the 'law' help to set the framework within which international cooperation can take place, Brown (2008: 35) asserts that 'it is the prevailing culture that actually sponsors co-operation in practice'. Brown uses the term 'culture' to refer specifically to two aspects of international policing cooperation. He (*ibid*) elaborates as follows:

> The culture factor comes into play in two respects: first, opportunities for sharing can be created, but officers must be both aware and willing to take advantage of them; second, in building co-operation, one partner has to be sensitive to the limitations on and the cultural preferences of the other. National cultures can be vastly different and such differences must be fully understood if any co-operative relationship is to be truly fruitful. Indeed, in many respects, culture is more significant as a factor than the other enablers in that it not only influences politicians and the drafting of the laws, but also disposes officers and prosecutors towards pursuing international lines of enquiry rather than settling for a quick result in the national courts.

The final enabling factor in international cooperation in policing according to Brown is that of a police organization's 'capacity'. As Brown (2008: 37) notes:

> All the political will, legal framework and enthusiasm in the world will come to nothing if the physical ability or actual capacity to implement the desired cooperation is lacking. Inadequate resources, training or funding in law enforcement generally will, of course, always result in the need for prioritisation, but where should international issues sit in the preferences? Reciprocity is a solid push factor in this regard, but will only operate where all parties concerned believe they stand to gain in the long run and are aware of the potential benefits of a continuing relationship.

Chapter 9: Future Policing of 'Organized Crime'

These four key factors—politics, law, culture, and capacity—that enable international cooperation between policing and law enforcement agencies are not equally weighted according to Brown (2008: 39) for:

> the existence of the right political will, the appropriate legal framework and a culture favourably disposed to international law enforcement supported by capacity, are each required for the propagation of successful cooperation, but these enablers also have to achieve a balance.

Moreover, achieving this balancing act between these four factors involves aligning the relative contribution of each factor and their interdependences as a structural whole. The following Figure 9.5 diagrammatically represents such a balanced alignment in the form of a molecular-type structure[2] for international cooperation in policing.

The dynamics of this molecular structure as presented in Figure 9.5 represent a balanced alignment in terms of the relative size of each factor and the interrelationships of one to the other. Also shown is the nature of the linkages between the factors. The structure works in the following manner.

If *politics* as the prerequisite factor for international cooperation is undermined by the political influences operating in a particular nation/state/country

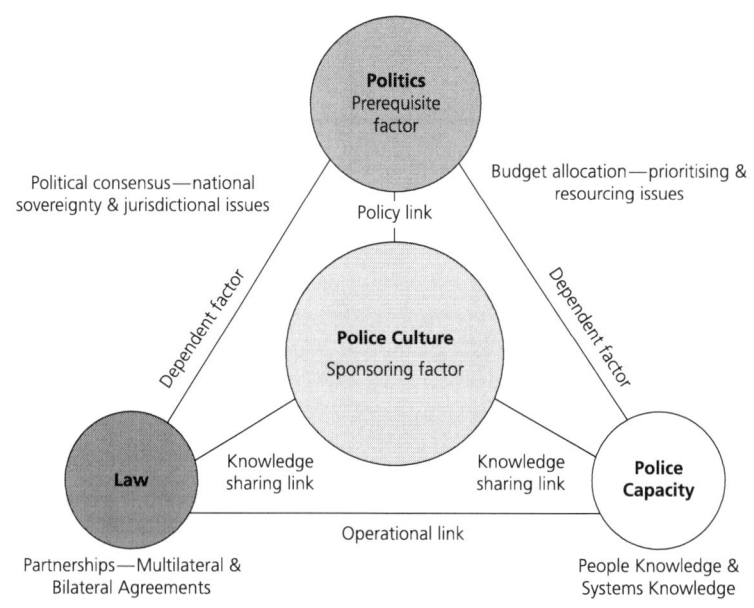

Figure 9.5 Balanced alignment of enabling factors in international cooperation

---

[2] The factors that enable international cooperation in policing have a similar structural arrangement to that of a molecule. In that, a molecule consists of 'one or more like atoms in the first case, and two or more different atoms in the second case' (Macquarie Dictionary, 1987: 1104).

being too strong against international police cooperation then that particular nation/state/country's decisions and choices on the dependent factors—*law* (eg sovereignty and jurisdictional issues, drafting of laws, etc) and *police capacity* (eg lack of provision in police budget for adequate resources like training, infrastructure etc) will be made according to expediency in support of the government's interest and mediated through *police culture* and its policy link to the government of the day. As Robinson (2000: 19) aptly puts it 'until the political will is strong enough, sovereignty will be the rope with which we tie law enforcement's hands behind its back'.

Moreover, if the influence of the *police culture* as a sponsoring factor for international police cooperation is too weak then as Brown (2008: 39) points out:

> investigators will be disinclined to engage with the laws and opportunities available, nothing will be shared and the investment in setting up the systems will be wasted; and where international law enforcement is inadequately resourced, investigators will struggle to meet the expectations of co-operating partners or to accomplish their duties.

Furthermore, even when there is political will for international police cooperation by a government, as the molecular structure makes plain, the dependent factors can still be rendered ineffectual. For instance, if the *law* is too prescriptive it will increase in size and become over-regulated. This will in effect decrease the opportunities for international cooperation because the field will become paralysed in trying to comply with conflicting legal approaches. Similarly, if the *capacity* of a police organization is increased but there is no corresponding development of enabling laws or the police culture of a particular nation/state/country is corrupted, then there is little value to be gained in pursing international cooperative agreements or partnership arrangements. In this regard a study by Dijk (2007) compared organized crime and the rule of law. He found that where police forces operate more professionally, levels of organized crime tend to remain relatively modest. Organized crime is more prevalent in countries where the rule of law is less well assured and vice versa. He found that the critical factor determining the extent of organized crime is the quality of institutions responsible for the rule of law, including competent police services and independent courts with standards of professional integrity.

Future Directions

This section offers some speculative thoughts of charting out the future direction of policing illegal business entrepreneurialism. To begin painting this picture, a snapshot by Robinson (2000: 19) sums up rather bleakly the future for policing entrepreneurially-driven organized criminality when he states:

> As long as we live in a world where a seventeenth-century philosophy of sovereignty is reinforced with an eighteenth-century judicial model, defended by a nineteenth-century concept of law enforcement that is still trying to come to

terms with twentieth-century technology, the twenty-first century will belong to transnational criminals.

How accurate this prediction about the global dominance of organized crime will prove to be in the foreseeable future is open to conjecture. What we do know is that the way policing business is done will have to change in some radically different ways, if we, as a global community, want to avoid the worst aspects of the rule of global criminality.

A starting point is to consider how policing and law enforcement has historically developed as a local solution to local crime problems. Historically, policing was, and is still, conceived as a statement of national sovereignty as represented by governments, and hence by definition confined by jurisdictional borders of a nation state. Moreover, it is the state that pays the lion's share of the policing budget in spite of some hybrid forms of public-private policing. As Robinson (2000: 18) notes:

> Boundaries and budgets rule. As a result, the state winds up with borders that must be respected and neither the authority nor the money to go beyond them. Criminals create wealth by purposely functioning beyond sovereign reach.

Therefore, it would seem to us that this present day reality of localized policing is outmoded. It no longer fits contemporary organized criminality. As a case in point take how money-laundering is now done by the Russians:

> In Cyprus, on the Greek side of the Green Line that divides the Mediterranean island into Greek and Turkish halves, more than $1 billion arrives every month from Russia, where it is washed through the nearly eight thousand Russian companies and banks that have been formed there since 1993. Another twenty-one to twenty-five thousand shell companies there belong, mostly, to Eastern Europeans. Once clean, some of that money goes to Britain. On the north side of the Green Line, Turkish heroin is bartered and sold like any commodity and monies from that market have also been traced to Great Britain. In today's global economy, the city of London is merely one blip on a computer screen away from Wall Street (Robinson, 2000: 19).

A complicating factor in all of this, without having to resort to the old chestnut of conspiracy theories, can clearly be discerned from the material presented in this work. In that, if there is any 'organization' behind global or transnational 'organized crime' it is one of international connectivity (Gasper, 2008: 19). 'Organized crime' is now globally wired. That is, there is international connectivity between diverse crime groups and networks of offenders each responsible for segments of one or more illicit crime markets. For instance, Robinson (2000: 18) again provides an entrepreneurially-driven innovative case example of such international criminal connectivity:

> In Ensenada, Baja California, Mexican traffickers and their Southeast Asian heroin-dealing partners–Thai and Laotian–worked out a drugs-by-mail scheme.

The gang in Mexico shipped bath products to Thailand, where the envelopes were intercepted by Thai gang members working inside the post office. They emptied out the bath products, refilled the envelopes with heroin and stamped them 'Undeliverable-Return to Sender.' The envelopes entered Mexico without customs inspection because it appeared that they'd originated in Mexico. Mexican gang members inside the Mexican postal service then delivered the drugs to their cohorts for smuggling into the United States.

As Gaspar (2008: 19) asserts policing and law enforcement agencies face new challenges that will involve them in thinking differently about how they go about the job of policing illegal business entrepreneurialism:

> In organised crime, the new challenge for investigators is to balance the energy put into the dismantling of domestic networks with that contributing to the removal of connecting networks in other countries.

Some may argue this is already being done with legal mutual assistance agreements and strategic partnerships. However, as Figure 9.3 makes clear there are a host of intervening variables and factors involved in getting international cooperation in policing to really work effectively and efficiently in practice across the globe. In this regard, Gaspar (2008: 27) makes a cogent argument that no matter how well developed law enforcement strategic partnerships are in terms of mutual assistance and information sharing all this is 'piecemeal' since 'there is no global doctrine on methodology' for policing transnational organized crime. Furthermore, 'National sovereignty sits firmly in the way of criminal justice even where countries have embarked on reducing barriers and borders'. These are big roadblocks to overcome. It will require extensive investment by governments in a whole-of-the-globe approach to 'organized crime' and resourcing police and their criminal justice partners in terms of new education and training initiatives that target 'organized crime' in the ways suggested by 'sector policing' and how best to strategically position policing agencies. Such roadblocks must be overcome—the alternative of Rule by Crime should not be an option for the global community.

A further complication in mapping out the future directions for policing is the 'marriage of convenience' with some 'legitimate' professionals like lawyers, bankers, accountants, property agents, and company formation agents who prepare the stage for global criminals. Without such 'legitimate business connections' organized criminal groups would not be able to function as successfully as they do in the global landscape. To successfully deal with decoupling this marriage of convenience between legitimate professionals and entrepreneurial criminals will require some revolutionary changes in law. Legal remedies that substantially penalize such professional involvement in illegal business enterprises have not occurred to date. With reference to this upperworld-underworld 'marriage of convenience' Robinson (2000: 338) sees this unholy partnership as one of the main stumbling blocks stopping the global community in coming to grips with 'organized crime' in its many forms. He asserts:

> The inability of modern society to deal with global crime has reached such overwhelming proportions that it is destined to be a defining issue for the twenty-first century much the way the cold war was for the twentieth and colonialism was for the nineteenth (*ibid*).

In conclusion, our assessment is that the odds are in favour of global crime becoming, if not the defining issue for the twenty-first century, a close second behind terrorism. Either way, taking first or second place provides little comfort. Jurisdictionally-based policing will have to remake itself as a global player. It will have to do better what 'organized crime' does well already. Policing must get internationally connected and wired into global responses and operations that target criminal organizations and their enabling 'legitimate' professionals. This will most certainly take courageous leadership and sustained commitment by governments, politicians, police executives, and a host of other institutions embedded in the justice field. To paraphrase a well-known observation—evil flourishes when good people do nothing.

References

Chapter 1

Aftenposten (22 May 2008). *Three young Norwegians jailed in Bolivia*. <http://www.aftenposten.no/english/local/article2438763.ece>. Accessed on 16 June 2009.

Audretsch, D. B. and Keilbach, M. (2007). 'The Theory of Knowledge Spillover Entrepreneurialism'. *Journal of Management Studies*, 44 (7): 1242–1254.

Barnes, T., Elias, R., and Walsh, P. (2001). *Cocky: the rise and fall of Curtis Warren, Britain's biggest drug baron*. Bury: Milo Books.

BBC (2009). *Accused 'Interpol's most wanted'*. <http://news.bbc.co.uk/2/hi/europe/jersey/8263205.stm>. Accessed on 10 April 2010.

Block, A. (1983). *East side-West side: Organizing Crime in New York, 1930–1950*. New Brunswick, NJ: Transaction Books.

Casson, M. and Godley, A. (2007). 'Revisiting the Emergence of the Modern Business Enterprise: Entrepreneurship and the Singer Global Distribution System'. *Journal of Management Studies*, 44 (7): 1064–1077.

Foss, K., Foss, N. J., Klein, P. G., and Klein, S. K. (2007). 'The Entrepreneurial Organisation of Heterogeneous Capital'. *Journal of Management Studies*, 44 (7): 1165–1186.

Grennan, S. and Britz, M. (2006). *Organized Crime: A Worldwide Perspective*. Upper Saddle River, New Jersey: Pearson, Prentice Hall.

Guardian (2009) [a]. *Curtis Warren 'ringleader of Jersey Smuggling gang'*. <http://www.guardian.co.uk/uk/2009/sep/18/curtis-warren-drug-trafficker>. Accessed on 29 October 2009.

Guardian (2009) [b]. *The life and times of Curtis Warren*. <http://www.guardian.co.uk/uk/2009/sep/18/ukcrime-jersey>. Accessed on 29 October 2009.

Guardian (2009) [c]. *Rich list criminal Curtis Warren was Jersey drug plotter, court hears*. <http://www.guardian.co.uk/uk/2009/sep/18/warren-jersey-drug-case>. Accessed on 29 October 2009.

Hsieh, C., Nickerson, J. A., and Zenger, T. R. (2007). 'Opportunity Discovery, Problem Solving and a Theory of the Entrepreneurial Firm'. *Journal of Management Studies*, 44 (7): 1255–1277.

Jacobides, M. G. and Winter, S. G. (2007). 'Entrepreneurialism and Firm Boundaries: The Theory of a Firm'. *Journal of Management Studies*, 44 (7): 1213–1241.

Kugler, M., Verdier, T., and Zenou, Y (2005). 'Organized crime, corruption and punishment'. *Journal of Public Economics*, 89: 1639–1663.

Langlois, R. N. (2007). 'The Entrepreneurial Theory of the Firm and the Theory of the Entrepreneurial Firm'. *Journal of Management Studies*, 44 (7): 1107–1124.

Lyman, M. and Potter, G. (2007). *Organized crime* (4th edn). Upper Saddle River, New Jersey: Pearson Prentice Hall.

References

Markovska, A. (2007). 'The bitter pill of a corrupt heritage: Corruption in Ukraine and developments in the pharmaceutical industry', in P. C. van Duyne, A. Maljevic, M. van Dijck, K. von Lampe, and J. Harvey (eds.), *Crime Business and Crime Money in Europe. The Dirty Linen of Illegal Enterprise*. Nijmegen, Netherlands: Wolf Legal Publishers, 227–246.

Markovski, S. and Hall, P. (2007). 'Public sector entrepreneurship and the production of defense'. *Public Finance and Management*, 7 (3): 260–294.

Milroy, A. (2007). Speech by CEO of the Australian Crime Commission on *Knowledge Based Approach to Policing* presented at the AIPIO Conference, 17–18 October, Melbourne. Australia.

Moles, P., and Terry, N. (1997). *Handbook of International Financial Terms*. Oxford Reference Online, Oxford University Press.

Small, K. and Taylor, B. (2006). 'State and local law enforcement response to transnational crime'. *Trends in Organised Crime*, 10 (2): 5–17.

Smith, D. C. (1974). *The Mafia Mystique*. New York: Basic Books.

Smith, D. C. (1994). 'Illicit enterprise: An Organized Crime Paradigm for the Nineties', in R. J. Kelly, K.-L. Chin, and R. Schatzberg (eds.), *Handbook of Organized Crime in the United States*. Westport, CT: Greenwood.

Symeonidou-Kastanidou, E. (2007). 'Towards a New Definition of Organised Crime in the European Union'. *European Journal of Crime, Criminal Law and Criminal Justice*, 83–103.

Times (2009). *British Drug Kingpin, Curtis 'Cocky' Warren, Found Guilty Of Smuggling*. <http://www.timesonline.co.uk/tol/news/uk/crime/article6864280.ece>. Accessed on 10 April 2010.

Times (2009). *British Drug Kingpin, Curtis 'Cocky' Warren, sentenced to 13 years*. <http://www.timesonline.co.uk/tol/news/uk/crime/article6943245.ece>. Accessed on 10 April 2010.

Thomas, A. and Mancino, A. (2007). 'The relationship between entrepreneurial characteristics, firms' positioning and local development'. *Entrepreneurship and Innovation*, 8 (2): 105–114.

Van Duyne, P. C. (2007). 'Crime finances and state of the art: Case for concern?', in P. C. van Duyne, A. Maljevic, M. van Dijck, K. von Lampe, and J. Harvey (eds.), *Crime Business and Crime Money in Europe—The Dirty Linen of Illicit Enterprise*. Nijmegen, Netherlands: Wolf Legal Publishers, 69–95.

VG. (2009). Vg.no. 12 June 2009. <http://www.vg.no/nyheter/utenriks/artikkel.php?artid=576139>. Accessed on 16 June 2009.

Von Lampe, K. (2007). 'Criminals are not alone. Some observations on the social microcosm of illegal entrepreneurs', in P. C. van Duyne, A. Maljevic, M. van Dijck, K. von Lampe, and J. Harvey (eds.), *Crime Business and Crime Money in Europe. The Dirty Linen of Illegal Enterprise*. Nijmegen, Netherlands: Wolf Legal Publishers, 131–156.

Witt, U. (2007). 'Firms as Realizations of Entrepreneurial Visions'. *Journal of Management Studies*, 44 (7): 1125–1140.

Zander, I. (2007). 'Do You See What I Mean? An Entrepreneurship Perspective on the Nature and Boundaries of the Firm'. *Journal of Management Studies*, 44 (7): 1141–1164.

Chapter 2

Black, J. (2002). *Dictionary of Economics*. Oxford Reference Online, Oxford University Press. <http://www.oxfordreference.com/views/ENTRY.html?subview=Main&entry=t19.e1697>. Accessed on 18 December 2008.

Buss, T. F. (2001). 'Exporting American economic development practice to Russia'. *Policy Studies Review*, 18 (3): 94–108.

Carter, D. L. (1997). 'International Organised Crime: Emerging Trends in entrepreneurial Crime', in P. J. Ryan and G. E. Rush (eds.), *Understanding Organised crime in Global Perspective*. Thousand Oaks: Sage.

Chang, J. J., Lu, H. C., and Chen, M. (2005). 'Organized Crime or Individual Crime? Endogeneous Size of a Criminal Organization and the Optimal Law Enforcement'. *Economic Inquiry*, 43 (3): 661–675.

Europol (2006). *OCTA: EU Organized Crime Threat Assessment 2006*. The Hague, Netherlands: European Police Office.

Europol (2007). *Organised Crime Threat Assessment* Report. <http://www.europol.europa.eu/publications/European_Organised_Crime_Threat_Assessment_(OCTA)/OCTA2007.pdf>. Accessed on 10 April 2010.

Fiorentini, G. and Peltzman, S. (eds.) (1995). *The Economics of Organised Crime*. Cambridge, UK: Cambridge University Press.

Griffiths, H. (2004). 'Smoking guns: European cigarette smuggling in the 1990s'. *Global Crime*, 6 (2): 185–200.

Gutauskas, A., Juska, A., Johnstone, P., and Pozzuto, R. (2004). 'Changing Typology of Organised Crime in Post-Socialist Lithuania (the late 1980s–Early 2000s)'. *Global Crime*, 6 (2): 201–221.

Kenney, M. (2007). 'The Architecture of Drug Trafficking: Network Forms of Organisation in the Colombian Cocaine Trade'. *Global Crime*, 8 (3): 233–259.

Levi, M. (2003). 'Organising Financial Crimes: Breaking the Economic Power of Organized Crime Groups?', in D. Siegel, H. van den, Bunt, and D. Zaitch (eds.), *Global Organized Crime Trends and Developments*. Dordrecht, The Netherlands: Kluwer.

Mack, J. A. and Kerner, H.-J. (1975). *The Crime Industry*. Westmead: Saxon House.

Macquarie Dictionary (1981). The Macquarie Library Pty Ltd. Australia.

Markina, A. (2007). 'Cigarette black market in Estonia', in P. C. van Duyne, A. Maljevic, M. van Dijck, K von Lampe, and J. Harvey (eds.), *Crime Business and Crime Money in Europe. The Dirty Linen of Illegal Enterprise*. Nijmegen, The Netherlands: Wolf Legal Publishers, 195–208.

Moore, M. (1987). 'Organised Crime as Business Enterprise', in H. Edelhertz (ed.), *Major Issues in Organised Crime Control*. Washington, DC: Government Printing Office.

Nelen, H. and Huisman, W. (2008). 'Breaking the Power of Organized Crime? The Administrative Approach in Amsterdam', in D. Siegel and H. Nelen (eds.), *Organized Crime: Culture, Markets and Policies*. New York, NY: Springer, 207–218.

Nicaso, A. and Lamothe, L. (2005). *Angels, Mobsters and Narco-Terrorists*: The Rising Menace of Global Criminal Empires. Canada: John Wiley & Sons.

Paoli, L. (October 2001). 'The "invisible hand of the market": the illegal drugs trade in Germany, Italy and Russia'. *Third Colloquium on Cross-border Crime*. Police Academy Bratislava, Slovak Republic, 19–38.

References

Pérez, N. (2007). *Crime Networks*. Job Market Paper, University of Maryland.

Reichel, P. (ed.) (2005). *Handbook of Transnational Crime and Justice*. Thousand Oaks, California: Sage Publications.

Reuter, P. (1983). *Disorganized Crime: Illegal Markets and the Mafia—The Economics of the Visible Hand*. Cambridge, MA: MIT Press.

Rubin, P. H. (1980). 'The Economics of Crime', in R. Andreano and J. Siegfried (eds.), *The Economics of Crime*. New York: John Wiley.

Ruggiero, V. (2000). *Crime and Markets: Essays in Anti-Criminology*. Oxford: Clarendon Press.

Ruggiero, V. and Khan, K. (2007). 'The Organisation of Drug Supply, South Asian Criminal Enterprise in the UK'. *Organised Crime in Asia: Governance and Accountability*. Symposium Proceedings, Queensland University of Technology and National University of Singapore, 61–74.

Scott, J. and Marshall G. (2005). *Dictionary of Sociology*. Oxford Reference Online, Oxord University Press. <http://www.oxfordreference.com/views/ENTRY.html?subview=Main&entry=t88.e1178>. Accessed on 18 December 2008.

Small, K. and Taylor, B. (2006). 'State and local law enforcement response to transnational crime'. *Trends in Organised Crime*, 10 (2): 5–17.

Tanev, T. A. (2001). 'Emerging from post-communism chaos: The case of Bulgaria'. *International Journal of Public Administration*, 24 (2): 235–248.

United Nations (2002). *Results of a pilot survey of forty selected organized criminal groups in sixteen countries*. United Nations, Office of Drugs and Crime.

Van Dijk, J. (2007). 'Mafia makers: assessing organised crime and its impact upon societies'. *Trends in Organised Crime*, 10: 39–56.

Van Duyne, P. C., von Lampe, K., van Dijck, M., and Newell, J. L. (eds.) (2005). *The Organized Crime Economy: Managing Crime Markets in Europe*. Nijmegen: Wolf Legal Publishers.

Chapter 3

Andreano, R. and Siegfried, J. (eds). *The Economics of Crime*. New York: John Wiley.

Australian Transaction Reports and Analysis Centre—AUSTRAC (2008). *Typologies and Case Studies Report 2008*.

Bannock, G., Davis, E., Trott, P., and Uncles, M. (2002). *The New Penguin Dictionary of Business*. London: Penguin Books.

Carter, D. L. (1997). 'International Organized Crime: Emerging Trends in Entrepreneurial Crime', in P. J. Ryan, and G. E. Rush (eds.), *Understanding Organized Crime in Global Perspective*. Thousand Oaks: Sage.

Coluccello, S. and Massey, S. (2007). 'Out of Africa: The human trade between Libya and Lampedusa'. *Trends in Organised Crime*, 10: 77–90.

Dietz, A. and Buttle, J. (2008). *Anti-Money Laundering Handbook*. Sydney: Lawbook Company.

EDGE (2005). *Final Results: Criminal Money Management—as a cutting Edge between Profit Oriented Crime and Terrorism*. European Interdisciplinary Analysis Project: AGIS Programme European Commission—Directorate-General Justice, Freedom and Security.

Grennan, S. and Britz, M. (2006). *Organized Crime: A Worldwide Perspective*. Upper Saddle River, New Jersey: Pearson, Prentice Hall.

Hancox, M. and Hackney, R. (2000). 'IT outsourcing: frameworks for conceptualizing practice and perception'. *Information Systems Journal*, 10: 217–237.

Jost, P. M. and Singh Sandhu, H. (2000). *The hawala alternative remittance system and its role in money laundering*. Lyon: Interpol General Secretariat. Accessed 3 May 2009.

Kaizen, J. and Nonneman, W. (2007). 'Irregular migration in Belgium and organized crime: An overview'. *International Migration*, 45 (2): 121–146.

Kosko, B. (1993). *Fuzzy Thinking: The New Science of Fuzzy Logic*. New York: Hyperion.

Madinger, J. (2006). *Money Laundering: A Guide for Criminal Investigators*. (2nd edn). Boca Raton: CRC Press: Taylor & Francis Group.

Markovska, A. (2007). 'The bitter pill of a corrupt heritage: Corruption in Ukraine and developments in the pharmaceutical industry', in P. C. van Duyne, A. Maljevic, M. van Dijck, K. von Lampe, and J. Harvey (eds.), *Crime Business and Crime Money in Europe. The Dirty Linen of Illegal Enterprise*. Nijmegen, The Netherlands: Wolf Legal Publishers, 227–246.

Markovski, S. and Hall, P. (2007). 'Public sector entrepreneurialism and the production of defense'. *Public Finance and Management*, 7 (3): 260–294.

McCusker, R. (2005). 'Underground Banking: Legitimate Remittance Network or Money Laundering System'. *Trends & Issues in Crime and Criminal Justice*. Australian Institute of Criminology: 300. <http://www.aic.gov.au/publications/tandi2/tandi300.pdf>. Accessed 10 April 2010.

McMullan, J. L. and Perrier, D. C. (2007). 'Controlling Cyber-Crime and Gambling: Problems and Paradoxes in the Mediation of Law and Criminal Organization'. *Police Practice and Research*, 8 (5): 431–444.

Nicaso, A., and Lamothe, L. (2005). *Angels, Mobsters and Narco-Terrorists: The Rising Menace of Global Criminal Empires*. Canada: John Wiley & sons.

Ortega, R. (2007). 'Defending the Corporate Crown Jewels from the Dangers that Lurk Within - Effective Internal Network Security Focuses on Behavior'. *Information Systems Security*, 16: 54–60.

Queensland Retired Police Association (2009). Personal communication from member via email on 25 May 2009.

Robinson, J. (2000). *The Merger: The Conglomeration of International Organized Crime*. Woodstock: the Overlook Press.

Rubin, P. H. (1980). 'The Economics of Crime', in R. Andreano and J. Siegfried (eds.), *The Economics of Crime*, New York: John Wiley.

Ruggiero, V. and Khan, K. (2007). 'The Organisation of Drug Supply, South Asian Criminal Enterprise in the UK'. *Organised Crime in Asia: Governance and Accountability*. Symposium Proceedings, Queensland University of Technology and National University of Singapore, 61–74.

Sheetz, M. (2004). 'Investigating Global Money Laundering'. *Law & Order*. 52 (1): 106–110.

Spapens, T. (2007). 'Trafficking in illicit firearms for criminal purposes within the European Union'. *European Journal of Crime, Criminal Law and Criminal Justice*, 15 (3): 359–381.

References

Stamp, J., and Walker, J. (2007). 'Money laundering through Australia, 2004'. *Trends & Issues in Crime and Criminal Justice.* Australian Institute of Criminology: <http://www.aic.gov.au/publications/tandi2/tandi300.pdf>. Accessed 10 April 2010.

United Nations (2002). *Results of a pilot survey of forty selected organised criminal groups in sixteen countries.* United Nations, Office of Drugs and Crime.

Van de Bunt, H. (2008). 'The Role of Hawala Bankers in the Transfer of Proceeds from Organised Crime', in D. Siegel and H. Nelen (eds.), *Organized Crime: Culture, Markets and Policies.* New York: Springer.

Van Dijk, J. (2007). 'Mafia makers: assessing organised crime and its impact upon societies'. *Trends in Organised Crime,* 10: 39–56.

Van Duyne, P. C. (2007). 'Crime finances and state of the art: Case for concern?', in P. C. van Duyne, A. Maljevic, M. van Dijck, K. von Lampe, and J. Harvey (eds.), *Crime Business and Crime Money in Europe—The Dirty Linen of Illicit Enterprise.* Nijmegen, Netherlands: Wolf Legal Publishers, 69–95.

White, R. (2007). *Anti-Gang Strategies and Interventions.* Australian Research Alliance for Children & Youth, University of Tasmania, Australia. <www.aracy.org.au>.

Williamson, O. E. (1979). 'Transaction-cost economics: The governance of contractual relations'. *The Journal of Law and Economics,* 22: 233–261.

Witt, U. (2007). 'Firms as Realizations of Entrepreneurial Visions'. *Journal of Management Studies,* 44: 7, 1125–1140.

Wright, A. (2006). *Organised Crime.* Devon, UK: Willan Publishing.

Zadeh, L. A. (1990). 'Fuzzy Logic', in P. Raeth (ed.), *Expert Systems: A Software Methodology for Modern Applications.* Los Alamitos, CA: IEEE Computer Society Press.

Zdanowicz, J. 'Detecting Money Laundering and Terrorist Financing via Data Mining'. *Communications of the ACM* in AUSTRAC, RMIT University and John Walker Crime Trends Analysis. *The Extent of Money Laundering in and through Australia in 2004.* Criminology Research Council. <http://www.criminologyresearchcouncil.gov.au/>. Accessed 10 April 2010.

Chapter 4

Commission on Police Integrity [Chicago] (1999). *Report of the Commission on Police Integrity.* Chicago, Illinois: Chicago Police Department.

Europol (2007). *Organised Crime Threat Assessment* Report. <http://www.europol.europa.eu/publications/European_Organised_Crime_Threat_Assessment_(OCTA)/OCTA2007.pdf>. Accessed on 10 April 2010.

Europol (2006). *OCTA: EU Organized Crime Threat Assessment 2006.* The Hague, Netherlands: European Police Office.

Gambetta, D. (1993). *The Sicilian Mafia: The Business of Private Protection.* Cambridge, MA: Harvard University Press.

Gerber, T. P. and Mendelson, S. E. (2008). 'Public Experiences of Police Violence and Corruption in Contemporary Russia: A Case of Predatory Policing?' *Law & Society Review,* 42 (1): 1–43.

Klerks, P. (2003). 'The network paradigm applied to organised crime', in A. Edwards and P. Gill (eds.), *Transnational Organised Crime: Perspectives on global security.* London: Routledge, 97–113.

New Zealand Police Association (2006a). 'The Lessons Canada can teach about dealing with gangs/organised crime'. *Police News*, 39 (3): 66–68.

New Zealand Police Association (2006b). 'The Changing Face of New Zealand Gangs'. *Police News*, 39 (3): 69.

New Zealand Police Association (2006c). 'Gang members/associates outnumber sworn police by nearly nine-to-one'. *Police News*, 39 (3): 71–72.

Nicaso, A., and Lamothe, L. (2005). *Angels, Mobsters and Narco-Terrorists: The Rising Menace of Global Criminal Empires*. Canada: John Wiley & Sons.

O'Connor, T. R. (2005). 'Police Deviance and Ethics', in, *MegaLinks in Criminal Justice*.< http://policecrimes.com/police_deviance.html >. Accessed on 10 April 2010.

Perry, F. (2001). 'Repairing Broken Windows – police corruption'. *FBI Law Enforcement Bulletin*, 70 (2): 23–27.

Punch, M. (2003). 'Rotten Orchards: "Pestilence", Police Misconduct And System Failure'. *Policing and Society*, 13 (2): 171–196.

Robinson, J. (2000). *The Merger: The Conglomeration of International Organized Crime*. Woodstock: the Overlook Press.

Ruggiero, V. and Khan, K. (2007). 'The Organisation of Drug Supply, South Asian Criminal Enterprise in the UK'. *Organised Crime in Asia: Governance and Accountability*. Symposium Proceedings, Queensland University of Technology and National University of Singapore, 61–74.

Serio, J. (2008). *Investigating the Russian Mafia*. North Carolina: Carolina Academic Press.

Van Duyne, P. C. (2000). 'Mobsters are human too: Behavioural science and organized crime investigation'. Crime, Law and Social Change, 34 (4): 369–390.

Wa, K. L. (2007). 'State Intervention and Social Change: An Account for the Decline of Triad Society in Hong Kong in post-1997 Era'. *Organised Crime in Asia: Governance and Accountability*. Symposium Proceedings, Queensland University of Technology and National University of Singapore, 218–145.

Zhang, S. X. and Pineda, S. L. (2008). 'Corruption as a Causal Factor in Human Trafficking', in D. Siegel and H. Nelen (eds.), *Organized Crime: Culture, Markets and Policies*. New York: Springer.

Chapter 5

Chu, K. Y. (2000). *The Triads as Business*. London: Routledge.

Financial Action Task Force (FATF). *Report on Money Laundering Typologies 1998–1999*, 29. <http://www.fatf-gafi.org/dataoecd/29/38/34038177.pdf>. Accessed on AUSTRAC website on 3 November 2008.

Financial Action Task Force (FATF). *Report on Money Laundering Typologies 2002–2003*, 16. <http://www.fatf-gafi.org/dataoecd/29/33/34037958.pdf>. Accessed on AUSTRAC website on 3 November 2008.

Gambetta, D. (1993). *The Sicilian Mafia: The Business of Private Protection*. Cambridge, MA: Harvard University Press.

Klerks, P. (2003). 'The network paradigm applied to organised crime', in A. Edwards and P. Gill (eds.), *Transnational Organised Crime: Perspectives on global security*. London: Routledge, 97–113.

References

Kugler, M., Verdier, T., and Zenou, Y. (2005). 'Organised crime, corruption and punishment'. *Journal of Public Economics*, 89: 1639–1663.

Nelen, H. and Lankhorst, F. (2008). 'Facilitating Organized Crime: The Role of Lawyers and Notaries', in D. Siegel and H. Nelen (eds.), *Organized Crime: Culture, Markets and Policies*. New York: Springer.

New Zealand Police Association (2006a). 'The Lessons Canada can teach about dealing with gangs/organised crime'. *Police News*, 39 (3): 66–68.

Nicaso, A. and Lamothe, L. (2005). *Angels, Mobsters and Narco-Terrorists: The Rising Menace of Global Criminal Empires*. Canada: John Wiley & Sons.

Robinson, J. (2000). *The Merger: The Conglomeration of International Organized Crime*. Woodstock: the Overlook Press.

Ruggiero, V. and Khan, K. (2007). 'The Organisation of Drug Supply, South Asian Criminal Enterprise in the UK'. *Organised Crime in Asia: Governance and Accountability*. Symposium Proceedings, Queensland University of Technology and National University of Singapore, 61–74.

Serio, J. (2008). *Investigating the Russian Mafia*. North Carolina: Carolina Academic Press.

Siegel, D. and Nelen, H. (2008). *Organized Crime: Culture, Markets and Policies*. New York: Springer.

Van Duyne, P. C. (2000). 'Mobsters are human too: Behavioural science and organized crime investigation'. *Crime, Law and Social Change*, 34 (4): 369–390.

Von Lampe, K. (2007). 'Criminals are not alone. Some observations on the social microcosm of illegal entrepreneurs', in P. C. van Duyne, A. Maljevic, M. van Dijck, K. von Lampe, and J. Harvey (eds.), *Crime Business and Crime Money in Europe. The Dirty Linen of Illegal Enterprise*. Nijmegen, Netherlands: Wolf Legal Publishers, 131–156.

Chapter 6

Audretsch, D. B. and Keilbach, M. (2007). 'The Theory of Knowledge Spillover Entrepreneurialism'. *Journal of Management Studies*, 44 (7): 1242–1254.

Chu, K. Y. (2000). *The Triads as Business*. London: Routledge.

Duyne, P. C. (2000). 'Mobsters are human too: Behavioural science and organized crime investigation'. *Crime, Law and Social Change*, 34 (4): 369–390.

Europol (2007). *Organised Crime Threat Assessment* Report. <http://www.europol.europa.eu/publications/European_Organised_Crime_Threat_Assessment_(OCTA)/OCTA2007.pdf>. Accessed on 18 December 2008.

Gambetta, D. (1993). *The Sicilian Mafia: The Business of Private Protection*. Cambridge, MA: Harvard University Press.

Grennan, S., and Britz, M. (2006). *Organized Crime: A Worldwide Perspective*. Upper Saddle River, New Jersey: Pearson, Prentice Hall.

Klerks, P. (2003). 'The network paradigm applied to organised crime', in A. Edwards and P. Gill (eds), *Transnational Organised Crime: Perspectives on global security*. London: Routledge, 97–113.

Mackenzie, S. (2002). *Organised Crime and common transit networks*. Canberra: Australian Institute of Criminology.

Markovski, S. and Hall, P. (2007). 'Public sector entrepreneurship and the production of defense'. *Public Finance and Management*, 7 (3): 260–294.

New Zealand Police Association (2006a). 'The Lessons Canada can teach about dealing with gangs/organised crime'. *Police News*, 39 (3): 66–68.

Nicaso, A., and Lamothe, L. (2005). *Angels, Mobsters and Narco-Terrorists: The Rising Menace of Global Criminal Empires*. Canada: John Wiley & Sons.

Parliamentary Joint Committee on the Australian Crime Commission (PJCACC) (2007). *Inquiry into the future impact of serious and organised crime on Australian Society*. Commonwealth of Australia.

Pérez, N. (2007). *Crime Networks*. Job Market Paper, University of Maryland.

Robinson, J. (2000). *The Merger: The Conglomeration of International Organized Crime*. Woodstock: the Overlook Press.

Serio, J. (2008). *Investigating the Russian Mafia*. North Carolina: Carolina Academic Press.

Thomas, A. and Mancino, A. (2007). 'The relationship between entrepreneurial characteristics, firms' positioning and local development'. *Entrepreneurship and Innovation*, 8 (2): 105–114.

Von Lampe, K. (2007). 'Criminals are not alone. Some observations on the social microcosm of illegal entrepreneurs', in P. C. van Duyne, A. Maljevic, M. van Dijck, K. von Lampe, and J. Harvey (eds.), *Crime Business and Crime Money in Europe. The Dirty Linen of Illegal Enterprise*. Nijmegen, Netherlands: Wolf Legal Publishers, pp 131–156.

Chapter 7

Brodeur, J. P. and Dupont, B. (2006). 'Knowledge Workers or "Knowledge" Workers?'. *Policing and Society*, 16 (1): 7–26.

Clarke Inquiry into the Case of Dr Mohamed Haneef (2008). *Report of the Inquiry into the Case of Dr Mohamed Haneef* (Volume One). Commonwealth of Australia. This report is available online at: <http://www.haneefcaseinquiry.gov.au/>. Accessed on 25 June 2009.

Davenport, T. H. and Prusak, L. (1998). *Working Knowledge*. Boston, MA: Harvard Business School Press.

Dean, G. and Gottschalk, P. (2007). *Knowledge Management in Policing and Law Enforcement: Foundations, Structures and Applications*. London: Oxford University Press.

Drucker, P. E. (1995). 'The Post Capitalistic Executive', in P. E. Drucker (ed.), *Management in a Time of Great Change*. New York: Penguin.

Findlay, M. (2007). 'Global Terror and Organised Crime: Symbiotic or synonymous?', in *Organised Crime in Asia: Governance and Accountability*. Symposium Proceedings, Queensland University of Technology and National University of Singapore, 46–60.

Flexner, A. (2001). 'Is social work a profession?'. *Research on Social Work Practice*, 11 (2): 152–165.

Freidson, E. (2001). *Professionalism: the third logic*. Chicago: University of Chicago Press.

Frické, M. (2009). 'The knowledge pyramid: a critique of the DIKW hierarchy'. *Journal of Information Science*, 35 (2): 131–142.

References

Gottschalk, P. (2005). *Strategic Knowledge Management Technology*. Hershey, PA, USA: Idea Group Publishing.

Grover, V. and Davenport, T. H. (2001). 'General Perspectives on Knowledge Management: Fostering a Research Agenda'. *Journal of Management Information Systems*, 18 (1): 5–21.

Herald Sun (2009). *Chronology of events in the Mohamed Haneef terrorism case*. <http://www.heraldsun.com.au/news/key-events-in-the-mohamed-haneef-case/story-e6frf7jo-1111118395365>. Accessed on 10 April 2010.

Krause, E. A. (1996). *Death of the guilds: Professions, states, and the advance of capitalism, 1930 to the present*. New Haven, CT: Yale University Press.

Kulick, O. A. (2006). 'Professionalism and OD: The Past, the Present, and Future Scenarios'. *Organisational Development Journal*, 24 (3): 20–33.

Lynch, A. (2009). 'Learning from Haneef'. *Inside Story—Current affairs and culture*. <http://inside.org.au/learning-from-haneef/>. Accessed on 25 June 2009.

Poston, R. S. and Speier, C. (2005). 'Effective Use of Knowledge Management Systems: A Process Model of Content Ratings and Credibility Indicators'. *MIS Quarterly*, 29 (2), 221–244.

Pugh, D. (1989). 'Professionalism in Public Administration: Problems, Perspectives, and the Role of ASPA'. *Public Administration Review*, 49 (1): 170–178.

Rowley, J. (2007). 'The wisdom hierarchy: representations of the DIKW hierarchy'. *Journal of Information Science*, 33 (2): 163–180.

Ryu, C., Kim, Y. J., Chaudhury, A., and Rao, H. R. (2005). 'Knowledge Acquisition via Three Learning Processes in Enterprise Information Portals: Learning-by-Investment, Learning-by-Doing, and Learning-from-Others'. *MIS Quarterly*, 29 (2): 245–278.

Sambamurthy, V. and Subramani, M. (2005). 'Special Issue on Information Technologies and Knowledge Management'. *MIS Quarterly*, 29 (1): 1–7; and 29 (2): 193–195.

Spiegler, I. (2000). 'Knowledge Management: A New Idea or a Recycled Concept?'. *Communications of the Association for Information Systems*, 3 (14).

Tanriverdi, H. (2005). 'Information Technology Relatedness, Knowledge Management Capability, and Performance of Multibusiness Firms'. *MIS Quarterly*, 29 (2): 311–334.

Thinkexist.com (2009). Einstein quotes. <http://www.thinkexist.com>. Accessed on 23 October 2009.

Wasko, M. M. and Faraj, S. (2005). 'Why Should I Share? Examining Social Capital and Knowledge Contribution in Electronic Networks of Practice'. *MIS Quarterly*, 29 (1): 35–57.

Wilensky, H. L. (1964). 'The professionalization of everyone?'. *The American Journal of Sociology*, 70: 137–158.

Chapter 8

Abadinsky, H. (2007). *Organised Crime*. Belmont, CA: Thomson Wadsworth.

Australian Crime Commission (2007). *Organised Crime in Australia*. Canberra: ACC Publication.

References

Bandidos (2009). *Bandidos Mototcycleclub Worldwide.* <http://www.bandidosmc.dk/>. Accessed on 6 February 2009.

Crime and Misconduct Commission (2000). 'Inside the Amphetamine Market in Queensland'. *CMC Bulletin* No. 2.

Europol (2007). *Organised Crime Threat Assessment* Report. <http://www.europol.europa.eu/publications/European_Organised_Crime_Threat_Assessment_(OCTA)/OCTA2007.pdf>.

Galeotti, M. (ed.) (2005). *Global Crime Today - The Changing Face of Organized Crime.* London: Routledge.

Gambetta, D. (1993). *The Sicilian Mafia: The Business of Private Protection.* Cambridge, MA: Harvard University Press.

Gilmour, S. (2008). 'Understanding Organized Crime: A Local Perspective'. *Policing: A Journal of Policy and Practice*, 2 (1): 18–27.

Guardian (2003). *Montenegrin PM accused of link with tobacco racket.* <http://www.guardian.co.uk/world/2003/jul/11/smoking.internationalcrime>. Accessed on 24 November 2008.

Harfield, C. (2008). 'Paradigms, Pathologies, and Practicalities—Policing Organized Crime in England and Wales'. *Policing: A Journal of Policy and Practice*, 2 (1): 63–73.

Hill, P. (2003). *The Japanese Mafia: Yakuza, Law and the State.* Oxford: Oxford University Press.

Huisman, S. (2008). 'Investigating Chinese Crime Entrepreneurs'. *Policing: A Journal of Policy and Practice*, 2 (1): 36–42.

Klerks, P. (2003). 'The network paradigm applied to organised crime', in A. Edwards and P. Gill (eds), *Transnational Organised Crime: Perspectives on global security.* London: Routledge, 97–113.

Moran, N. (2002). 'Emerging Trends: Transnational Drug Production and Trafficking'. *Crime and Justice International*, 18 (63): 5–6.

National Alliance of Gang Investigators Association (NAGIA) (2009). <http://www.nagia.org/Home/tabid/36/Default.aspx>. Accessed on 8 February 2009.

New Zealand Police Association (2005). 'How organised crime controls the meth market'. *Police News*, 38 (1): 12–15.

New Zealand Police Association (2006a). 'The Lessons Canada can teach about dealing with gangs/organised crime'. *Police News*, 39 (3): 66–68.

New Zealand Police Association (2006b). 'The Changing Face of New Zealand Gangs'. *Police News*, 39 (3): 69.

New Zealand Police Association (2006c). 'Gang members/associates outnumber sworn police by nearly nine-to-one'. *Police News*, 39 (3): 71–72.

Nicholas, R. (2006). 'The current amphetamine situation in Australasia—implications for policing'. *Australasian Centre for Policing Research (ACPR) Discussion Paper.* Marsden: South Australia.

Norwegian Police University College (2008). *Personal communication*, Detective Superintendent of Police for Organised Crime, Oslo, Norway.

Paoli, L. (2003). *Mafia Brotherhoods: Organized Crime, Italian Style.* New York: Oxford University Press.

Richter, M. (2000). 'Outlaw Motorcycle Gangs: Alliance and Expansion'. *Crime and Justice International*, 14 (42/43): 7–8.

Ridley, N. (2008). 'Organized Crime, Money Laundering, and Terrorism'. *Policing: A Journal of Policy and Practice*, 2 (1): 28–35.

Roberti, F. (2008). 'Organized Crime in Italy: The Neapolitan Camorra Today'. *Policing: A Journal of Policy and Practice*, 2 (1): 43–49.

Shelley, L. (2003). 'Trafficking in Women: The Business Model Approach'. *The Brown Journal of World Affairs*, Vol. X Issue 1: 119–131.

Siegel, D. and Nelen, H. (eds.) (2008). *Organized Crime: Culture, Markets, and Politics*. New York: Springer.

Wikipedia (2009). <http://en.wikipedia.org/wiki/Milo_Dukanovic>. Accessed on 2 December 2009.

Zhang, S. X. and Pineda, S. L. (2008). 'Corruption as a Causal Factor in Human Trafficking', in D. Siegel. and H. Nelen (eds.), *Organized Crime: Culture, Markets, and Politics*. New York: Springer.

Chapter 9

Abadinsky, H. (2007). *Organized Crime* (8th edn). Belmont, CA: Thomas Wadsworth.

Albanese, J. S. (2004). *Organized crime in our times* (4th edn). LexisNexis Group, Cincinnati, Ohio: Anderson Publishing.

Bennet, A. and Bennet, D. (2005a). 'Designing the Knowledge Organization of the Future: The Intelligent Complex Adaptive System', in C. W. Holsapple (ed.), *Handbook of Knowledge Management*. Netherlands: Springer Science & Business Media, Vol 2: 623–638.

Bennet, A. and Bennet, D. (2005b). 'The Rise of the Knowledge Organization', in C. W. Holsapple (ed.), *Handbook of Knowledge Management*. Netherlands: Springer Science & Business Media, Vol 1: 5–20.

Biloslavo, R. (2005). 'Use of knowledge management framework as a tool for innovation capability audit'. *International Journal of Innovation and Learning*, 2 (4): 402–424.

Black, J. (2002). *Dictionary of Economics*. Oxford Reference Online, Oxford University Press. <http://www.oxfordreference.com/views/ENTRY.html?subview=Main&entry=t19.e1697>. Accessed on 18 December 2008.

Bock, G. W., Zmud, R. W., and Kim, Y. G. (2005). 'Behavioral intention formation in knowledge sharing: examining the roles of extrinsic motivators, social-psychological forces, and organizational climate'. *MIS Quarterly*, 29 (1): 87–111.

Brown, S. (2008). 'Ready, willing and enable: A theory of enablers for international co-operation', in S. Brown (ed.), *Combating International Crime: The Longer Arm of the Law*. London: Routledge-Cavendish.

Chen, H., Schroeder, J., Hauck, R. V., Ridgeway, L., Atabakhsh, H., Gupta, H., Boarman, C., Rasmussen, K., and Clements, A. W. (2002). 'COPLINK Connect: information and knowledge management for law enforcement'. *Decision Support Systems*, 34: 271–285.

David, E., and Bamford, J. (June 2005). 'Your Alliances are Too Stable'. *Harvard Business Review*.

Gasper, R. (2008). 'Tackling international crime: Forward into the third era', in S. Brown (ed.), *Combating International Crime: The Longer Arm of the Law*. London: Routledge-Cavendish.

Grennan, S. and Britz, M. (2006). *Organized Crime: A Worldwide Perspective*. Upper Saddle River, New Jersey: Pearson, Prentice Hall.

Harfield, C. (2008). 'Paradigms, Pathologies, and Practicalities—Policing Organized Crime in England and Wales'. *Policing: A Journal of Policy and Practice*, 2 (1): 63–73.

Hughes, V. and Jackson, P. (2004). 'The Influence of Technical, Social and Structural Factors on the Effective use of Information in a Policing Environment'. *The Electronic Journal of Knowledge Management*, Vol 2 (1): 65–76.

Kark, R. and van Dijk, D. (2007). 'Motivation to lead, motivation to follow: the role of the self-regulatory focus in leadership processes'. *Academy of Management Review*, 32 (2): 500–528.

Leong, A. (2007). *The Disruption of International Organised Crime: An Analysis of Legal and Non-legal Strategies*. Aldershot: Ashgate.

Liebowitz, J. (2004). 'Will knowledge management work in the government?'. *Electronic Government: An International Journal*, 1 (1): 1–7.

Liu, C. C. and Chen, S. Y. (2005). 'Determinants of knowledge sharing of e-learners'. *International Journal of Innovation and Learning*, 2 (4): 434–445.

Lyman, M. and Potter, G. (2004). *Organized crime*. Upper Saddle River, New Jersey: Pearson Prentice Hall.

Macquarie Dictionary (2nd revision) (1987). New South Wales, Australia: The Macquarie Library.

Owen, L., Goldwasser, C., Choate, K., and Blitz, A. (2008). 'The power of many: ABCs of collaborative innovation', in M. Chapman, S. Berman and A. Blitz (eds.), *Rethinking Innovation: Insights from the World's Leading CEOs*. Artarmon, NSW, Australia: Fast Thinking Books.

Rawlinson, P. (2008). 'Mission Impossible? Researching Organized Crime', in R. King and E. Wincup (eds.), *Doing Research on Crime and Justice*. Oxford: Oxford University Press, 291–313.

Reichel, P. (ed.) (2005). *Handbook of Transnational Crime and Justice*. Thousand Oaks, California: Sage Publications.

Robinson, J. (2000). *The Merger: The Conglomeration of International Organized Crime*. Woodstock: the Overlook Press.

Serious Organised Crime Agency (2006). *The United Kingdom Threat Assessment of Serious Organised Crime 2006/7*. London: SOCA.

Serious Organised Crime Agency (2009). <http://www.soca.gov.uk/aboutUs/index.html>. Accessed on 19 October 2009.

Siegel, L. (2008). *Criminology: The Core* (3rd edn). Belmont, CA: Thomson-Wadsworth.

Smith, D. C. (1994). 'Illicit enterprise: An Organized Crime Paradigm for the Nineties', in R. J. Kelly, K.-L. Chin, and R. Schatzberg (eds.), *Handbook of Organized Crime in the United States*. Westport, CT: Greenwood.

Van den Hooff. B. and Huysman, M. (2009). 'Managing knowledge sharing: Emergent and engineering approaches'. *Information & Management*, 46 (1): 1–8.

Van Dijk, J. (2007). Mafia makers: assessing organised crime and its impact upon societies. *Trends in Organised Crime*, 10: 39–56.

Von Lampe, K. (2008). 'Organized Crime in Europe: Conceptions and Realities'. *Policing: A Journal of Policy and Practice*, 2 (1): 7–17.

Index

accounting
  Crime Money Management (CMM) 52
Albania
  Crime Money Management
      (CMM) 111
  impenetrability of groups 116
  mafia command structure 111
  organized crime 109, 111
  specialists 111
all expenses holiday offers
  drug trafficking 4
Alternative Money Remittance
    Systems (AMRS) 53
anti-policing countermeasures
  knowledge 11
anti-surveillance technologies
  knowledge 11
Asia
  syndicated criminal networks 91–92
  Triads 91
  violence 73, 74, 75
asset specificity 51
  cost of redeploying asset to
      alternative uses 51
Australia
  derivatives market 98–99
  GPS, hijacking technology of 48
  money laundering 98–99
  organized crime 48, 55, 95, 98–99
  policing 145
  publicly traded company shares
      scam 95
  smurfing 55
Australian Crime Commission
  organized crime 6

Bandidos (Norway) 156–166
Bandolo, Giovanni 49–50
banking
  Alternative Money Remittance Systems
      (AMRS) 53
  Crime Money Management
      (CMM) 53
  informal banking systems (IBS) 53
  Niue 170
  Russian scam 93–94
banks
  funding 9

Belgium
  human trafficking 59
Big Circle Boys (BCB) 91–92
boot tracing 58
  accessing a computer's back-up
      memory 58
branding
  Mafia 75, 116
bribery
  cooperation 12
  corruption 76
  pharmaceutical industry corruption
      (Ukraine) 54
  standard operating procedures 12
business connections
  banking scam (Russian) 93–94
  Big Circle Boys (BCB) 92
  case studies/examples
    banking scam (Russian) 93–94
    Big Circle Boys (BCB) 92
    Crime Money Management
        (CMM) 99–100
    lawyers as enablers of human
        trafficking (Italy) 97–98
    lawyers as go-betweens (Italy) 96
    Mafiaocracy (Post-Soviet Russia) 97
    money laundering via derivatives
        market (Australia) 98–99
    publicly traded company shares
        scam (Australia) 95
    stock market 98–99
    Tongs 94–95
    Triads 94–95, 98
    turf wars 90–91
  Crime Money Management
      (CMM) 99–100
  criminal 90–93
  human trafficking 97–98
  influential people 96–100
  lawyers 96–98
  legitimate 93–95
  money laundering via derivatives
      market (Australia) 98–99
  Outlaw Motorcycle Gangs (OMCGs) 91
  stock market 98–99
  Tongs 94
  Triads 94–95, 98
  turf wars 90–91

Index

business development model
  see also consolidating crime business; establishing crime business; expanding crime business; positioning crime business
  case studies/examples 23–24
  competition 24–28
  consolidating phase 20, 21, 87–102
  diagram 20
  disruption strategies 22
  establishing phase 20, 21–22
  expanding phase 20, 22, 68–86
  generally 19
  Mafia type depictions 21
  management of business 20
  markets
    competition 24–28
    generally 24
    summary 40
  operating framework 19–22
  organisation of business 20, 22
  phases 20–21
    see also consolidating crime business; establishing crime business; expanding crime business; positioning crime business
    consolidating phase 20, 21, 87–102
    establishing phase 20, 21–22
    expanding phase 20, 22, 68–86
    interrelationship 20–21
    meaning 20
    nature 21
    positioning phase 20, 22, 103–119
    sequential 20
    tandem phases 20
  policing 143–144
  positioning phase 20, 22, 103–119
  resources 21–22
  starting up business 20, 21–22
  strategic value 19–20
  sustaining business 20, 22
  temporary ventures 22
  tracking evolution of crime groups 22
Business Enterprise (BE) paradigm
  see also business development model
  meaning 5–6
  origins 6
business intelligence
  assessment of market potential 71
  brokering street war (Canada) 72
  case studies/examples
  brokering street war (Canada) 72
  patching over business strategy 71
  competition 71–72
  expanding crime business 69
  meaning 70–71
  Outlaw Motorcycle Gangs (OMCGs) 71
  patching over business strategy 71
business planning
  meaning 48–49
  transaction costs 50, 51
  opportunity costs 50, 51
Canada
  brokering street war 72
  criminal heaven for organized crime 60
  cybercrime 58
  drug markets 60
  fake Versace jackets (Italian Camorra in Canada) 50
  Hells Angels'
    drug trade 90
    price fixing 115
    surveillance program 82
  operational logistics 60
  Outlaw Motorcycle Gangs (OMCGs) 82, 90
capabilities
  consolidating crime business 87–89
  decision-making under uncertainty 6, 7, 10–11
  diagram 7
  establishing crime business 44–45
  expanding crime business 68–70
  generally 6–7
  interrelationship 6, 14–17
  opportunity perspective 6, 7–8
  people cooperation 6, 7, 11–12
  profit maximization 6, 7, 12–14, 105–107
  resources mobilization 6, 7, 8–10, 55–62
  structure 7
  temporal order 6–7
capital
  acquisition 56
  bankrolling 56
  establishing crime business 44, 56–57
  funding 56–57
  participation in small-scale ventures 56
  pooling resources 57
  resources 9, 56–57

Index

car dealing
   case studies/examples 46–47
   Verhagen Group (Dutch) 46–47
case studies/examples
   Albanian organized crime 109
   Bandidos (Norway) 156–166
   banking scam (Russian) 93–94
   Big Circle Boys (BCB) 92
   branding strategy (Sicilian Mafia) 75
   brokering street war (Canada) 72
   business connections
      banking scam (Russian) 93–94
      Big Circle Boys (BCB) 92
      Crime Money Management (CMM) 99–100
      lawyers as enablers of human trafficking (Italy) 97–98
      lawyers as go-betweens (Italy) 96
      Mafiaocracy (Post-Soviet Russia) 97
      publicly traded company shares scam (Australia) 95
      stock market 98–99
      Tongs 94–95
      Triads 94–95, 98
      turf wars 90–91
   business development model 23–24
   business intelligence
      brokering street war (Canada) 72
      patching over business strategy 71
   business planning
      fake Versace jackets (Italian Camorra in Canada) 50
      illegal immigration (Chinese) 49
      'Red Daisy' fraud 49
   car dealing 46–47
   cigarette smuggling 38–39, 57
   civil wars 114
   computer chips (Vietnam) 47
   consolidating crime business
      business connections 90–91, 92, 93–94, 95
      influential people connections 96, 97, 98–100
      lawyers 96, 97
   corruption
      corrosive agent, corruption as 80–81
      systemic corruption (Post-Soviet Russia) 77, 79
      Vladimir 'The Poodle' Podatiev 79
   counter-intelligence
      hash-smuggling (Netherlands) 82

Crime Business Analysis Matrix (CBAM) 154, 156–166
Crime Money Management (CMM) 99–100
criminal entrepreneurship 14–17
criminal heaven for organized crime (Canada) 60
cuckoo smurfing 55
decentralized command structure 111
deportation of gang members 109–110
entrepreneurial vision
   computer chips (Vietnam) 47
   hijacking technology (Australia) 48
   Verhagen Group (Dutch) 46–47
expanding crime business
   business intelligence 71, 72
   corruption 77, 79, 80–81
   counter-intelligence 82
   violence 73–74, 75–76
failed states 114
fake Versace jackets (Italian Camorra in Canada) 50
hash-smuggling (Netherlands) 82
hijacking technology (Australia) 48
human resources 61
human trafficking 59, 146–150
illegal firearms' trafficking 59
illegal immigration (Chinese) 49
impenetrability, ensuring 116
Knowledge-Managed Policing (KMP) 133–142
lawyers
   go-betweens (Italy) 96
   human trafficking (Italy) 97
Lithuania, organized crime in 23–24, 36
little and often principle 112
low profile, keeping 116
Mafiaocracy (Post-Soviet Russia) 97
money laundering via derivates market (Australia) 98–99
Montenegro 152–153
networking 113
Nigerian crime groups 110
Nigerian scams 112
one way Russian style joint ventures 107
Operation Kronos: human smuggling (United Kingdom) 74
operational logistics
   criminal heaven for organized crime (Canada) 60
   cybercrime (Canada) 58
   human trafficking (Belgium) 59
   illegal firearms' trafficking 59

205

Index

case studies/examples (*cont.*)
  Outlaw Motorcycle Gangs (OMCGs) 71, 154, 156–166
  patching over business strategy 71
  pharmaceutical industry corruption (Ukraine) 54
  police crackdowns 115
  pooling resources 57
  positioning crime business
    Albanian organized crime 109, 111
    civil wars 114
    decentralized command structure 111
    deportation of gang members 109–110
    failed states 114
    impenetrability, ensuring 116
    little and often principle 112
    low profile, keeping 116
    MS-13 (Salvadorans) 108
    networking 113
    Nigerian crime groups 110
    Nigerian scams 112
    one way Russian style joint ventures 107
    police crackdowns 115
    specialists, use of 111, 112
    strategic alliances 115
  publicly traded company shares scam (Australia) 95
  'Red Daisy' fraud 49
  reputational violence 75
  smurfing (Europe and Australia) 55
  specialists, use of 111, 112
  strategic alliances 115
  terrorism 133–142
  Tongs 94–95
  Triads 94–95, 98
  Verhagen Group (Dutch) 46–47
  violence
    branding strategy (Sicilian Mafia) 75
    indirect brutal violence (Chinese) 73–74
    Operation Kronos: human smuggling (United Kingdom) 74
    reputational violence 75
    Vietnam 75–76
  Warren, Curtis 'Cocky' 14–17
  young women as drug mules 3–4
CBAM *see* Crime Business Analysis Matrix (CBAM)
China
  fe ich'ien system 53
  illegal immigration 49
  indirect brutal violence 73–74
  Tongs 94–95
  Triads 94–95
  violence 73–74
cigarette smuggling
  case studies/examples 38–39, 57
  Estonia 38–39
  Europe 57
  financial backing 57
  markets 38–39
  Montenegro 153
  Netherlands 38
civil wars
  positioning crime business 113–114
CMM *see* Crime Money Management (CMM)
Colombia
  drug markets 27
communication skills
  cooperation 11, 12
competition
  business development model 24–28
  business intelligence 71–72
  drug markets 26–27
  illegal markets 24–28
  invisible hand 24–25, 27
  key factors 26
  legal markets 24–28
  markets 24–28
  profits 13, 106
  supply and demand 27–31
  visible hand 25
connections
  criminal business connections 90–93
  legitimate business connections 93–95
consolidating crime business
  business connections
    see also **business connections**
    criminal 90–93
    influential people 96–100
    lawyers 96
    legitimate 93–95
  capabilities 87–89
  case studies/examples
    banking scam (Russian) 93–94
    Big Circle Boys (BCB) 92
    lawyers as go-betweens (Italy) 96
    publicly traded company shares scam (Australia) 95
    Tongs 94
    turf wars 90–91

206

Index

communication skills 89
cooperation 87–88, 89–90
criminal business connections 90–93
fuzzy mapping 100–102
generally 87
lawyers 96–98
legitimate business connections 93–95
management 87, 89–90
summary 102
syndicated criminal networks 91–92
Triads 91
turf wars 90–91
contacts
familial entrepreneurial culture 8
cooperation
bribery 12
co-opting 11
communication skills 11, 12
connections 11
consolidating crime business 87–88, 89–90
corruption 11, 12
entrepreneurialism 11–12
expanding crime business 69
influential people 11
misinformation 11
people 6, 7, 11–12
relationship-building 11
resources 9
scams 11
securing 11
social microcosm 12
violence 11–12
corruption
bribery 76
case studies/examples
  corrosive agent, corruption as 80–81
  systemic corruption (Post-Soviet Russia) 77, 79
  Vladimir 'The Poodle' Podatiev 79
cooperation 11, 12
corrosive agent, corruption as 80–81
Crime Money Management (CMM) 54–55
drug trade 77
entrepreneurialism 9
Europe 76
expanding crime business 69, 76–81
honey traps 9, 76
kick-backs to police 76
law enforcement 77–80
New Zealand 80

pharmaceutical industry (Ukraine) 54
police 77, 78–80
purpose 9
resources 9
Russia 77, 79
standard operating procedures 12
systemic corruption (Post-Soviet Russia) 77, 79
uses 9, 76
Vladimir 'The Poodle' Podatiev 79
counter-intelligence
case studies/examples
  hash-smuggling (Netherlands) 82
communications 81
education 82–83
expanding crime business 69, 81–83
law enforcement 81–82
Outlaw Motorcycle Gangs (OMCGs) 82
proactive measures 81, 82
reactive measures 81
techniques 81
Crime Business Analysis Matrix (CBAM)
benefits 154
case studies/examples 154, 156–166
diagram 154, 155
fuzzy mapping 154
Outlaw Motorcycle Gangs (OMCGs) 154, 156–166
purpose 143, 154
Crime Money Management (CMM)
accounting 52
Albania 111
Alternative Money Remittance Systems (AMRS) 53
banking 53
business connections 99–100
case studies/examples 99–100
cash 54
concept 52
corruption 54–55
fe ich'ien system (China) 53
funds transfer 53–54
Hawala money remittance scheme (India) 53
Hundi funds transfer scheme (Pakistan) 53
informal banking systems (IBS) 53
informal funds transfer schemes 53
investment 52
money cycle 52–53
money laundering 52, 53
Netherlands 99–100

207

Crime Money Management
    (CMM) (cont.)
  pharmaceutical industry (Ukraine) 54
  smurfing 55
  use of term 52
cuckoo smurfing 55
cybercrime
  boot tracing 58
  Canada 58
  definition 169–170
  gambling machines 58
  machine code monitor 58
  organized crime 169
Czech Republic
  Triads 98

decision-making
  control structure 10
  entrepreneurialism 6, 7, 10–11
  expanding crime business 70
  judgment 10
  knowledge 11
  risk assessment 51
  risk-taking 10
  uncertainty, under 6, 7, 10–11, 70
derivatives market
  Australia 98–99
  money laundering 98–99
disruption strategies
  business development model 22
drug mules
  young women 3–4
drug trade
  see also **drug trafficking**
  Canada 60
  Colombia 27
  competition 26–27
  corruption 77
  Germany 26–27
  human resources 62
  Italy 26–27
  Netherlands 82
  Outlaw Motorcycle Gangs (OMCGs) 71
  pooling resources 57
  Russia 26–27
  United Kingdom 57
drug trafficking
  see also **drug trade**
  all expenses holiday offers 4
  entrapment 4
  luggage used for courier 4
  victims 5

Warren, Curtis 'Cocky' 14–17
young women used as drug mules 3–4

economic crime 169
education
  counter-intelligence 82–83
enterprise crime 169, 170
entrapment
  drug trafficking 4
entrepreneurial criminality
  social harm 5
entrepreneurialism
  case study 14–17
  cooperation 11–12
  corruption strategies 9
  decision-making under uncertainty
    6, 7, 10–11
  definition 6–7
  familial entrepreneurial culture 8
  flair 17
  individual capabilities
    decision-making under uncertainty
      6, 7, 10–11
    diagram 7
    establishing crime business 44–45
    generally 6–7
    interrelationship 6, 14–17
    opportunity perspective 6, 7–8,
      45–55
    people cooperation 6, 7, 11–12
    profit maximization 6, 7, 12–14
    resources mobilization 6, 7, 8–10,
      55–62
  structure 7
  temporal order 6–7
  innovation 9–10
  judgment 10
  knowledge 11
  opportunity perspective 6, 7–8, 45–55
  people cooperation 6, 7, 11–12
  policing 173–174
  profit maximization 6, 7, 12–14
  resources mobilization 6, 7, 8–10,
    55–62
  risk-taking 6
  summary 17–18
environmental crimes 169
equipment
  resources 9
establishing crime business
  asset specificity 51
  business modelling phase 43–45

business planning 44, 48–52
capabilities 44–45
capital 44, 56–57
case studies/examples
    cigarette smuggling 57
    computer chips (Vietnam) 47
    cuckoo smurfing 55
    fake Versace jackets (Italian Camorra in Canada) 50
    hijacking technology (Australia) 48
    illegal immigration (Chinese) 49
    pharmaceutical industry corruption (Ukraine) 54
    pooling resources in drug trade (United Kingdom) 57
    'Red Daisy' fraud 49
    Verhagen Group (Dutch) 46–47
crime money management *see* **Crime Money Management (CMM)**
cuckoo smurfing 55
diagram 44
entrepreneurial vision 44, 46–48
extortion rackets 49
factors 44–45
fuzzy mapping 63–67
generally 43
hijacking technology (Australia) 48
human resources 44, 60–62
illegal immigration (Chinese) 49
interrelationship with other business phases 43–44
operational logistics 44, 57–60
opportunity 45–55
opportunity cost 51
planning 48–52
'Red Daisy' fraud 49
resources mobilization
    capital 56–57
    generally 55
    operational logistics 44, 57–60
summary 67
transaction costs 50, 51
transaction frequency 51
unknown costs 51–52
Verhagen Group (Dutch) 46–47
Estonia
cigarette smuggling 38–39
ethnicity
human resources 61
role in criminal enterprises 92

Europe
cigarette smuggling 57
corruption 76
illegal firearms' trafficking 59
policing 145
smurfing 55
expanding crime business
business intelligence 69, 70–72
business modelling phase 68–70
capabilities 68–70
case studies/examples
    business intelligence 71, 72
cooperation 69
corruption 69, 76–81
counter-intelligence 69, 81–83
decision-making 70
fuzzy mapping 83–86
generally 68
people cooperation 69
resource mobilization 68–69
risk management 70
summary 86
violence 69, 73–76
extortion rackets
establishing crime business 49

failed states
positioning crime business 113–114
familial entrepreneurial culture
entrepreneurialism 8
fe ich'ien system 53
Felix, Ramon Arellano 21
firearms
illegal firearms' trafficking (Europe) 59
fuel taxes
'Red Daisy' fraud 49
funding
banks 9
capital 56–57
crime money 9
long-term 9
long-term credit 9
ownership equity 9
short-term 9
working capital 9
funds transfer
Crime Money Management (CMM) 53–54
fe ich'ien system (China) 53
Hawala scheme (India) 53
Hundi scheme (Pakistan) 53

fuzzy mapping
  consolidating crime business 100–102
  Crime Business Analysis Matrix (CBAM) 154
  establishing crime business 63–67
  expanding crime business 83–86
  meaning 63
  positioning crime business 117–119

gambling machines
  cybercrime 58
gangs
  culture 8
  opportunity 8
Germany
  drug markets 26–27
globalisation
  criminal industries 37–39
  market share 109–110
  policing 150–153
GPS
  hijacking technology (Australia) 48

'Hawala' money remittance scheme 53
hash-smuggling
  Netherlands 82
high-end organized crime
  meaning 3
honey traps 9, 76
Hong Kong
  Triads 91
  violence 75
human needs
  manipulation for profit 5
human resources
  associates 61
  case studies/examples 61
  cost/benefit analysis 62
  drug trade 62
  establishing crime business 44, 60–62
  ethnicity 61
  family members 61
  gangs 61
  kinship 61
  meaning 60–61
  recruitment 61–62
  risk reduction strategies 62
  start-up crime businesses 62
human trafficking
  Belgium 59
  business connections 97–98
  case studies/examples 59, 146–150

  lawyers' involvement 96–97
  United Kingdom 74
'Hundi' funds transfer scheme 53

IBS (Informal Banking Systems) 53
illegal firearms' trafficking
  Europe 59
illegal immigration
  China 49
India
  'Hawala' money remittance scheme 53
individual capabilities
  entrepreneurialism 6–7
influential people
  business connections 96–100
informal banking systems (IBS) 53
innovation
  entrepreneurialism 9–10
  resources 9–10
  strong sense 13
  weak sense 13
intelligence *see* **business intelligence**
international crime 169
investment
  Crime Money Management (CMM) 52
invisible hand 24–25, 27
Italy
  drug markets 26–27

judgment
  decision-making 10
  entrepreneurialism 10

KMP *see* **Knowledge-Managed Policing (KMP)**
knowledge
  see also **Knowledge-Managed Policing (KMP)**
  administrative 126
  analytical 126
  anti-policing countermeasures 11
  anti-surveillance technologies 11
  categories 126
  characteristics 124
  competency 130–131
  cube 123, 129, 130–142
  decision-making 11
  depth of police knowledge 127–130
  hierarchy 124
  insight 130
  intelligence 124, 126
  know-why 123, 131

ladder 124
legal 126
levels of police knowledge 126–127
new 125
operational 126
perception 130
policing 126
sharing 168, 178–182
strategic 11
technical 126
understanding 130, 131
uses 124–125
Knowledge Cube (KC)
Knowledge-Managed Policing (KMP) 123, 129, 130–142
theoretical cube 131, 132
Knowledge-Managed Policing (KMP)
administrative knowledge 126
analytical knowledge 126
application of knowledge in policing 123–126
aspects 125
balance between knowledge and systems 125
case study 133–142
categories of knowledge 126
competency knowledge 130–131
depth of knowledge 127–130
entrepreneurialism, policing 173–174
generally 123
insight knowledge 130
intelligence 124
know-why knowledge 123, 131
knowledge 123–126
Knowledge Cube (KC) 123, 129, 130–142
knowledge ladder 124
legal knowledge 126
levels of police knowledge 126–127
meaning 125
operational knowledge 126
people 125
perception knowledge 130
professionalism knowledge 127, 131
professionalizing 127
sharing knowledge 168, 178–182
summary 142
systems 125
technical knowledge 126
terrorism 133–142
training 127
understanding knowledge 130, 131
validated information 124

law enforcement
consequences 110
corruption 77–80
counter-intelligence 81–82
lawyers
business connections 96–98
case studies/examples
go-betweens (Italy) 96
human trafficking (Italy) 97
legitimacy
cloak of 5
Lithuania
markets 36
organized crime 23–24, 36
logistics *see* **operational logistics**
long-term credit
funding 9
long-term funds
resources 9

Mafia
Albania 111
Bandolo, Giovanni 49–50
branding 75, 116
Calabrian 21
Camorra 21, 49–50
Italian 21
protection rackets 75, 116
reputational violence 116
risk estimation 51
Sacra Corona 21
Sicilian 21, 75
violence 116
marketplace crimes 169
markets
business development model
competition 24–28
generally 24
summary 40
cigarette smuggling 38–39
competition 24–28
criminal markets
generally 33
global spheres of influence 33–34
push-pull factors 35–37
elasticity 29, 30
global nature of criminal industries 37–39
impact of law enforcement 31
imperfections 13–14
invisible hand 24–25
key factors 26

Index

markets (*cont.*)
  Lithuania 36
  market elasticity 29–30
  market price 28
  profits 13–14
  push-pull factors 35–37
  Russia 36
  share 31–33
  size 31–33
  Smith, Adam 25
  supply and demand 27–31
  supply gaps 31
  visible hand 25
  volatility 14
media profile
  positioning crime business 116
Mexico
  Felix, Ramon Arellano 21
  Tijuana Cartel 21
  Zambada-Garcia, Ismael 13, 21, 31
mobile phones
  PIN numbers, use in ascertaining 48
money laundering
  see also **Crime Money Management (CMM)**
  Australia 98–99
  back-door 53
  concept 52
  cuckoo smurfing 55
  derivatives market 98–99
  front-door 53
  informal banking systems (IBS) 53
  integration 53
  layering 53
  placement 53
  smurfing 55
  stages 53
Montenegro
  case studies/examples 152–153
  cigarette smuggling 153
MS-13 (Salvadorans) 108

necessity
  opportunity 8
Netherlands
  cigarette smuggling 38
  Crime Money Management (CMM) 99–100
  drug trade 82
  hash-smuggling 82
  Verhagen Group (Dutch) 46–47

networking
  positioning crime business 113
New Zealand
  corruption 80
  Outlaw Motorcycle Gangs (OMCGs) 72
Nigeria
  organized crime 5, 110, 112–113, 169
  scams 5, 112–113, 169
Niue
  banking 170
Norway
  sex industry 31–32

OMGCs *see* **Outlaw Motorcycle Gangs (OMCGs)**
Operation Kronos: human smuggling (United Kingdom) 74
operational logistics
  Canada 60
  case studies/examples
  criminal heaven for organized crime (Canada) 60
  cybercrime (Canada) 58
  human trafficking (Belgium) 59
  illegal firearms' trafficking 59
  criminal heaven for organized crime (Canada) 60
  cybercrime (Canada) 58
  establishing crime business 44, 57–60
  human trafficking (Belgium) 59
  illegal firearms' trafficking 59
  meaning 58
  resources 9, 57–60
opportunity
  capability 7–8
  costs 50, 51
  entrepreneurial vision 46–48
  entrepreneurialism 6, 7–8
  establishing crime business 45–55
  exploitation 8
  familial entrepreneurial culture 8
  gangs 8
  identification 8
  necessity 8
  perspective 6, 7–8
  "seeing" 8
  sources 7–8
opportunism
  key concept 51
  explanatory mechanism 52
organized crime
  Albania 109, 111

Australia 48, 55, 95, 98–99
Australian Crime Commission 6
Belgium 59
Canada 19–20, 21, 22, 103–119
China 49, 53, 73–74, 94–95
Colombia 27
Czech Republic 98
definition 6, 169–171
Estonia 38–39
Europe 55, 57, 59, 76
Germany 26–27
Hong Kong 75, 91
Italy 26–27
Lithuania 23–24, 36
Mexico 13, 21, 31
morphing 169–171
Netherlands 38, 46–47, 82, 99–100
New Zealand 72, 80
Nigeria 5, 110, 112–113, 169
Norway 31–32
Pakistan 53
Russia 26–27, 36, 49, 77, 79, 93–94, 107
subject-matter 3
Sweden 31
Ukraine 54
United Kingdom 57, 74
victims 5
Vietnam 47, 75–76
Outlaw Motorcycle Gangs (OMCGs)
Bandidos (Norway) 156–166
business connections 91
business intelligence 71
Canada 82, 90
case studies/examples 71, 154, 156–166
counter-intelligence 82
Crime Business Analysis Matrix (CBAM) 154, 156–166
drug trade 71
New Zealand 72
surveillance of police 82
ownership equity
funding 9

paedophile networks
online grooming 5
Pakistan
'Hundi' funds transfer scheme 53
partnerships
policing 178–182
patching over business strategy 71

petty crimes
familial entrepreneurial culture 8
pharmaceutical industry
corruption (Ukraine) 54
PIN numbers
mobile phone names used to ascertain 48
planning
establishing crime business 48–52
Podatiev, Vladimir 79
police
corruption 77, 78–80
crackdowns 115
Hells Angels' surveillance (Canada) 82
policing
see also **Crime Business Analysis Matrix; Knowledge-Managed Policing (KMP)**
context 143–144
Australia 145
business development model 143–144
competitive 177
criminal businesses
Australia 145
case study 146–150
context of policing 143–144
cultural variations 146–150
Europe 145
generally 143
global spheres of influence 150–153
Montenegro case study 152–153
networks 145
oriented clusters of criminal groups 145
structure of criminal organisations 144–145
UK approach 171–173
cultural variations 146–150
directions for future 185–188
disadvantaged 176
entrepreneurialism 173–174
Europe 145
future
directions 185–188
generally 168
international cooperation 182–185
intervention strategies 177–178
knowledge sharing 178–182
morphing of organized crime 169–171
global partnerships 178–182
globalisation 150–153
hierarchical crime structures 145

213

Index

policing (*cont.*)
  international cooperation 182–185
  intervention strategies 177–178
  local partnerships 178–182
  Montenegro case study 152–153
  oriented clusters of criminal groups 145
  partnerships 178–182
  positioning of police sector 174–177
  random 175–176
  Serious Organised Crime Agency (SOCA) 144, 171–172
  structure of criminal organisations 144–145
  summary 166–167
  targeted 176
  threat level 145
  UK approach 171–173
positioning crime business
  Albanian organized crime 109
  business development model 103–104
  case studies/examples
    Albanian organized crime 109, 111
    civil wars 114
    decentralized command structure 111
    deportation of gang members 109–110
    failed states 114
    impenetrability, ensuring 116
    little and often principle 112
    low profile, keeping 116
    MS-13 (Salvadorans) 108
    networking 113
    Nigeria 110, 112
    one way Russian style joint ventures 107
    police crackdowns 115
    specialists, use of 111, 112
    strategic alliances 115
  civil wars 113–114
  command structure 111
  competitive advantages 111–117
  decentralized command structure 111
  deportation of gang members 109–110
  failed states 113–114
  fuzzy mapping 117–119
  generally 103
  global market share 109–110
  impenetrability, ensuring 116
  local market share 107–108
  low profile, keeping 116
  market share

  global 109–110
  local 107–108
  media profile 116
  MS-13 (Salvadorans) 108
  networking 113
  Nigerian crime groups 110, 112
  one way Russian style joint ventures 107
  opportunistic exploitation 114–115
  police crackdowns 115
  price fixing 115
  profit maximization 104–107
  stability of crime leadership 114–115
  strategic alliances 115
  summary 119
premises
  resources 9
price fixing 115
profits
  aggression 13
  competition 13, 106
  entrepreneurialism 6, 7, 12–14
  global market share 109–110
  human needs manipulated for 5
  local market share 107–108
  market context 13, 106
  maximization 5, 6, 7, 12–14, 105–107
  supply and demand 106–107
  time factor 12–13
protection rackets
  Mafia 75
  Triads 116

relationship-building
  cooperation 11
reputational violence 75
resources
  see also **human resources**
  business development model 21–22
  capital 9, 56–57
  cooperation 9
  corruption 9
  entrepreneurialism 6, 7, 8–10
  equipment 9
  funding 9
  innovation 9–10
  logistics support 9, 57–60
  long-term funds 9
  mobilization 6, 7, 8–10, 55–62
  operational logistics 9, 57–60
  ownership equity 9
  pooling 57

214

premises 9
short-term funding 9
transport 9
working capital 9
risk assessment
business planning 51
'write off' costs 51
risk-taking
decision-making 10
entrepreneurialism 6
human resources 62
Russia
banking scam 93–94
corruption 77, 79
drug markets 26–27
Mafiaocracy 97
markets 36
one way Russian style joint ventures 107
'Red Daisy' fraud 49
violence 73, 75

scams
cooperation 11
Nigerian 5, 112
publicly traded company shares scam (Australia) 95
'Red Daisy' fraud 49
Serious Organised Crime Agency (SOCA) 144, 171–172
sex industry
Norway 31–32
Sweden 31
sex trafficking
victims 5
Smith, Adam
markets 25
smurfing
Australia 55
Crime Money Management (CMM) 55
Europe 55
SOCA (Serious Organised Crime Agency) 144, 171–172
social harm
entrepreneurial criminality 5
victimless crimes 5
social microcosm
criminal underworld 12
SOP *see* **standard operating procedures**
standard operating procedures
bribery 12
corruption 12

stock market
business connections 98–99
strategic alliances
positioning crime business 115
supply and demand
competition 27–28, 27–31
graphs 28–31
profits 106–107
Sweden
sex industry 31
syndicated criminal networks
Asia 91–92
Big Circle Boys (BCB) 91–92
Triads 91–92

terrorism
case studies/examples 133–142
Knowledge-Managed Policing (KMP) 133–142
Tijuana Cartel 21
Tongs 94–95
training
Knowledge-Managed Policing (KMP) 127
transaction costs
establishing crime business 50, 51
transaction frequency
cost of occasional and recurrent transactions 51
transnational crime 169
transport
resources 9
Triads
business connections 94–95, 98
case studies/examples 94–95
China 94–95
Czech Republic 98
Hong Kong 91
meaning 91
protection rackets 116
turf wars
business connections 90–91
consolidating crime business 90–91

Ukraine
pharmaceutical industry, corruption in 54
uncertainty
'unknown' costs of transaction 51
United Kingdom
drug markets 57
human trafficking 74

215

Index

Verhagen Group (Dutch)
  establishing crime business 46–47
victimless crimes
  social harm 5
victims
  drug trafficking 5
  invisible 5
  organized crime 5
  sex trafficking 5
Vietnam
  computer chips case study 47
  violence 75–76
violence
  Asia 73, 74, 75
  case studies/examples
    branding strategy (Sicilian Mafia) 75
    indirect brutal violence
      (Chinese) 73–74
    Operation Kronos: human smuggling
      (United Kingdom) 74
    reputational violence 75
    Vietnam 75–76
  China 73–74, 74
  cooperation 11–12
  expanding crime business 69, 73–76

  expressive purpose 73
  Hong Kong 75
  human trafficking 74
  indirect brutal violence
    (Chinese) 73–74
  instrumental purpose 73
  Mafia 116
  Operation Kronos: human smuggling
    (United Kingdom) 74
  purposes 73
  reputational violence 75, 116
  Russia 73, 75
  Vietnam 75–76
visible hand of market 25

Warren, Curtis 'Cocky' 14–17
white collar crime 169, 170
working capital
  funding 9

young women
  drug mules 3–4

Zambada-Garcia, Ismael 13, 21, 31